IN CHAMBERS

ASPEN COURSEBOOK SERIES

IN CHAMBERS

A Guide for Judicial Clerks and Externs

Jennifer Sheppard
Associate Professor of Law
Mercer University, Walter F. George School of Law

Wolters Kluwer
Law & Business

> Wolters Kluwer Law & Business
> Attn: Order Department
> PO Box 990
> Frederick, MD 21705

Printed in the United States of America.

1 2 3 4 5 6 7 8 9 0

ISBN 978-1-4548-0289-1

Library of Congress Cataloging-in-Publication Data

Sheppard, Jennifer L.
  In chambers : a guide for judicial clerks and externs / Jennifer Sheppard.
    p. cm. — (Aspen coursebook series)
  Includes bibliographical references and index.
  ISBN 978-1-4548-0289-1
  1. Law clerks — United States. 2. Clerks of court — United States. I. Title.
  KF8807.S54 2012
  347.73′16 — dc23
                                                              2012000725

About Wolters Kluwer Law & Business

Wolters Kluwer Law & Business is a leading global provider of intelligent information and digital solutions for legal and business professionals in key specialty areas, and respected educational resources for professors and law students. Wolters Kluwer Law & Business connects legal and business professionals as well as those in the education market with timely, specialized authoritative content and information-enabled solutions to support success through productivity, accuracy and mobility.

Serving customers worldwide, Wolters Kluwer Law & Business products include those under the Aspen Publishers, CCH, Kluwer Law International, Loislaw, Best Case, ftwilliam.com and MediRegs family of products.

CCH products have been a trusted resource since 1913, and are highly regarded resources for legal, securities, antitrust and trade regulation, government contracting, banking, pension, payroll, employment and labor, and healthcare reimbursement and compliance professionals.

Aspen Publishers products provide essential information to attorneys, business professionals and law students. Written by preeminent authorities, the product line offers analytical and practical information in a range of specialty practice areas from securities law and intellectual property to mergers and acquisitions and pension/benefits. Aspen's trusted legal education resources provide professors and students with high-quality, up-to-date and effective resources for successful instruction and study in all areas of the law.

Kluwer Law International products provide the global business community with reliable international legal information in English. Legal practitioners, corporate counsel and business executives around the world rely on Kluwer Law journals, looseleafs, books, and electronic products for comprehensive information in many areas of international legal practice.

Loislaw is a comprehensive online legal research product providing legal content to law firm practitioners of various specializations. Loislaw provides attorneys with the ability to quickly and efficiently find the necessary legal information they need, when and where they need it, by facilitating access to primary law as well as state-specific law, records, forms and treatises.

Best Case Solutions is the leading bankruptcy software product to the bankruptcy industry. It provides software and workflow tools to flawlessly streamline petition preparation and the electronic filing process, while timely incorporating ever-changing court requirements.

ftwilliam.com offers employee benefits professionals the highest quality plan documents (retirement, welfare and non-qualified) and government forms (5500/PBGC, 1099 and IRS) software at highly competitive prices.

MediRegs products provide integrated health care compliance content and software solutions for professionals in healthcare, higher education and life sciences, including professionals in accounting, law and consulting.

Wolters Kluwer Law & Business, a division of Wolters Kluwer, is headquartered in New York. Wolters Kluwer is a market-leading global information services company focused on professionals.

I dedicate this book to my professor and mentor, the late Max Kravitz. You showed me not only how to practice law but how to pursue justice. You are missed.

Summary of Contents

Contents

Acknowledgments

Just as it takes a village to raise a child, it seems like it took a village to assist me in drafting this book. I thank all those who helped me during the drafting process. I thank Professor David Ritchie for asking me to teach a class preparing the judicial externs at Appalachian School of Law for their summer externships. That experience was the impetus for this book. Additionally, I thank Professors Suzanne Cassidy, Linda Edwards, Jim Fleissner, David Hricick, Pat Longan, and Suzianne Painter-Thorne for the advice they provided on various chapters and sample documents. Their suggestions greatly improved earlier drafts of the book. Further, I thank my research assistants, Adrienne Bershinsky and Pamela "Krisi" Hartig, for their assistance. My puny timelines are now beautiful flowcharts thanks to Krisi's efforts. And Adrienne's editing suggestions improved the organization and substance of the book. Finally, I thank Harry Pregerson, Circuit Judge for the U.S. Court of Appeals for the Ninth Circuit; the late John D. Holschuh, U.S. District Judge for the Southern District of Ohio; the Honorable Norah McCann King, Magistrate Judge for the Southern District of Ohio; and Lisa Woodward, law clerk to Judge Holschuh, for providing samples of various documents for inclusion in this book. The contribution of each of these individuals was invaluable, and I am wholeheartedly grateful for their help.

IN CHAMBERS

Introduction: What Do Judicial Externs and Clerks Do?

A judicial clerkship provides direct insight into the inner workings of the court and is one of the most rewarding professional experiences a new lawyer can have. The judicial clerk[1] gains practical experience and learns how the court operates from inside the judge's chambers. Witnessing firsthand how the court operates will make the clerk a better lawyer because he or she has insight into how a judge thinks and what will persuade a judge. While a judicial clerkship is highly desired because of its potential as a phenomenal learning experience, one question looms before a newly employed judicial clerk: What exactly do judicial clerks do? What will the judge expect you, as either an unpaid extern or a paid judicial law clerk, to do during your time in chambers?

It is difficult to generalize about the role of a judicial clerk. The duties of a judicial clerk are not defined in any policy manual but, rather, are determined by the individual judge. A judicial clerk essentially does whatever the judge asks. While individual judges vary greatly in what they ask of their clerks, some commonalities exist. Generally, judicial clerks conduct legal research, review the record before the court, check citations to authority in the litigants' briefs, and draft documents, including bench memoranda and first drafts of orders and opinions. Clerks may also be asked to proofread the judge's orders and opinions, cite check, assist the judge during courtroom proceedings, serve as a "sounding board" for the judge, play devil's advocate, and serve as the judge's confidant. Furthermore, while not nearly as exciting as the clerk's other duties, a

---

1. References to "judicial clerks" include both judicial externs and paid judicial clerks unless otherwise distinguished.

judicial clerk may be asked to perform tasks such as maintaining the chambers' library or performing other administrative tasks. Thus, judicial clerks "are not just secretaries"[2] or mere "errand runners."[3] They are the judge's right hand. Judicial clerks serve an integral role in the decision-making process and, as such, are indispensable to a judge.

Given that a judicial clerk is essentially an extension of his or her judge, the actions of a clerk reflect on the judge. Thus, it is important that the clerk act professionally in all matters and refrain from embarrassing the judge in any fashion. This means that, inter alia, the clerk's work product should be beyond reproach and that the clerk should maintain all personal and judicial confidences. To assist judicial clerks with accomplishing these important goals, this book attempts to provide information that clerks will need to hit the ground running and to succeed. It addresses basic information about the court, including courthouse personnel (who the different courthouse actors are and what they do) and other common practical matters, like how to read a docket sheet and work with a case file. Furthermore, this book provides an overview of civil and criminal procedure, the ethical requirements of judicial clerks, legal research and citation, standards of review, and drafting specific documents for the court.

Additional Resources

- ◆ Federal Law Clerk Info. Sys., *https://lawclerks.ao.uscourts.gov/employinfo.htm*.
- ◆ Jefferson Lankford, *Judicial Law Clerks: The Appellate Judge's "Write Hand,"* in Judging: A Book for Student Clerks (LexisNexis 2002).
- ◆ Gerald Lebovits, *Judges' Clerks Play Varied Roles in the Opinion Drafting Process*, 76 N.Y. St. B.J. 34 (July/Aug. 2004).
- ◆ Eugene A. Wright, *Observations of an Appellate Judge: The Use of Law Clerks*, 26 Vand. L. Rev. 1179 (1973).

---

2. Eugene A. Wright, *Observations of an Appellate Judge: The Use of Law Clerks*, 26 Vand. L. Rev. 1179, 1181 (1973).

3. Gerald Lebovits, *Judges' Clerks Play Varied Roles in the Opinion Drafting Process*, 76 N.Y. St. B.J. 34, 34 (July/Aug. 2004).

1 Basic Information to Get You Started

When you first begin working in the judge's chambers, whether as an extern or a paid law clerk, there will be a lot to learn. You will be expected to learn ethical standards that affect your behavior as well as substantive areas of law, some of which you will be familiar with and some of which you will not be familiar with. You will be required to master many skills, including legal research, legal writing, and legal citation. To make the situation even more difficult, you will likely be out of your element. Many law students and recent graduates have spent little time in a courthouse. They are unfamiliar with the rules governing behavior in the courtroom and judge's chambers, the personnel working in the courthouse, the meaning of terms traditionally used by the court and practitioners, the docket system used by the court, and case files.

When all the things you have to learn quickly coalesce, you may feel a little overwhelmed. To help you ease into your externship or clerkship more readily, this chapter identifies courthouse personnel and explains their job duties, defines the meanings of confusing terms used by the court and practitioners, and explains how to use the docket system and work with a case file.

I. Court Personnel

There are many people, both lawyers and laypersons, who work for the court and make it run efficiently. Each individual has an important role, and as a representative of the judge, it is your duty to treat everyone with respect.

The actors at the state and federal level are often the same or similar. However, when these individuals are referred to differently or have different functions, this section will highlight the differences and explain them.

A. District Court

1. JUDGES

Federal district court judges derive their authority from Article III of the U.S. Constitution. District court judges are appointed by the president with the advice and consent of a majority of the Senate. Once the Senate confirms a district court judge, he or she is appointed to the bench for life, unless impeached.

State trial court judges come to the bench in a variety of ways. In some states, the governor appoints judges to the bench. Such appointments do not tend to be lifetime appointments but are for shorter terms. In other states, the public elects trial court judges for specific periods of time.

a. Chief Judge

There is only one chief judge in each trial court. The chief judge is responsible for the administration and management of the court. The chief judge oversees the clerk of court's office, the pretrial services office, the probation office, and the magistrates or magistrate judges. In addition to ensuring that these offices run properly, the chief judge is also responsible for ensuring that work is assigned to all the judges in accordance with the court's rules.

b. Senior Judges

In federal court, judges who are age 65 or older are eligible for either retirement or senior status when their age plus their time on the bench equals 80 (the "rule of 80"). The decision to take senior status is entirely at the judge's discretion. While senior judges essentially share the same duties as active judges, senior judges may elect to carry a reduced caseload or decline to hear certain types of cases, such as criminal cases or Social Security appeals. As long as a senior judge maintains a certain minimum of courtroom hours, he or she maintains a full staff; however, the judge may have to share a courtroom and a courtroom manager.

There is no state counterpart for a senior judge. In state court, when a judge retires, he or she does not seek reappointment or reelection.

c. Active Judges

Active judges are all judges other than the chief judge or senior judges.

d. Magistrates or Magistrate Judges

Magistrates and magistrate judges are somewhat different. In state courts, magistrates may or may not be required to have a law degree. Although their responsibilities vary widely from state to state,[1] magistrates often have authority to handle applications for bail, arrest and search warrants, the adjudication of petty or misdemeanor criminal offenses, and the trials of civil cases up to a certain dollar amount.

In federal court, magistrate judges are Article I judicial officers who can perform any of the functions of a district court judge in a civil case. District court judges appoint magistrate judges to terms of eight or four years. They are required to have been a practicing lawyer for at least five years before they can be appointed as a magistrate judge. The primary purpose for creating the position of magistrate judge was to provide district courts with an additional judicial resource whose services could be used in the manner most helpful to the individual district court. Magistrate judges are assigned to handle those matters where the need is greatest in the individual district court. The specific duties assigned to the magistrate judge may be determined by reviewing the district court's local rules, which are located on the district court's website.

With regard to criminal matters, magistrate judges handle all the preliminary phases of a felony criminal case to arraignment. Magistrate judges issue arrest and search warrants, conduct initial appearances and preliminary hearings, set bond or order detention without bond, conduct preliminary probation or supervised release revocation hearings, receive grand jury returns of indictments, and arraign defendants (only those entering not guilty pleas). They also try petty offenses, vehicular citations, and, with the consent of the defendant, any other misdemeanor cases. The decision of the magistrate judge in a misdemeanor case may be appealed to the district court judge.

In civil matters, magistrate judges may handle most pretrial matters. Magistrate judges rule on nondispositive motions, including motions to amend the pleadings, for more definite statement, for extension of time or change of counsel, and those arising in discovery disputes. Magistrate judges also hold preliminary pretrial hearings, status conferences, and

---

1. For instance, in Ohio, the judges of many state trial courts appoint magistrates. These magistrates are required to be attorneys and do almost everything that a judge does. On the other hand, in Georgia, magistrates are elected by the public and are not required to be attorneys. Consequently, their responsibilities are much more limited than their Ohio counterparts. Georgia magistrates are authorized to hold preliminary hearings in criminal cases, conduct bench trials for certain misdemeanor offenses, grant bail, and preside over small claims court, where the amount in controversy does not exceed $15,000.

settlement conferences. When the case is ready for trial, the magistrate judge reports this information to the district court judge.

A district court judge may refer case-dispositive motions to a magistrate judge for report and recommendation. Case-dispositive motions include motions for injunctive relief, summary judgment, and to dismiss. The parties may file objections to the magistrate judge's report and recommendation with the district court judge. The district court judge may adopt, reject, or adopt in part and modify the report and recommendation. Additionally, if all the parties consent, a magistrate judge may try any civil case (in either a jury or bench trial). Appeals of civil cases heard by the magistrate judge are appealed directly to the court of appeals.

With regard to specific types of civil litigation, the magistrate judge has specific responsibilities. In prisoner litigation — where conditions of confinement are being challenged — and Social Security appeals, the magistrate judge rules on nondispositive motions and issues a report and recommendation for the disposition of case-dispositive motions. With regard to prisoner habeas corpus cases, the pro se law clerk (described below) prepares a draft decision, which the magistrate judge reviews before forwarding it to the district court judge.

2. Law Clerks

a. Law Clerks, Generally

"The law clerk is the judge's attorney."[2] The law clerk advises the judge on matters and handles many other tasks, including researching cases and writing drafts of documents for the judge. In federal district court, each district judge is entitled to a minimum of two law clerks. The chief judge for each district may employ an additional clerk. Magistrate judges generally are permitted to employ one clerk.

In state courts, the number of law clerks that a judge may have varies depending on the jurisdiction and the availability of resources. Some states permit a judge only one law clerk, whereas others permit more. Some states allow a court a particular number of law clerks and require the judges in the court to share those clerks.

While some judges fill one or all of their positions with permanent clerks, most judicial clerkships are for a set term of one or two years. The terms of the two clerks may run in tandem, but if a judge employs clerks for two-year terms, the terms may be staggered a year apart so that there is a "senior" clerk in chambers. The length of the terms and whether to stagger them is entirely within the judge's discretion.

b. Pro Se Law Clerks

District courts with heavy prisoner litigation may appoint pro se law clerks to review civil cases filed by prisoners, including petitions for a writ

---

2. Calvert G. Chipchase, *Federal District Court Law Clerk Handbook* 10 (ABA 2007).

of habeas corpus and complaints for violations of civil rights under 42 U.S.C. §1983. In some district courts, there may even be a law clerk who is assigned solely to death penalty habeas corpus cases. Pro se law clerks screen the complaints and petitions for substance, analyze their merits, and prepare draft opinion and orders regarding resolution of the cases. Once the pro se law clerk prepares the draft opinion and order, he or she submits it for review to the magistrate judge assigned to the case.

3. Other Courthouse Personnel

a. Judicial Assistants

All district court judges and most magistrate judges are entitled to a judicial assistant. The judicial assistant is the judge's legal secretary or administrative assistant. The judicial assistant performs administrative functions, including answering phones, greeting visitors in the office, and scheduling appointments for the judge. Although the judicial assistant works primarily for the judge, the assistant sometimes aids the law clerk when necessary. The judicial assistant is a valuable source of information regarding how the courthouse operates.

In federal court, judges may opt to substitute their judicial assistant with another law clerk. If a judge has opted for an additional law clerk, the law clerks will share the administrative duties for which the judicial assistant would have been responsible.

b. Deputy Clerks

Deputy clerks are sometimes referred to as "courtroom deputies," "case managers," "courtroom managers," or "scheduling clerks." Although technically an employee of the clerk's office, a deputy clerk serves the judge to whom he or she has been assigned and often has a desk in chambers. Deputy clerks are responsible for scheduling hearings, trials, and other proceedings. They keep the judge abreast of the calendar. While their primary duty is to keep the courtroom operating smoothly, deputy clerks also fulfill several other responsibilities, including calling cases, administering oaths to witnesses and jurors, maintaining custody of trial exhibits, entering in the permanent record of the clerk's office a description of all relevant actions taken in open court or in chambers, serving as a liaison between the judge's chambers and the clerk's office, and managing juries.

c. Clerk of Court

The clerk of court is the chief operating officer of the court and the head of the clerk's office. The clerk of court is responsible for implementing district policies. The clerk of court's primary responsibilities include developing and maintaining a record management system (docketing system) that keeps track of court records and case files; managing the jury selection process; and hiring, training, and managing the staff in the clerk's office.

d. Filing Clerks

Filing clerks are staff in the clerk's office. They manage the case files for every case in the courthouse.

e. Court Reporter

Court reporters are employed by the court and record all court proceedings verbatim, whether by shorthand or mechanical means. They are also responsible for preparing a transcript of the proceedings at the request of the judge or any of the parties to the proceeding. If the court reporter provides a transcript to the parties, the reporter charges a fee. The court reporter must file a copy of every transcript with the clerk of court, which is a public record available to the public without charge.

Trial court judges may require that the record be taken by electronic sound recording rather than by a court reporter. In this situation, an employee of the clerk of court, usually the deputy clerk, is responsible for operating the equipment and seeing to the preparation of any requested transcript.

f. Librarians

The librarian maintains the courthouse library, which is maintained primarily for use by judges and their staff. The courthouse library may also be open to employees of other governmental agencies, members of the bar, and the public. The library has one or two staff members with special training in legal research who can assist law clerks and judges in research.

g. Probation and Pretrial Services Officers

Probation and pretrial services officers are appointed by the court. Probation officers are responsible for conducting presentence investigations; preparing presentencing reports; supervising probationers; and completing investigations, evaluations, and reports to the parole commission when parole is being considered for an offender or when an offender allegedly violates parole. The pretrial services officers evaluate persons proposed for pretrial release, monitor and assist those released, and report to the court on these activities. Smaller courts offer pretrial services through their probation offices; larger courts have separate pretrial offices.

h. Courthouse Security

In federal court, the U.S. Marshals Service is responsible for courthouse security. U.S. Marshals transport prisoners and provide security for the courthouse. The marshals transport the prisoners and remain near the prisoners in the courtroom. The Marshals Service also oversees the courtroom security officers (CSOs), to whom specific courthouse security functions may be assigned. CSOs often man the security checkpoints at the entrances to the courthouse and have other security responsibilities.

In state court, sheriff's office deputies often serve the same functions as the U.S. Marshals and the CSOs. Sheriff's deputies are responsible for the transport of the prisoners and the security of the courthouse. A deputy will often be present in the courtroom during hearings and trials.

B. Appellate Court

Appellate courts have several of the same personnel as trial courts. For example, appellate judges have judicial assistants, law clerks, and externs. These individuals serve similar functions as their trial court counterparts; therefore, those positions will not be examined in further detail. However, those personnel who do not have a trial court counterpart are discussed below.

1. JUDGES

a. Circuit Judges

A circuit judge may be either an active or senior judge. If the judge has senior status, he or she may have a reduced caseload; however, the judge may be subject to some limitations with regard to voting.

b. Chief Judge

The chief judge, in addition to the regular active circuit judge duties, is responsible for the administration of the circuit court.

c. Presiding Judge

The presiding judge is generally the most senior, active judge on the three-judge panel. The presiding judge's primary responsibility is to preside over oral argument. The presiding judge is also responsible for managing the post-argument conference in which the judges debate the issue and for assigning the duty to write the majority opinion to one of the judges on the panel.

d. Judge Sitting by Designation

A judge sitting by designation is not a member of the circuit court, but is a judge from another court who is invited to participate in hearing oral arguments. The judge may be a circuit judge from another circuit or a district court judge from within the circuit. A judge sitting by designation is authorized to participate in the decision-making process and in writing the opinion.

2. OTHER COURTHOUSE STAFF

a. Staff Lawyers

The staff attorney's office functions as the court's central legal staff, serving the court at large rather than individual judges. Staff attorneys assist the court by initially screening the appeals filed for the purpose of determining jurisdiction. Additionally, staff attorneys help the court in refining the issues on appeal; determining which cases require oral argument; and aiding the court in the consideration of many motions, including the determination of in forma pauperis status, certificates of appealability, transcripts at government expense, and to withdraw or substitute counsel.

b. Clerk of Court

The clerk of court, along with the chief judge, plays a significant role in the administration of the court. Furthermore, the clerk's office serves as the chief repository for the trial records for cases being appealed, and all official court correspondence moves through the clerk's office.

c. Records Clerk

If the court grants a petition to appeal, the trial court record will be transferred to the appellate court. The records clerk is responsible for ordering, receiving, and distributing the records from the lower courts.

II. Confusing Terminology

Law students and recent graduates are often unfamiliar with the subtle shades of difference in meaning enjoyed by some specific terms traditionally used by courts and practitioners. Consequently, judicial externs and clerks sometimes misuse these terms. This section identifies some of the terms that commonly cause confusion and explains the differences.

A. Appellant/Petitioner and Appellee/Respondent

Law students and young lawyers tend to use appellant and petitioner and appellee and respondent interchangeably. Though these terms mean something similar, they have subtle differences in meaning. For instance, at the circuit court, or the intermediate appellate court level, *appellant* refers to the party who was unsuccessful in district court and brought the appeal. *Appellee* refers to the party who is defending the district court's decision. However, if the original action arose in an agency context, the party challenging the action below is the *petitioner* and the party defending that action is the *respondent*.

To make matters even more confusing, when the U.S. Supreme Court grants certiorari in a case, it refers to the parties as the *petitioner* and the *respondent*, but the terms mean something different than they meant at the circuit court. At this level of appellate review, the term *petitioner* refers to the party challenging the circuit court's decision. *Respondent* refers to the party defending the circuit court's decision.

B. Opinion, Holding, Judgment, and Decision

Although law students usually understand that an opinion, a holding, a judgment, and a decision are not the same thing, they often have difficulty articulating the difference between these court dispositions. An *opinion* resolves the legal issues in a case and articulates the reasoning employed by the court to reach that decision. It identifies and explains the governing law and applies that law to the facts of the case. The *holding* in a case is the specific part of the opinion that resolves the legal question that was before the court. The *judgment*, which is typically located at the end of the opinion, states the court's procedural disposition of the case. *Decision*, on the other hand, is a less precise term than the other three. In fact, one can use *decision* to refer to an opinion, a holding, or a judgment.

C. Reverse, Vacate, and Overrule

Law students and young lawyers tend to use the terms *reverse*, *vacate*, and *overrule* interchangeably. These terms do not share the same meaning. A *reversal* is an appellate court's disposition of an appeal. To *reverse* a decision means that a higher-level court rejects the lower court's *holding in the same litigation*. For instance, when a party appeals a trial court's decision and the appellate court disagrees with the trial court's holding, it *reverses* that holding. That reversal affects the same parties and concerns the same issues as the lower court's decision. *Vacatur*, on the other hand, is slightly more expansive. Like reversal, vacatur occurs at the appellate stage and involves the same parties and issues as the lower court decision. However, an appellate court *vacates* a lower court's entire underlying decision when the appellate court rejects that decision and sets it aside. That decision then becomes void and without effect.

On the other hand, two separate litigations are involved when a court *overrules* a legal principle from a prior case. A court in the *subsequent* litigation *overrules* a rule of law that was announced in an *earlier* litigation that involved different parties and different issues.

III. How to Read a Docket and Work with a Case File

A. The Docket System

The docket system provides comprehensive case information about all cases that have been litigated in a specific court since a particular date. A reader can locate information pertaining to a particular case—the docket for that case—if he knows the case number (a.k.a. the docket number), the plaintiff's name, or the defendant's name.

The docket for each case lists all the parties to the case, the judge assigned to the case, the magistrate or magistrate judge assigned to the case (if applicable), and the attorneys for each party. The docket identifies the nature of the suit (i.e., whether it is a civil lawsuit, a criminal case, a bankruptcy case, etc.). Additionally, the docket identifies the general causes of action asserted by the plaintiff. Furthermore, the docket for a particular case records all documents filed in the litigation (along with a brief description of each document) or entered into the record by the court, and any court conferences, hearings, or trials that have taken place during the litigation. The docket also provides the date on which each document was filed and the dates on which the conferences, hearings, or trial were held.

B. Case Files

A case file (or a court file) is the official record of the court for a case and includes all of the pleadings, motions, exhibits, orders, and verbatim testimony that took place during the trial or in depositions. Not every court file contains each item mentioned above. For example, discovery documents, such as transcripts of depositions, written interrogatories, answers to written interrogatories, or written admissions, would not appear in the case file as exhibits unless one of the parties submitted those documents to the court as evidence in support of an argument in a brief.

Each document filed in a case is assigned a number in the file. The docket number will be recorded somewhere on the first page of the document, usually at the bottom right-hand corner. Additionally, when reviewing the docket for the case, the docket number assigned to a particular document will be listed beside the title of that document.

In the file folder containing the case, some information that is not part of the official court record may be kept. These documents may include correspondence received by the judge or the court regarding the litigation; the judge's handwritten notes concerning pretrial conferences, which may later be typed; or a log of telephone calls regarding the litigation. This information is likely to be attached to the back of the front cover of the folder, so that when you open the folder, it is on the left. You will be able to discern that these documents are not part of the official court record because they will not be docketed and will not have a number written on them to identify their location in the case file. These documents, which are not docketed and not part of the "official" court record, should not be considered when resolving a pending motion.

Furthermore, it is important to note that the documents in a case file are arranged in reverse chronological order. When you open the file folder, the document filed most recently will be the first one you see. As you leaf back through the file, you will locate documents filed before the most recent one was filed in reverse chronological order. The last document you generally will see in the case file is the complaint that initiated the litigation.

C. Tips for Working with a Case File

When you first receive an assignment requiring you to work with a particular case file, collect the file, either from the judge or from the clerk's office. Once you have retrieved the file, print the docket sheet for the case. Look at the docket sheet to see what has happened in the course of the litigation and to see what motions, responses to motions, replies in support of motions, orders, and various other documents have been filed during the litigation. Essentially, use the docket sheet to get a feel for the case. Then, if the judge has requested that you draft an opinion and order concerning a particular motion, review the docket sheet to identify every document concerning that motion. You should search for the motion itself and the brief filed in support of that motion, the nonmoving party's brief responding to that motion, and the moving party's reply. In regard to several types of motions — for instance, motions to dismiss, for summary judgment, or an injunctive order — you will also need to examine the complaint and answer. Remember, however, that an answer may not have been filed if you are working on a motion to dismiss the claim.

It is extremely important that you review the entire case file when completing any assignment for a judge. It is especially important when writing an opinion and order resolving a motion to think about what other documents in the file might affect the outcome of the motion on which you are working. You must take this step before you start researching the matter and writing an opinion. If you fail to do so, and there is a motion pending that would affect the outcome of the motion you are working on, you will have wasted not only your time but also that of the court. For instance, if you are working on a motion to dismiss the action for failure to state a claim, which is decided on the pleadings, would it be necessary to first resolve a pending motion to amend the complaint, the initial pleading in the litigation? Of course it would be necessary to resolve that motion before you could resolve the motion to dismiss! The motion to amend the complaint seeks to alter the allegations in the complaint, the same allegations that the defendant is challenging as being deficient in the motion to dismiss. If you fail to resolve the motion to amend the complaint before resolving the motion to dismiss, you will likely resolve the motion to dismiss based on the wrong allegations.

Additional Resources

- Calvert G. Chipchase, *Federal District Court Law Clerk Handbook* (ABA 2007).
- Federal Judicial Center, *Chambers Handbook for Judges' Law Clerks and Secretaries* (West 1994)
- Joseph L. Lemon, Jr., *Federal Appellate Court Law Clerk Handbook* (ABA 2007).

2

Civil Litigation Process

I. Introduction

Civil litigation involves disputes between parties over virtually any matter that is not governed by an administrative body and that is not a crime. At this point in your legal education, you have likely completed a course on civil procedure. If you have completed such a course, this chapter will serve as a streamlined review of the civil litigation process. If you have not yet completed a course on civil procedure, this chapter provides an overview of the civil litigation process.

📖 FOR YOUR LIBRARY

In federal court, civil litigation is governed by several sets of rules that, collectively, set forth the procedure that lawyers must follow during litigation. In addition to these rules, courts commonly recognize certain secondary sources as authoritative with regard to particular legal areas. Judges often rely on such resources when resolving issues and sometimes even cite these resources in their opinions. These sources include:

- Federal Rules of Civil Procedure
- Federal Rules of Appellate Procedure
- Federal Rules of Bankruptcy Procedure
- Federal Rules of Evidence
- Local rules of the particular district in which the case is being litigated
- Rules of the individual court in which the case is being litigated

---

continues on next page

> • *Moore's Federal Practice*[1]
> • Wright and Miller's *Federal Practice and Procedure*[2]
> • *Weinstein's Federal Evidence*[3]
> • Pattern jury instructions — most of the federal courts of appeal have their own such instructions, which are found on the court's website

---

◈ STATE COURT ALERT!

The procedural rules followed in many state courts are quite similar to those followed in federal courts, but others differ drastically. Consequently, you must consult the appropriate rules for the state jurisdiction in which the case is situated.

A. The Civil Litigation Process

While this chapter sets forth the steps in the civil litigation process, it must be noted that in any given case some steps may be omitted due to court order or inaction by or agreement of the parties. It should also be noted that other parties begin negotiations in an attempt to resolve the dispute before the commencement of the litigation. Negotiations may continue throughout the litigation and into the appellate process. To facilitate settlement, the parties may utilize different forms of alternative dispute resolution, including arbitration or mediation.

1. COMMENCEMENT OF THE ACTION: THE COMPLAINT AND SUMMONS

The filing of a *complaint* commences a civil lawsuit. In the complaint, the plaintiff will identify the parties to the lawsuit, establish that the court has jurisdiction over the subject matter, establish that the lawsuit has been brought in the proper venue, identify the causes of action, and request specific relief.

When the complaint is filed, the clerk of court assigns the case a "case" or "docket" number, which consists of three parts. The first part of the docket number is an abbreviation that establishes whether the case is a civil or criminal case: "C.A." or "Cr.," respectively. The second part of the number consists of the last two digits of the year in which the lawsuit was filed. The third part is a number that is assigned consecutively as suits are filed in each calendar year, usually starting with 101. Therefore, the 97th civil case filed in 2007 would be assigned the

---

1. James William Moore, Daniel R. Coquillette, Gregory P. Joseph, Sol Schrieber, Jerold Solovy & Georgene Viaro, *Moore's Federal Practice* (3d ed., Matthew Bender 1997).
2. Charles Alan Wright et al., *Federal Practice and Procedure* (West 2010).
3. Joseph M. McLaughlin, *Weinstein's Federal Evidence* (2d ed., Matthew Bender 1997).

number CA-07-197. After assigning a case number, the clerk then assigns the case to a judge for management and disposition. Sometimes, judges have their initials included at the end of the case number.

Once the complaint is filed, the court issues a *summons*, which is an order by the clerk made upon the filing of the complaint that requires a response by the defendant. The plaintiff must deliver, or serve, the complaint and summons on the other party to the lawsuit within a specific period of time following the filing of the complaint and in a particular manner that is reasonably calculated to provide the defendant with notice of the suit. Delivering the complaint and summons to the defendant is referred to as "service of process."

Rather than attempting to serve the defendant with the complaint and summons, the plaintiff may provide the defendant with a written notice of the lawsuit and a request that the defendant waive service of process so that the plaintiff may avoid the costs associated with service. If the plaintiff requests waiver of service, and provides the defendant with proper notice of the request and lawsuit, the defendant has a duty to avoid the unnecessary costs associated with serving process. If the defendant is in the United States and refuses to waive service, the court will impose the costs incurred by the plaintiff in effecting service on the defendant. The purpose of service of process or filing a waiver of service is to establish the court's jurisdiction over the defendant and to provide the defendant with notice of the lawsuit.

Rule 4 of the Federal Rules of Civil Procedure regulates the manner in which service of process may be effected on individuals located in the United States, individuals located in a foreign country, corporations and associations, the United States, state and local governments, and foreign states. While the plaintiff is responsible for effecting service of process on the defendant, the plaintiff cannot personally serve the defendant with the documents. Rather, the plaintiff must get another person, who is at least 18 years old and who is not a party to the suit, to serve the documents to the defendant. Once service of process has been completed, the plaintiff will file a notice of process with the court. However, if the plaintiff fails to successfully serve the defendant within the required period of time, the court can dismiss the action without prejudice, or, if the plaintiff can demonstrate good cause for the failure to serve process, the judge may direct that service be accomplished within a specific additional period of time.

2. DEFENDANT'S RESPONSE TO THE COMPLAINT: DEFAULT, ANSWER, OR MOTION TO DISMISS

Upon receipt of service of process, the defendant has several options. The defendant can default on the action, file a motion to dismiss the action, or file an answer.

A *default* occurs if the defendant receives notice of the lawsuit and does nothing, failing to defend against the lawsuit within the appropriate period of time. If the defendant fails to take appropriate action with regard to the lawsuit, the clerk of court may note the default on the record. The default is not actually effective until the judge who is assigned to the case enters the default judgment pursuant to Rule 55 of the Federal Rules of Civil Procedure.

However, if the defendant chooses to take steps to defend against the action, the defendant can file either a motion to dismiss one or more claims or an answer. If the defendant responds to the complaint by filing a *motion to dismiss* one or more claims, the defendant would request that the court dismiss the action based on a variety of grounds, including the court's lack of subject-matter jurisdiction over the claim(s) or personal jurisdiction over the defendant, improper venue, insufficiency of process, insufficiency of service of process, failure to state a claim upon which relief can be granted, and failure to join a necessary party.

The two most common motions to dismiss filed at this stage of the litigation are based on the court's lack of subject-matter jurisdiction and the plaintiff's failure to state a claim. A motion to dismiss for lack of subject-matter jurisdiction maintains that the court lacks the constitutional or statutory authority to hear the claim brought by the plaintiff. The parties cannot waive a lack of subject-matter jurisdiction. If the court lacks subject-matter jurisdiction over the claim, that claim will be dismissed.

A motion to dismiss for failure to state a claim upon which relief can be granted under Federal Rule of Civil Procedure 12(b)(6) maintains that no legal claim exists for the facts alleged in the complaint. Such a motion requests that the lawsuit be dismissed because even if all the facts alleged by the plaintiff are true, they do not prove a wrong that is remedied by the law. If the court grants the motion, the defendant wins on the merits of the claim. However, if the court denies a defendant's motion to dismiss, the defendant must file an *answer* to the complaint. Federal Rule of Civil Procedure 12(a)(4) requires that the answer be filed within 14 days of the court's denial of the motion to dismiss.

If the defendant does not move to dismiss, or if the defendant files a motion to dismiss that is denied by the court, the defendant must file an answer responding to the complaint within a specific time following service of process. An answer is a response to the merits of the complaint. In the answer, the defendant must respond to the allegations, assert any affirmative defenses, and assert any counterclaims against the plaintiff or cross-claims against other defendants. When responding to each allegation in the complaint, the answer should repeat the number of each paragraph of the complaint and either admit or deny each allegation. If the defendant is unable to admit or deny an allegation due to insufficient information, the defendant may respond by stating that the defendant lacks sufficient information on which to either admit or deny the allegation. Thus, the answer will look like a list of numbered paragraphs followed by "admit," "deny," or "defendant lacks sufficient information on which to either admit or deny the allegation."

In addition to admitting or denying each factual allegation in the complaint, the defendant may include affirmative defenses in the answer. The defendant may provide more facts and assert that the plaintiff should not prevail based on those facts. Examples of affirmative defenses that the defendant can include in the answer include defenses based on the statute of limitations and the court's lack of personal jurisdiction over the defendant. Some objections, such as to the court's jurisdiction over the defendant, must be made in either the answer or in a motion to dismiss, or they are waived.

Finally, in the answer, the defendant may assert a counterclaim against the plaintiff or a cross-claim against another defendant. In a counterclaim, the defendant asserts claims against the plaintiff. When the defendant asserts a counterclaim against the plaintiff, they "switch places" with regard to that claim. Thus, the plaintiff becomes the defendant and the defendant becomes the plaintiff, but only in relation to the counterclaim. If the defendant asserts a counterclaim against the plaintiff, then the plaintiff must file a *reply* to the counterclaim (which essentially serves as the plaintiff's answer to the allegation). In a cross-claim, the defendant asserts a claim against another defendant to the litigation. Finally, a defendant may include a third party on the theory that the third party will be liable to the defendant for any judgment that may result from the litigation.

The complaint, answer, counterclaims, cross-claims, and third-party complaints include all the allegations made by the parties to the litigation and constitute the *pleadings* in the case. The pleadings may be altered by motion to amend the pleadings or to add new claims or parties.

3. Discovery: The Fact-Finding Process

Discovery is the process by which the parties to litigation investigate the facts of the case and exchange information under the supervision of the court. The main purpose of discovery is to allow the parties to obtain evidence relevant to the claims or defenses that have been pled from other parties and, in some instances, nonparties. The information obtained during the discovery process also may be used for strategic purposes, such as assessing the likelihood of success and the propriety of settling the case, preparing for trial, exposing weaknesses in the opponent's position, and imposing costs on the opponent.

Rule 26 of the Federal Rules of Civil Procedure provides general rules governing discovery. The rules require the automatic disclosure of certain basic information and documents pertaining to the case that can substantiate disputed facts alleged with particularity in the pleadings. With regard to obtaining information that is not automatically disclosed by the parties, there are several forms of discovery techniques, including depositions, written interrogatories, requests for admissions, requests for the production of documents and things, medical examinations, and requests for permission to enter upon land and property for inspection purposes.

Third parties who are not party to the litigation may be compelled by subpoena to produce documents and physical evidence, deposition testimony, and testimony at trial.

Depositions are governed by Rule 30 of the Federal Rules of Civil Procedure. In a deposition, lawyers examine a party or witness. The witness or party is questioned verbally before a court reporter, who records both the questions and the answers. The person being deposed, or the deponent, is under oath during the deposition.

Interrogatories are governed by Rule 33 of the Federal Rules of Civil Procedure. Interrogatories are written questions presented by one party to another party; interrogatories may not be served on nonparties. The rules generally limit the number of interrogatories that a party may serve on another. Finally, the person at whom the questions are directed must answer the questions in writing under penalty of perjury, or under oath.

Written *requests for admissions* are governed by Rule 36 of the Federal Rules of Civil Procedure. The number of admissions that can be requested are also limited. Failure to admit or deny the requests for admission in writing within a particular period of time will result in the requests being deemed admitted.

Requests for the production of documents and things are governed by Rule 34 of the Federal Rules of Civil Procedure. Requests for the production of documents and things are written requests to produce documents and other items related to the litigation. Requests for documents cannot simply be a fishing expedition that requests all documents that may be relevant to the suit. Rather, the requests for documents must seek specific documents or a specific category of documents.

Medical examinations are governed by Rule 35 of the Federal Rules of Civil Procedure. Medical examinations can be requested by motion to the court when physical or mental conditions are in controversy. If the court finds good cause, the court may order a party or a person under the control of a party to submit to a physical or medical examination.

Parties are obligated to comply with discovery requests. Therefore, in routine cases, counsel for the parties conduct discovery with little involvement of the court. While the court will schedule dates for the completion of pretrial steps, including discovery, generally, that will be the extent of the court's involvement in the discovery process. However, if a party refuses to comply with discovery requests, or if a party's discovery requests are burdensome, the opposing party may seek court aid. If the party refuses to comply with the discovery requests, the opposing party may seek assistance from the court by filing a *motion to compel discovery*. A motion to compel discovery seeks a court order requiring the recalcitrant party to respond to the discovery request. The court may impose sanctions on a party for refusing to comply with a discovery request. Nonparties may be compelled by subpoena to produce documents and physical evidence as well as to testify at deposition.

On the other hand, if the party or nonparty to whom the discovery request is directed believes that the requests are burdensome or harassing, the party may file a *motion for a protective order*, which asks the court to allow that party not to respond to a discovery request. A request for a protective order may be based on a number of grounds, including undue harassment or unreasonable demands, or to avoid the disclosure of confidential or privileged information. Privileged information includes attorney-client or doctor-patient information, or materials created by attorneys in anticipation of litigation, known as attorney work product.

4. PRETRIAL MOTIONS: MOTION FOR SUMMARY JUDGMENT AND MOTIONS IN LIMINE

Not only are discovery-related motions filed during the pretrial stage of the litigation, but many other types of motions may also be filed. The most common motion that is filed once discovery has commenced is a *motion for summary judgment*, which is governed by Rule 56 of the Federal Rules of Civil Procedure. A motion for summary judgment asks the court to dismiss a claim on its merits for lack of production of evidence sufficient for a jury to find in favor of the nonmoving party. Because no reasonable jury could find for the nonmoving party given that the material facts are not in dispute, there is nothing for a jury to decide. Any party to the litigation may file a motion for summary judgment. Such a motion may relate to the entire case, or it may relate to specific claims or defenses. If a motion for summary judgment on the entire case is granted, the moving party wins the case on the merits. If summary judgment is granted in regard to specific claims or defenses, the remainder of the case is set for resolution at trial.

Because a motion for summary judgment is asking a judge to render a decision by applying the applicable law to the undisputed facts of the case, the moving party must provide the court with the necessary evidence by submitting it with the motion. The judge cannot render a decision on the motion if the evidence has not been provided.

Other motions, called *motions in limine*, can be filed with the court regarding the admissibility of evidence. A motion in limine requests that the court prohibit opposing counsel from referring to or offering evidence on matters considered by the moving party to be so highly prejudicial to it that the moving party wants to avoid any exposure of that evidence to the jury.

5. THE PRETRIAL CONFERENCE AND ORDER STAGE

Within 120 days of any defendant being served with the complaint or 90 days of any defendant appearing in the case, whichever is earlier, the court must issue a scheduling order. The scheduling order sets deadlines for joining other parties, amending the pleadings, completing discovery, and filing motions. The scheduling order will also set dates for a pretrial conference and the trial, modify the deadline for disclosures under Rule of Federal Procedure 26 or the extent of discovery, and address any other appropriate matters.

The court may also hold one or more pretrial conferences to deal with a variety of preliminary matters that may aid the just, speedy, and inexpensive disposition of the action. These preliminary matters include eliminating frivolous claims or defenses, formulating the issues for trial, amending the pleadings if needed, setting deadlines for the filing of motions for summary judgment, scheduling additional pretrial and settlement conferences and the trial, disposing of pending motions, finalizing discovery procedures, and referring matters to a magistrate judge. After any pretrial conference, the court should issue an order reciting the actions taken during the conference.

The court will also hold a final pretrial conference. This conference must be held as close to the start of trial as possible. The purpose of the pretrial conference is to create a trial plan, including a plan to facilitate the admission of evidence. With regard to evidentiary matters, the court will rule in advance on the admissibility of evidence, obtain admissions and stipulations as to uncontested evidence, require the parties to exchange lists of witnesses and documents, limit the number of expert witnesses, mark exhibits, and establish a reasonable limit on the time allowed to present evidence. The final pretrial order, which the court issues following this conference, may be altered only to prevent manifest injustice.

6. TRIAL STAGE

At trial, counsel for the parties presents the evidence to a fact finder, which may be either the judge or a jury. While juries are the fact finder in many trials, and the right to a jury trial is present in the Seventh Amendment, if the parties agree to a "bench trial," the judge will serve as the fact finder. If the parties choose a jury trial, the jury is selected during a process called "voir dire." During voir dire, the judge, the attorney, or both will question the prospective jurors about their ability to decide the case fairly. Each party may challenge jurors for *cause*, claiming that information about a prospective juror suggests that the juror lacks the ability to be impartial. Each party is also permitted a specific number of *peremptory challenges*, which allow the discharge of prospective jurors without any explanation.

Once the jury has been selected, the trial begins. The trial proceeds in the following manner:

1. The plaintiff and defendant give their opening statements.
2. The plaintiff presents its case to the jury.
3. The defendant presents its case.
4. The plaintiff and defendant give their closing statements.
5. The plaintiff gives a rebuttal to defendant's closing statement.
6. The judge instructs the jury.
7. The jury deliberates on the matter and issues a verdict.

In their opening statements, attorneys for the parties simply tell the jury what they believe the evidence will show during the trial. During the presentation of the plaintiff's and defendant's cases, the parties present evidence through testimony and documentary evidence. When a party calls a witness, the questioning of that witness is referred to a *direct examination*. The opposing party then questions that witness during *cross-examination*. The attorney who originally called the witness may *redirect examination*, while the opposing party is given the opportunity to *recross-examine* the witness. During closing statements, the plaintiff and defendant present their arguments regarding what the evidence presented during the trial means.

During the course of the trial, each party may file a motion seeking to end the case in whole or in part. A motion requesting *judgment as a matter of law*, which was formerly known as a directed verdict, requests that the judge enter judgment for the moving party on the grounds that "no legally sufficient evidentiary basis [exists] for a reasonable jury to find for that party on that issue."[4] A motion for judgment as a matter of law can be filed only after a certain point in the trial. Once the plaintiff has presented its case in chief and rested, the defendant can make such a motion, asserting that, based on the evidence presented by the plaintiff, no reasonable jury could find in favor of the plaintiff. Such a motion is often denied. When the defendant has presented its case in chief and rested, but before closing arguments, either the plaintiff or defendant can request judgment as a matter of law. Again, these motions are usually denied. The judge will then instruct the jury on the law governing the dispute, and the jury will deliberate on the matter and reach a verdict. Even though preverdict judgment non obstante veredicto (JNOV) motions are often denied, they are constitutionally required predicates for any post-judgment motion for JNOV.

Once the parties have presented their cases, the judge will *charge* the jury by providing instructions meant to guide jury deliberations. The judge will instruct the jury with regard to the law governing the dispute. The judge prepares these instructions with the assistance of counsel. For more information on jury instructions, see Chapter 10.

The jury will then retire to *deliberate* in secret. Once it has applied the law to the facts presented at trial, the jury will return a *verdict*. The verdict may be a *general verdict* that simply addresses liability, or a *special verdict* that answers questions that are intended to clarify the factual basis underlying its decision. For more information regarding verdicts, see Chapter 10.

7. Posttrial Motions

Posttrial motions challenge the sufficiency of the evidence on which the verdict is based. After the jury has issued the verdict, a party may renew

---

4. Fed. R. Civ. P. 50(a) (2009).

its motion for judgment as a matter of law; in addition, it may request a new trial. A renewed motion for judgment as a matter of law, which was formerly known as a motion for judgment notwithstanding the verdict, asserts that the jury verdict lacked sufficient basis in the law. This motion is granted only where the judge previously denied an earlier motion for judgment as a matter of law that should have been granted. This motion is granted or denied on a claim-by-claim, defense-by-defense basis. If not, the judge will enter the jury's verdict as a judgment.

8. Appellate Review

An appeal must be based on an alleged error of law, not fact. Appellate courts will not review factual issues. However, they will review the sufficiency of the factual evidence. Furthermore, a litigant generally cannot file an appeal whenever the court takes action that the litigant believes to be error. Under the *final judgment rule*, a litigant may only appeal after the entry of final judgment. Appeals can be taken interlocutorily, or while the case is pending, when they involve issues that cannot be effectively reviewed at the conclusion of the case, such as appeals contesting the grant or denial of preliminary injunctive relief.

Once judgment has been entered, an aggrieved party has the right to appeal. To commence an appeal, a party must file a *notice of appeal* with the district court within a specific period of time following entry of judgment. A party's failure to file a notice of appeal in a timely fashion constitutes a waiver of the right to appeal. The purpose of a notice of appeal is to inform opposing counsel and the court that an appeal is being taken and to establish appellate jurisdiction.

When a notice of appeal is filed, the district court will then forward a copy of the notice to the clerk of the court of appeals. If the petition to appeal is granted, the district court record will be transferred to the appellate court and the appeal will be docketed. The parties will file briefs in support of their positions on appeal, and the court may hold oral argument to enable the judges to question the attorneys. The court will deliberate on the matter, issue an opinion, and issue a mandate.

The appellant is responsible for getting the record sent from the district court to the appellate court within a specific amount of time. The record consists of all documents and exhibits filed by the parties, all transcripts of relevant proceedings, all court orders, and anything else that was before the court when it made the decision that is the subject of the appellate review. While the district court clerk will gather most of the documents that constitute the record on appeal, the appellant is responsible for ordering, and paying for, a transcript of relevant proceedings. Once the record has been transferred to the appellate court, the appellant must docket the appeal. This process is completed in the clerk's office. Once the appellant pays a fee, the clerk of the appellate court opens a case file and sends notice of the appeal to the parties.

The parties to the appeal will then file written briefs in which they present their legal and factual arguments to the court. The appellant files the opening brief because it bears the burden of establishing that the trial court erred. The appellee files a responding brief, and the appellant then may file a reply brief responding to new matters raised in the appellee's brief. The Federal Rules of Appellate Procedure set forth standards governing the format of the brief, color of the cover, content, method of reproduction, number of copies, and deadlines for filing the briefs. The local rules of that circuit and, at times, of the individual court may impose additional requirements regarding the brief.

When drafting the briefs, the parties are required to determine which portions of the record on appeal are relevant to the issues raised, and the appellant must include reproductions of them in a joint appendix. However, if relevant material is omitted from the joint appendix, the court may refer to the original record.

The court may, and often does, dispense with oral argument if it can resolve the appeal based solely on the briefs and the record. However, if the court is unable to decide the appeal based solely on the briefs and the record, the court will hold oral arguments. During oral arguments, the parties have the opportunity to present their arguments to the court, and the court has the opportunity to question the parties regarding concerns that were not fully addressed by the briefs. A panel of three judges initially decides cases.

After the court deliberates on the matter, it will reach a decision and issue a written opinion. The court may affirm, or uphold, the decision of the district court in whole or in part. If the appellate court affirms the trial court's decision only in part, it may modify that decision so that it is consistent with the law as determined by the appellate court. Alternatively, the appellate court may reverse, or reject, the district court's holding and remand the case to the judge who erred at trial. A case is usually remanded for additional findings of fact or for other resolution consistent with the appellate decision.

The party who loses the appeal may file a *petition for rehearing* within a specific period of time following the issuance of the judgment. A petition for rehearing attempts to persuade the court to withdraw its decision and reconsider the matter. The party that prevailed on appeal may not respond to the petition unless requested to do so by the court. Most petitions for rehearing are denied.

Some cases are heard en banc by all the active judges on the court and any senior judges who sat on the panel that originally heard the case. A majority of the active judges on the court may order that a case be heard en banc to maintain uniformity of decisions or when a case involves an extremely important question.

Unless a petition for rehearing en banc has been filed, the clerk of court will issue the *mandate* within a specific period following the entry of judgment. The mandate is the formal order of the appellate court; upon its issuance, the appellate court's decision has the force and effect of law. Additionally, the mandate notifies the district court of its decision, directs it to take any action or enter a specified disposition, and confers jurisdiction back to the district court for any proceedings that may be necessary.

The losing party may request that the court stay issuance of the mandate while an application for a *writ of certiorari* to the U.S. Supreme Court remains pending. However, if the losing party chooses not to seek certiorari, the mandate is the final stage in the appellate process.

Figure 2-1 shows the civil litigation process.

Additional Resources

- ◆ Federal Judicial Center, *Chambers Handbook for Judges' Law Clerks and Secretaries* (West 1994).
- ◆ Toni M. Fine, *American Legal Systems: A Resource and Reference Guide* (Anderson 1997).
- ◆ Judith Resnick, *Processes of the Law: Understanding Courts and Their Alternatives* (Foundation Press 2004).

Figure 2-1. CIVIL LITIGATION PROCESS

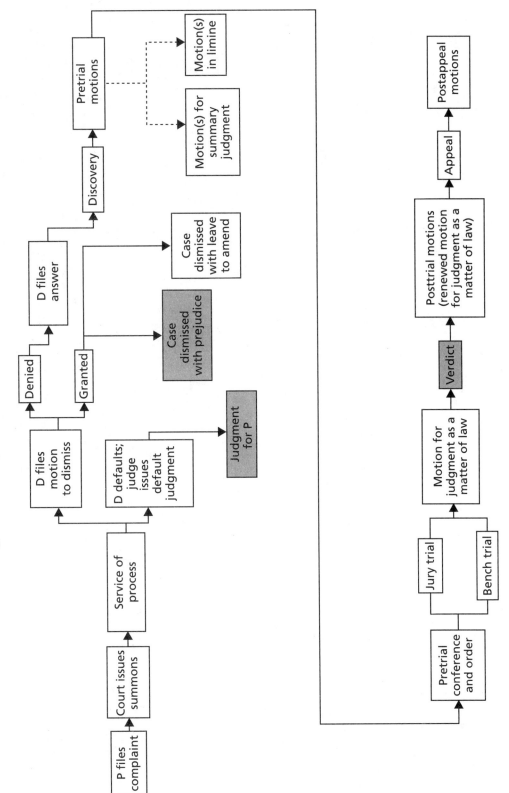

3 Criminal Litigation Process

I. Introduction

Criminal actions are initiated by federal, state, or local governments to punish individuals or entities for crimes defined in the jurisdiction's criminal code. In federal court, litigation is governed by the Federal Rules of Criminal Procedure and each individual court's local rules. Each state has its own version of the rules of criminal procedure that governs procedure in that jurisdiction. These rules essentially set forth the procedure that the litigants must follow during the litigation process. The procedural rules followed in many state courts are quite similar to those followed in federal courts.

At this point in your legal education, you have likely completed a course on criminal law. Additionally, you may or may not have completed a course on criminal procedure. If you have completed such a course, this chapter will serve as a streamlined review of criminal procedure. If you have not yet completed such a course, this chapter will provide a basic overview of the law governing criminal investigations and the criminal litigation process.

📖 FOR YOUR LIBRARY

In federal court, criminal litigation is governed by several constitutional amendments, statutes, and procedural rules that, collectively, set forth the procedure that lawyers must follow during litigation. In addition to these rules, courts commonly recognize certain secondary sources as authoritative with regard to particular legal areas. Judges often rely on such resources when resolving issues and sometimes even cite these resources in their opinions. These sources include:

- Fourth, Fifth, Sixth, and Eighth Amendments to the U.S. Constitution
- Federal Rules of Criminal Procedure
- Bail Reform Act, 18 U.S.C. §§3141-3150
- Speedy Trial Act of 1974, 18 U.S.C. §§3161-3174
- Federal Sentencing Guidelines
- Federal Rules of Appellate Procedure
- Federal Rules of Evidence
- Local rules of the particular district in which the case is being litigated
- Rules of the individual court in which the case is being litigated
- *Moore's Federal Practice*[1]
- Wright and Miller's *Federal Practice and Procedure*[2]
- *Weinstein's Federal Evidence*[3]
- Pattern jury instructions — most of the federal courts of appeal have their own such instructions, which are found on the court's website

---

⚠️ STATE COURT ALERT!

The procedural rules followed in many state courts are quite similar to those followed in federal courts, but others differ drastically. Consequently, you must consult the appropriate rules for the state jurisdiction in which the case is situated.

II. Sources of Federal Criminal Procedure

A. Constitutional Rights and Protections in Criminal Actions

The U.S. Constitution imposes limits on the government's power to investigate and prosecute crimes. The Fourth, Fifth, Sixth, and Eighth

---

1. James William Moore, Daniel R. Coquillette, Gregory P. Joseph, Sol Schrieber, Jerold Solovy & Georgene Viaro, *Moore's Federal Practice* (3d ed., Matthew Bender 1997).
2. Charles Alan Wright et al., *Federal Practice and Procedure* (West 2010).
3. Joseph M. McLaughlin, *Weinstein's Federal Evidence* (2d ed., Matthew Bender 1997).

Amendments govern actions by law enforcement personnel, including prosecutors, and provide most of the protections for criminal defendants.[4]

The Fourth Amendment protects individuals from unreasonable searches and seizures by law enforcement. This essentially means that law enforcement must justify any arrest or search of an individual or his property with probable cause. Thus, to arrest an individual, law enforcement must show probable cause that the individual has committed a crime. Additionally, before law enforcement can lawfully search the property of an individual, it must establish that evidence of a crime may be found there. When law enforcement has probable cause to believe that evidence of a crime may be found in or on the property of an individual, the officer must generally obtain a search warrant. There are several exceptions to the warrant requirement for searches. The most common exceptions include when the individual consented to the search, the evidence was in "plain view," "exigent circumstances" existed (otherwise known as "hot pursuit"), and the search of the individual was incident to a lawful arrest. Furthermore, when an officer stops an individual to investigate a suspicion of criminal activity, the officer need only have reasonable suspicion (as opposed to the higher probable cause standard) that a crime is being committed to conduct a brief investigatory stop and, if there is reasonable suspicion of danger, a protective pat-down search for weapons.

The Fifth Amendment requires indictment by grand jury and the provision of due process. It also prohibits compelled self-incrimination and double jeopardy. The most well-known Fifth Amendment case is *Miranda v. Arizona*.[5] In *Miranda*, the U.S. Supreme Court interpreted the Fifth Amendment to mean that law enforcement must give certain warnings, later known as *Miranda* warnings, to the suspect before custodial interrogation can lawfully occur. Double jeopardy means that a defendant cannot be tried or punished twice for the same offense.

The Sixth Amendment requires a public trial, a trial by a jury of one's peers, a speedy trial, notification of the charges issued against a defendant, the ability to confront witnesses against one, and the right to counsel in serious criminal offenses. The speedy trial provision of the Sixth Amendment imposes time limits on the criminal pretrial process. The Speedy Trial Act of 1974, 18 U.S.C. §§3161-3174, provides for specific time constraints and thus has an impact on criminal proceedings. Under the act, the prosecution must file an indictment or information within a specific

---

4. While the Fourth, Fifth, Sixth, and Eighth Amendments apply only to the federal government, the Due Process Clause of the Fourteenth Amendment incorporates them by reference and makes them applicable to state actors. Furthermore, individual state constitutions may provide additional protections to criminal defendants.

5. 384 U.S. 436 (1966). Under *Miranda*, a suspect must be warned that he has the right to remain silent, that any statement he makes may be used as evidence against him, and that he has the right to an attorney, and that if he cannot afford an attorney, one will be appointed to him. *Id.* at 444. While a suspect may waive rights, that waiver must be made voluntarily, knowingly, and intelligently. *Id.*

period of time,[6] and the court must set the case for trial "at the earliest practicable time."[7] Under 18 U.S.C. §3162, failure to meet the speedy trial requirements results in dismissal of the charge, although dismissal is almost never with prejudice.

The Eighth Amendment prohibits the federal government from imposing excessive bail, excessive fines, or cruel and unusual punishment. The U.S. Supreme Court has held that the cruel and unusual clause of the Eight Amendment applies to the states as well as the federal government. The Eighth Amendment completely prohibits certain punishments regardless of the crime. Additionally, the Eighth Amendment prohibits other punishments that are excessive when considered in light of the crime or when considered in light of the defendant's competence. For instance, capital punishment cannot be imposed for rape, whether of an adult woman or a child. Furthermore, the mentally disabled and juveniles under 18 years of age are not subject to capital punishment.

B. Other Sources

While the Fourth, Fifth, Sixth, and Eighth Amendments govern actions by law enforcement personnel and provide most of the protections for criminal defendants, criminal litigation is governed by several other sources of law as well. These sources govern all aspects of the criminal litigation process, including procedure, evidence, sentencing, and appeal.

Procedural matters, though governed by a variety of sources, are governed primarily by the Federal Rules of Criminal Procedure. These rules address every stage of a criminal litigation, from the preliminary procedures to postconviction procedures. The preliminary proceedings govern, among other things, the initial filing of a complaint or indictment, arraignment and initial appearance, and bail. The rules also address pretrial proceedings, which govern discovery and pretrial motions concerning, inter alia, the severance of charges or codefendants, discovery of grand jury materials, further specificity from the prosecution in the form of a bill of particulars, the suppression of evidence, or dismissal of the action. The rules also govern the guilt stage, which includes guilty pleas and trial. Postconviction procedures address posttrial motions and sentencing.

Important federal statutes supplement the procedural rules, such as the Bail Reform Act, which regulates the detention and release of criminal defendants during the litigation process, and the Federal Sentencing Guidelines, which provide courts with guidance when determining the length of a convicted defendant's sentence.

Evidentiary issues are governed by those Federal Rules of Evidence that apply to criminal litigation, including rules on hearsay, witnesses, opinions and expert testimony, privileges, and authentication and identification. One important rule is Rule 403, which governs the admissibility of

6. 18 U.S.C. §3161(b) (2008).
7. 18 U.S.C. §3161(a).

some evidence by allowing the trial judge to balance the probative value of the evidence with other competing concerns. Rule 403 allows for the exclusion of relevant evidence "if its probative value is substantially outweighed by the danger of unfair prejudice, confusion of the issues, or misleading the jury, or by considerations of undue delay, waste of time, or needless presentation of cumulative evidence." Rule 404 also applies to criminal litigation and governs the inferences jurors can draw from character evidence or from evidence of other crimes or wrong acts.

Additionally, in a particular jurisdiction, the Federal Rules of Criminal Procedure, the procedure mandated by federal statutes, and the Federal Rules of Evidence may be supplemented by local court rules, which individual district courts may adopt. Finally, the Rules of Appellate Procedure govern criminal appeals.

When resolving an issue arising from a federal criminal case, it is important that you consider which of the sources of law identified above to consult. If you are in a state jurisdiction, it is equally true that you should determine which sources to consult. States have adopted their own rules of criminal procedure, evidence, sentencing, and appeal. While the rules in many states are derived, at least in part, from the federal rules, this is not true in every state. Even in those states that have essentially adopted the federal rules, the rules may be different in some regards. You must be sure to consult the rules of the particular jurisdiction to ensure accuracy.

III. Stages in a Criminal Action

While this chapter sets forth the major stages in a federal criminal case, it is important to note that this discussion is a generalization meant to aid understanding of the process. Under the Federal Rules of Criminal Procedure, several different procedures may be used to initiate a criminal case. The federal rules allow for a criminal case to be initiated by a complaint, a grand jury indictment, or an information. A complaint is a preliminary charge based on probable cause. It may either precede or follow an arrest. A complaint must be followed by an indictment. The government may also skip the filing of the complaint and simply issue an indictment. Or, if the defendant waives indictment, the case may proceed by way of an information. The manner in which the case is initiated also controls whether the defendant is entitled to an arraignment or an initial appearance and a preliminary hearing. Further, cases may end at different stages in the process due to a guilty plea, a court-ordered dismissal of the indictment, or a jury's acquittal of the defendant.

A. Preliminary Proceedings

Under the Federal Rules of Criminal Procedure, there are several procedures for initiating criminal proceedings. The federal rules allow criminal proceedings to be initiated by the filing a complaint, which is a preliminary charge based on probable cause. The rules also allow criminal proceedings to be initiated by a grand jury indictment or a prosecutor's information.

1. GRAND JURY

The Fifth Amendment guarantees an individual charged with a federal crime the right to have the charge presented to a grand jury for indictment. However, if an individual who is entitled to be prosecuted by grand jury indictment waives that right, the individual may be prosecuted by an information.[8] Under the Speedy Trial Act, 18 U.S.C. §3161(b), the prosecution must file an indictment or an information within 30 days of arrest or service of summons. An additional 30 days is granted only if no grand jury has met in the district within the first 30-day period.

The grand jury, which is impaneled by the district court, is "a body of citizens who listen to evidence of criminal allegations and determine whether there is probable cause to believe the offense was committed."[9] To facilitate its decision, the grand jury has subpoena power to command individuals to attend the proceedings and offer testimony or produce documents. While grand juries hear testimony and review documents, it is important to note that grand jury proceedings are not like a trial. Grand jury proceedings are generally secret, the accused has no right to be present at the proceedings or to present information designed to persuade the grand jury that probable cause of the offense does not exist. Furthermore, neither the accused nor witnesses are entitled to have an attorney with them inside the grand jury room.

During deliberation and voting, only members of the grand jury may be present. If 12 or more grand jury members are persuaded that probable cause exists to believe the accused committed the crime, then the grand jury will issue an indictment in open court.

The grand jury requirement of the Fifth Amendment has not been incorporated into the Fourteenth Amendment and, as such, is not applicable to the states.[10] Nevertheless, all but two states authorize prosecuting a defendant via grand jury indictment.[11] That does not mean, however, that indictment by grand jury is the primary means of prosecuting a defendant in each of those states. Twenty-eight states allow a prosecution to be brought by an information as well as by grand jury indictment.[12] In many of those states, routine cases are prosecuted by an information rather than indictment.[13]

---

8. Fed. R. of Crim. P. 7(b).
9. Calvert G. Chipchase, *Federal District Court Law Clerk Handbook* 100 (ABA 2007).
10. *Hurtado v. California*, 110 U.S. 516 (1884); *Gerstein v. Pugh*, 420 U.S. 103, 118-119 (1975); *Gaines v. Washington*, 277 U.S. 81, 86 (1928); *Lem Woon v. Oregon*, 229 U.S. 586 (1913).
11. Wayne R. LaFave et al., *Criminal Procedure* 3, §8.1(a) (2009).
12. *Id.*
13. *See id.*

2. ARRAIGNMENT OR INITIAL APPEARANCE

Once an individual has been arrested, the defendant must be brought without unnecessary delay before a judge to hear the charges against him or her and to enter a plea to those charges. This initial encounter between the defendant and a judge is called an *arraignment* when the defendant was arrested following issuance of an information or indictment and is called an *initial appearance* when the defendant was arrested in the absence of an information or indictment.

The defendant may plead guilty, not guilty, or nolo contendre. A plea of nolo contendre, or no contest, means that a defendant does not admit guilt but does not contest the entry of judgment against him or her. If a defendant enters a plea of guilty or nolo contendre, a judge may refuse to accept the plea if the judge believes that the defendant did not enter the plea voluntarily or understand the nature of the charges or the possible penalties. However, if a defendant pleads not guilty and does not later change the plea, the case will proceed to trial.

Additionally, during this initial hearing, the judge must inform the defendant how to request bail and of the right to request counsel.

3. BAIL

The defendant may file a motion seeking pretrial release from jail on bail. The Bail Reform Act of 1984, 18 U.S.C. §§3141-3150, governs the release of defendants on bail. The act requires the judge to grant the pretrial release of a defendant unless the defendant is a flight risk or poses a danger to the community. Pursuant to 18 U.S.C. §3142(f), only defendants who fall into certain categories are subject to detention without bail. These categories include defendants charged with a violent crime, an offense for which the maximum sentence is life imprisonment or death, certain drug offenses for which the maximum offense is greater than ten years, or repeat felony offenders. A hearing must be held to determine whether the defendant fits within these categories; anyone not within them must be granted release on bail. The only exception to this is if the defendant poses a serious risk of flight or obstruction of justice. If there is a serious risk that the defendant will flee or seek to obstruct justice, the defendant may be detained.

A defendant may be released from jail based on his own recognizance or on a bond, which may be either secured or unsecured. Additionally, if a judge believes that a defendant is a flight risk or may be a danger to others, the judge may subject the defendant's release to a variety of conditions meant to reduce the risk of flight or of harm to others.

4. PRELIMINARY HEARING

A defendant is entitled to a *preliminary hearing*, or preliminary examination, when arrested in the absence of an indictment (and in some states even when an indictment has been returned). A preliminary hearing is held in addition to the initial appearance. A preliminary hearing is designed to serve the same function as a grand jury — to require the government to establish probable cause before an independent third party.

During a preliminary hearing, a judge conducts an examination and determines whether there is probable cause to bind over a defendant to answer to the charges. If a judge determines that probable cause does not exist, the defendant is discharged.

B. Pretrial Proceedings

1. DISCOVERY

Discovery in criminal actions is much narrower than in civil litigation. The pertinent rules do not require expansive disclosure of information in criminal actions. Furthermore, if the defendant fails to request discovery from the prosecution, the prosecution is entitled to a very limited amount of discovery.

In a criminal action, both the prosecution and the defense are required to produce prior witness statements. The Jencks Act, 18 U.S.C. §3500, requires that the prosecution provide the prior statements of witnesses to the defense. Federal Rule of Criminal Procedure 26.2 conversely requires that the defense provide the prior statements of its witnesses to the prosecution. With regard to witness statements, it is important to note that the parties need only produce the statements of witnesses who will testify at trial. Furthermore, only those statements that relate to the witness's testimony at trial must be produced.

In addition to prior witness statements, *Brady v. United States* requires that the prosecution provide to the defendant any important (or "material") exculpatory evidence. Rule 16 of the Federal Rules of Criminal Procedure also requires that the prosecution produce the defendant's prior statements and information concerning the defendant's criminal record. Under certain circumstances, the prosecution must allow the defense to inspect all documents that it plans to introduce at trial.

Rules 12.1 and 12.2 of the Federal Rules of Criminal Procedure require the defendant to provide the prosecution with notices of alibis and of insanity defenses. Additionally, once the defendant requests certain types of information from the prosecution, the defendant must reciprocate subject to claims of privilege, such as the Fifth Amendment protection against self-incrimination.

2. PRETRIAL MOTIONS

A defendant may file several types of motions prior to trial. The motions seek a wide variety of outcomes, including release on bail, severance of charges or codefendants, discovery of grand jury materials, further specificity from the prosecution in the form of a bill of particulars, the suppression of evidence, or dismissal of the action. Some of these motions will be discussed in more detail below.

First, when a defendant is indigent, the defendant may file motions requesting that counsel be appointed to represent the defendant or expert services be provided at the government's expense.

Second, the defendant may file a motion to suppress evidence (including defendant's own statements and witness identifications) on the ground that it was obtained in a manner that violated the defendant's constitutional rights. For instance, the defendant may argue that law enforcement obtained evidence pursuant to an unreasonable search of the defendant's person or property in violation of the Fourth Amendment to the U.S. Constitution. Or the defendant could argue that law enforcement obtained an involuntary confession from the defendant in violation of the Fifth Amendment.

Finally, the defendant may file a motion to dismiss the charges,[14] challenging the sufficiency of the indictment or information. Indictments and informations are required to be sufficiently specific to provide the defendant with fair notice of the crimes with which he or she has been charged. Thus, the indictment or information must specifically identify the statutes the defendant allegedly violated and state the elements of the charged crime.[15] Errors, or other inadequacies, in indictments or informations are grounds for dismissal only when they mislead a defendant to his or her prejudice. Additionally, the court construes the indictment or information in a manner that favors validity.

Some other grounds on which a defendant may base a motion to dismiss the charges include defects in jurisdiction, prosecutorial misconduct, or violations of grand jury secrecy.

C. Guilt Stage

1. GUILTY PLEAS

a. Generally

A defendant may plead not guilty, guilty, or nolo contendre. When the defendant pleads not guilty, the case moves on to trial. However, when the defendant pleads guilty or nolo contendre, the court must accept the plea before it can be entered. A plea of nolo contendre is essentially an admission of guilt that subjects the defendant to punishment by the court but allows the defendant to deny the alleged facts in other proceedings. Because a plea of nolo contendre is essentially an admission of guilt, references to "guilty pleas" in the remainder of this chapter will refer to pleas of both guilty and nolo contendre.

---

14. In some states, such motions are sometimes called motions to quash the indictment or demurrers. The Federal Rules of Criminal Procedure have abandoned those labels for a motion to dismiss an indictment.

15. Fed. R. Crim. P. 7(c)(1).

The court must take certain steps before it may accept a plea of guilty. First, the court should advise the defendant of his rights and the consequences of his guilty plea, and determine that the defendant understands these rights and consequences. The court should inform the defendant that he has the right to

1. plead not guilty,
2. a jury trial,
3. representation by an attorney that the court will appoint if the defendant cannot afford one,
4. confront and cross-examine adverse witnesses,
5. refrain from compelled self-incrimination,
6. testify and present evidence on his behalf, and
7. compel the attendance of witnesses.

In addition to informing the defendant of his rights, the court should explain that the defendant waives these rights if the court accepts his guilty plea. Furthermore, the court should inform the defendant of the nature of each charge to which the defendant is pleading; the maximum possible sentence; any mandatory minimum sentence; the court's obligation when determining the sentence to consider the applicable sentence range under the sentencing guidelines, possible departures from that range, and any other relevant factors; the court's authority to order restitution; any applicable forfeiture; and the terms of any plea-agreement provision waiving the right to appeal or to collaterally attack the sentence.

If the court determines that the defendant understands his rights and the consequences of pleading guilty, the court must determine whether the defendant voluntarily pleads guilty or does so due to force, threats, or promises (aside from promises in a plea agreement). If the defendant has entered a guilty plea due to force, threats, or promises, the court may not accept the guilty plea and must enter a plea of not guilty.

Finally, before a court can accept a defendant's guilty plea, the court must determine that a factual basis exists for entering the plea. If there is no factual basis suggesting the defendant is guilty of the crime charged, then the court should reject the guilty plea. Consider the following example. A criminal defendant is charged with a crime and agrees to a plea bargain presented by the prosecutor. When the judge asks the defendant how he pleads, the defendant responds, "Guilty." However, when the judge asks the defendant if he did it (i.e., the act with which he has been charged), the defendant says, "No." When the defendant will not admit guilt on the facts, there is not a sufficient factual basis on which the judge can accept the guilty plea.

b. Guilty Pleas Pursuant to a Plea Agreement

Defendants often enter guilty pleas pursuant to a plea agreement with the prosecutor. The prosecutor may agree to certain conditions in exchange for a defendant's guilty plea to the charged offense or to a lesser or related offense. The prosecutor may agree to not file other charges or to move to dismiss other charges. The prosecutor may also agree that a specific sentence or sentencing range is appropriate, or that a particular provision, policy statement, or sentencing factor of the sentencing guidelines does or does not apply. Finally, the prosecutor may agree only to recommend, or agree not to oppose the defendant's request, that a specific sentence or sentencing range is appropriate or that a particular provision, policy statement, or sentencing factor of the sentencing guidelines does or does not apply.

When the prosecutor agrees to dismiss charges, agrees that a specific sentence or sentencing range applies, or agrees that a particular provision, policy statement, or sentencing factor is or is not applicable to the case before the court, such agreements bind the court once the court accepts the plea agreement. However, if the court refuses to accept the plea agreement, it must inform the parties of its rejection and advise the defendant that the court is not required to follow the plea agreement. The court must also inform the defendant that if he does not withdraw the guilty plea, the court may dispose of the case less favorably toward the defendant than the plea agreement contemplated and provide the defendant an opportunity to withdraw the plea.

On the other hand, if the prosecutor simply agrees to recommend, or agrees not to oppose the defendant's request that a specific sentence or sentencing range is appropriate or that a particular provision, policy statement, or sentencing factor of the sentencing guidelines does or does not apply, such a recommendation or request does not bind the court. Consequently, if the prosecutor agrees only to recommend (or not oppose a defendant's request for) a particular sentence or provision of the sentencing guidelines, the court must advise the defendant that the he has no right to withdraw the guilty plea if the court refuses to follow the prosecutor's recommendation.

2. TRIAL

A criminal trial proceeds in much the same manner as a civil trial. A complete criminal trial proceeds in six primary stages. First, except in rare cases that are heard only by a judge (a nonjury trial), most trials begin with voir dire, or jury selection. The jury in a criminal matter, or petit jury, generally consists of 12 jurors and some alternate jurors. During voir dire, the judge, prosecution, and defendant question the pool of potential jurors. The questions may be general or of a more specific nature. The more specific questions will pertain to the particular case before the court — the judge, prosecution, or defendant may ask the potential jurors about their personal ideological predispositions or about life experiences that may pertain to the case. Following the questioning, the judge may excuse potential jurors based on their answers. Furthermore, the prosecution and the defendant may exclude a number of potential jurors through challenges "for cause" or "peremptory challenges." A challenge for cause is used to exclude jurors who have demonstrated that they cannot be objective in deciding the case. For instance, if a potential juror indicates a bias against the law, the prosecution could dismiss that potential juror for cause. Peremptory challenges, on the other hand, allow a party to exclude a potential juror for any nondiscriminatory reason. In a federal misdemeanor case, each party is granted only three peremptory challenges. In a typical federal felony case, the prosecution is granted six peremptory challenges, and the defendant is granted ten such challenges. In a capital case, however, both parties are granted 20 peremptory challenges. The parties may be granted additional peremptory challenges when selecting alternate jurors. The number of such challenges varies depending on the number of alternate jurors being selected. The number of peremptory challenges granted to each party for a particular type of case may vary in state courts.

After the jury is impaneled, the parties present their opening statements. Because the prosecution bears the burden of proof regarding the defendant's guilt, it presents its opening argument first. In that argument, the prosecution relates the facts of the case and explains what it will prove. The defendant may then present his or her opening argument or may wait to present that argument until the close of the prosecution's case-in-chief. In either situation, the defendant's opening argument presents his or her interpretation of the facts, begins to rebut the prosecution's key evidence, and presents any legal defenses to the crimes charged.

Following opening statements, the prosecution presents its case-in-chief, which is when it presents its key evidence in an attempt to convince the jury beyond a reasonable doubt that the defendant is guilty of the crime charged. During its case-in-chief, the prosecution will call its eyewitnesses and expert witnesses to testify. The prosecution will question each witness during its "direct examination"; following the prosecution's questioning of a witness, the defendant will have the opportunity to "cross-examine" that witness. The prosecution then is given the opportunity to "redirect," meaning that it may again question its witness to rehabilitate any weaknesses that may have appeared in the witness's credibility or testimony as a result of cross-examination. During its case-in-chief, the prosecution may also present physical evidence, including documents, medical reports, and photographs. Once the prosecution has completed its case-in-chief, the defendant may present his or her case. It is important to note, however, that the defendant may choose not to present a case-in-chief. Rather, the defendant may instead choose to make its points through the cross-examination of the prosecution's witnesses and through its challenges to the prosecution's evidence.

Once all the evidence has been presented, the parties give their closing arguments. Closing argument is a party's last opportunity to address the jury. As such, closing argument is used to summarize the evidence and the party's case. The prosecution gives its closing argument first, explaining how the evidence demonstrates the defendant's guilt beyond a reasonable doubt. The defendant, in his or her closing argument, attempts to show how the prosecution's evidence has fallen short of meeting its burden of proof and explains to the jury that it must find the defendant not guilty of the charged crimes (or of any lesser included offenses). The prosecution, following the defendant's closing argument, is permitted an opportunity to rebut the defendant's arguments.

After the parties have finished their closing arguments, the judge instructs the jury on the law necessary to determine the defendant's guilt or innocence. While the judge determines what law applies to the case based on the crimes charged and the evidence presented at trial, the prosecution and defense are permitted to submit suggestions to the court and to challenge certain instructions. More information is provided in Chapter 10 regarding the process for creating jury instructions and drafting jury instructions.

Once the judge has charged the jury, the jury retires to deliberate. During deliberations, the jury may reach a verdict either acquitting the defendant or finding the defendant guilty. The jury may find the defendant guilty of the crime charged, an attempt to commit the charged crime, any lesser offense necessarily included in the charged crime, or an attempt to commit any lesser included offense. Most jurisdictions, including the federal government and many states, mandate that a jury's verdict in a criminal case be unanimous. Thus, if the jury is unable to agree on a verdict (known as a hung jury), the court declares a mistrial. In the event of a mistrial, the judge orders a new trial. When a defendant is charged with multiple counts (or crimes), the jury must return a verdict on those counts on which it was able to reach agreement. The judge may declare a mistrial with regard to the remaining counts.

During the course of the trial, the defendant can file a variety of motions, the most significant of which is a motion for a judgment of acquittal, which challenges the sufficiency of the prosecution's evidence and requests dismissal of the case. A defendant may seek dismissal of the case following the prosecution's case-in-chief, following the defendant's case-in-chief, or following the verdict. To prevail on such a motion, the defendant must show that the evidence is insufficient to sustain a verdict.

D. Posttrial Stage

1. Posttrial Motions

Following a criminal trial, the defendant may file motions requesting that the court grant a new trial, arrest the judgment due to errors, correct or reduce the sentence, or vacate the sentence.

Under Rule 33 of the Federal Rules of Criminal Procedure, a defendant must file a motion for a new trial within seven days following the verdict. However, the defendant may file such a motion based on newly discovered evidence up to three years following the verdict. A judge may grant a motion for a new trial only if the "interests of justice" require it.

Under Rule 34 of the Federal Rules of Criminal Procedure, a motion to arrest judgment must be filed by the defendant within seven days of the verdict. The court may "arrest" a judgment only when the indictment or bill of information fails to charge an offense or the court lacks jurisdiction over the charged offense.

2. SENTENCING

a. The Law

Several statutes and guidelines govern sentencing and sentencing procedures in the federal courts. Titles 18 and 21 of the U.S. Code and the Sentencing Reform Act of 1984 are the primary statutes that govern sentencing. Titles 18 and 21 prescribe statutory minimum and maximum sentences for offenses. The federal sentencing guidelines also govern sentencing. The Federal Rules of Criminal Procedure govern sentencing procedures. Rule 32 concerns sentencing and judgment, whereas Rule 35 limits the court's authority to correct or reduce the sentence.

The Sentencing Reform Act of 1984 created the U.S. Sentencing Commission, a judicial agency, and directed it to create sentencing guidelines. These federal sentencing guidelines are found in the U.S. Sentencing Guidelines Manual. The Sentencing Reform Act also authorized the commission to issue policy statements explaining the guidelines and their application. In addition to the guidelines and the policy statements authorized by the Sentencing Reform Act, the commission also provided commentary and application notes to further explain the guidelines and their application. Though when initially promulgated, the federal sentencing guidelines and the commission's policy statements and commentaries had the force of law, following the U.S. Supreme Court's decision in *United States v. Booker*,[16] the guidelines are simply advisory. While, as a practical matter, judges must continue to use the sentencing guidelines to calculate sentencing ranges, they are not obligated to follow the sentencing guidelines.

b. Sentencing Procedure

If the defendant pleads guilty or a jury convicts the defendant, then the defendant must be sentenced. Sentencing occurs after an abbreviated fact-finding process. In addition to considering evidence presented at trial, the court may also consider evidence that was inadmissible as long as it has "probable accuracy."[17]

The court will usually order a probation officer to prepare a presentence report. This report is the best tool for determining the appropriate sentence. The report presents the facts relevant to sentencing, explains the

---

16. 543 U.S. 220 (2005).
17. U.S. Sentencing Guideline Manual §6A1.3(a).

officer's application of the sentencing guidelines to those facts, and offers the officer's sentencing recommendation. The report may contain additional information regarding statements in the report that a party has objected to and the officer's comments regarding those objections. The presentence report must be disclosed to the defendant within a specific period of time before the sentencing hearing. This period of time varies from jurisdiction to jurisdiction.

The court may wish to hold an evidentiary hearing before imposing a sentence if factual issues that could affect the sentence are in dispute. Additionally, if the correct interpretation of the guidelines is unclear, the court may hear arguments from the attorneys on this matter. After resolving all disputes, the court imposes a sentence on the defendant, stating the reasons for the sentence on the record.

A motion to correct the sentence must be filed within 14 days following the verdict and can only be granted based on mathematical or technical errors. Furthermore, Rule 35 of the Federal Rules of Criminal Procedure severely limits the court's authority to reduce the sentence. Sentences can be reduced only when the defendant provides "substantial assistance" to the government in investigating or prosecuting another individual.

3. APPEAL

Just as in civil matters, the parties may appeal criminal cases. However, while the defendant may appeal the guilty verdict rendered by the jury as well as his sentence, the prosecutor's options are more limited. The prosecutor may appeal a trial court's dismissal of indictments and directing verdicts of acquittal, and the defendant's sentence. The prosecutor generally may not appeal an acquittal of a defendant. The Fifth Amendment's prohibition of double jeopardy, or trying a defendant more than once for the same offense, limits the prosecutor's ability to appeal judgments of acquittal. The prosecution may appeal an acquittal of a defendant only when the jury has returned a guilty verdict and the judge has entered a postconviction motion for judgment for an acquittal under Rule 29.

The Federal Rules of Appellate Procedure govern appellate procedure in criminal appeals as well as in appeals of civil cases. Rule 4 of the Federal Rules of Appellate Procedure requires a defendant to file a criminal appeal within 14 days of his conviction, whereas the prosecution is allowed 30 days in which to file an appeal. On appeal, the evidence is viewed in the light most favorable to the prosecution. Furthermore, a defendant cannot appeal an issue not raised at trial unless that issue constitutes "plain error," or an extraordinary mistake affecting substantial rights held by the defendant.[18] Defects that do not affect substantial rights are considered harmless errors and are not sufficient bases to justify reversal of

---

18. Federal R. App. P. 52.

a conviction. If on appeal, the appellate court affirms the decision of the trial court, the defendant may seek review by the U.S. Supreme Court by filing a petition for a writ of certiorari.

After defendants have exhausted all appellate avenues, they may request reconsideration of their convictions through habeas corpus, which challenges the legality of a detention on the grounds that conviction was obtained in violation of federal constitutional rights.

While there is an extensive body of law regarding habeas corpus petitions that is beyond the scope of this chapter, please note that the procedure that must be used to file a petition for habeas corpus is slightly different if the conviction originated in federal rather than state court. Under 28 U.S.C. §2254, prisoners convicted in state courts must exhaust all other state remedies before a petition for habeas corpus will be reviewed. However, federal prisoners seek release from custody under 28 U.S.C. §2255. Proceedings under this act are treated as a continuation of the original criminal action; thus, prisoners are required to file their petitions in the sentencing court rather than in the court with jurisdiction over the prisoner's place of incarceration.

Figure 3-1 shows the criminal litigation process.

IV. The Role of the Law Clerk

Where criminal cases are concerned, just as with civil cases, the work of a judicial clerk varies depending on the judge. Clerks may be needed to conduct legal research with regard to evidentiary questions or motions filed by the parties, either pretrial or posttrial, to assist the judge in drafting jury instructions, to attend the trial, or to aid in sentencing.

Most district court judges, as well as state court judges, have their clerks assist in drafting jury instructions. As previously indicated, while it is the jury's duty to decide the facts and reach a verdict, the judge's duty is to determine the rules of law that govern those facts. It is in determining the law that governs the case and in drafting the jury instructions that the judge will read to the jury that the judge requires the clerk's assistance. For more instructions on drafting jury instructions, see Chapter 10.

District court judges vary greatly with respect to what they require their law clerks to do regarding sentencing matters. Many judges do not require much assistance from their law clerks with regard to sentencing. However, issues may occasionally arise during sentencing that require legal research, and the judge may ask his or her law clerk to conduct such research and prepare a memorandum explaining the answer.

However, some judges ask their clerks to assist in determining the appropriate sentencing range under the sentencing guidelines. This is an extremely complex process, and if asked to assist, a judicial clerk should

Figure 3-1. CRIMINAL LITIGATION PROCESS

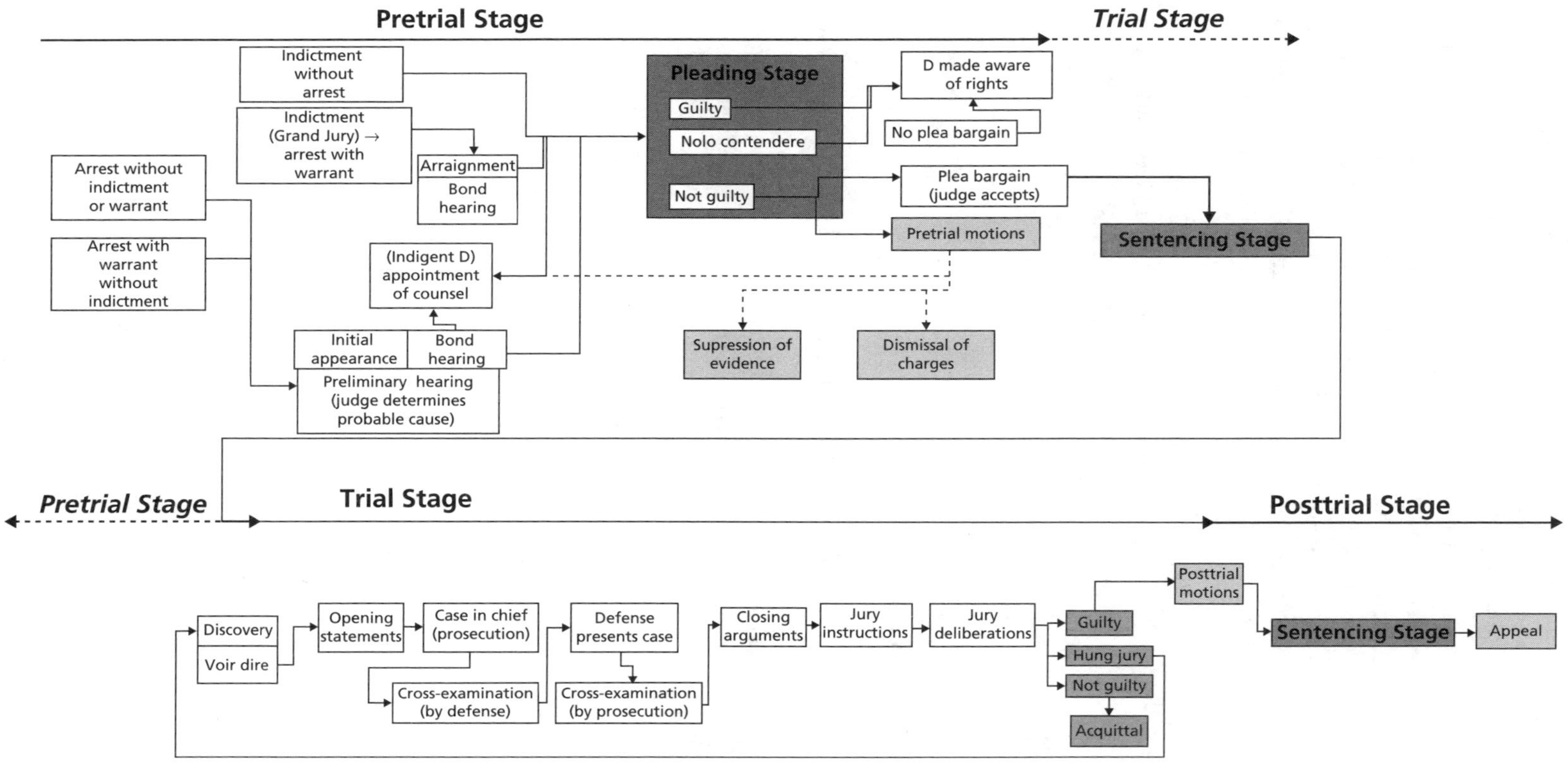

Pretrial Stage
Trial Stage
Indictment without arrest
Indictment (Grand Jury) → arrest with warrant
Arrest without indictment or warrant
Arrest with warrant without indictment
Arraignment
Bond hearing
(Indigent D) appointment of counsel
Initial appearance
Bond hearing
Preliminary hearing (judge determines probable cause)
Pleading Stage
Guilty
Nolo contendere
Not guilty
D made aware of rights
No plea bargain
Plea bargain (judge accepts)
Pretrial motions
Supression of evidence
Dismissal of charges
Sentencing Stage
Pretrial Stage
Trial Stage
Posttrial Stage
Discovery
Voir dire
Opening statements
Case in chief (prosecution)
Cross-examination (by defense)
Defense presents case
Cross-examination (by prosecution)
Closing arguments
Jury instructions
Jury deliberations
Guilty
Hung jury
Not guilty
Acquittal
Posttrial motions
Sentencing Stage
Appeal

familiarize herself with the U.S. Sentencing Guidelines Manual (including the guidelines, policy statements, and commentary) and the circuit's case law interpreting those guidelines. Furthermore, to determine the proper sentencing range under the sentencing guidelines, one must be familiar with the entire structure of the guidelines and not attempt to apply them in a piecemeal fashion. For example, simply consulting the guidelines for the type of offense in question will rarely yield a correct result. Other factors must be taken into account, including the nature of the offense, the defendant's prior criminal history, conduct that might result in a reduction or enhancement of the sentence, or extraordinary circumstances that might justify a downward departure from the minimum sentence.

Whenever determining the appropriate sentencing range under the sentencing guidelines, remember to pay close attention to the date the criminal acts occurred and the effective dates for the legislative and guideline provisions to ascertain which provisions apply to the offense in question.

Additional Resources

◆ Calvert G. Chipchase, *Federal District Court Law Clerk Handbook* (ABA 2007).
◆ Judith Resnick, *Processes of the Law: Understanding Courts and Their Alternatives* (Foundation Press 2004).

CHAPTER

4

Professionalism and Ethics for Judicial Clerks

Judges are required to act both professionally and ethically. Given that judicial clerks are the trusted agents of judges and that their conduct reflects on the judge, judicial clerks have a "derivative duty" to act both professionally and ethically.[1]

I. Professional Conduct in the Courtroom and in Chambers

A. Attire

Most judges do not have a formal dress code. However, given that you are a representative of the judge, it is important that you dress in a professional manner when at the courthouse or on court business. In this environment, professional means business professional. Thus, men should wear suits or, at a minimum, slacks and a sports jacket. Ties are a must. Women's attire is a little more varied and depends largely on the particular judge's or the legal community's expectations. However, in general, women should wear a business suit or at least a business skirt and blouse. Their attire should be tasteful and conservative. Women should also wear pantyhose with skirts or dresses.

---

1. John Paul Jones, *Some Ethical Considerations for Judicial Clerks*, 4 Geo. J. Legal Ethics 771, 772, 775 (1990-1991).

Once you get to the courthouse, you may realize that the standard for business professional in your community is a little more lax than that detailed above. If that is the case, you may choose to relax your standards somewhat. However, since your behavior reflects on the judge, erring on the side of caution is always best. If you have some doubt as to the hemline of a skirt or the neckline of a shirt, wear something else that you have no doubt is appropriate.

B. Conduct

1. TIMELINESS

Timeliness is a must when clerking for a court. If you are scheduled to be in chambers at a particular time, you should be there on time. If you cannot avoid being late, you should call the judge's chambers and let someone know that you have been detained and will be arriving later than expected. Furthermore, if you are ill or cannot be at work for some other reason, call the judge's chambers and let someone know that you will not be coming to work that day. You should do this for each day that you are absent from work.

2. LANGUAGE

Your language should be professional at all times. You should employ language that demonstrates respect for everyone you meet in the courthouse or speak with on the telephone. You should not use profane language. You should not tell sexist, racist, or otherwise raunchy jokes. Your behavior reflects on the judge. Your primary obligation to the judge is to refrain from embarrassing him or her or otherwise engaging in behavior that raises the appearance of impropriety. If you will not refrain from cursing or telling inappropriate jokes because *that is just who you are*, then you should not work for a judge.

📖 FOR YOUR LIBRARY

Given that this chapter cannot hope to address every ethical situation that may arise, it may be necessary to consult other resources that govern the ethical obligations of judicial clerks and externs. These sources include:

- Code of Conduct for Judicial Employees, *http://www.uscourts.gov/Viewer. aspx?doc = /uscourts/RulesAndPolicies/conduct/Vol02A-Ch03.pdf*
- *Maintaining the Public Trust: Ethics for Federal Judicial Law Clerks, http:// ftp.resource.org/courts.gov/fjc/ethics01.pdf*
- Volume II of the *Guide to Judiciary Policies and Procedures* (the *Guide*)

The *Guide* provides information used by the judiciary in its day-to-day operations and focuses on ethics. The *Guide* contains the Code of Conduct for

Judicial Employees, the Ethics Reform Act of 1989 and the Judicial Conference regulations promulgated under the act, published advisory opinions of the Codes of Conduct Committee, and the Compendium of Selected Opinions of the Codes of Conduct Committee and a new Compendium of Selected Employee Opinions. With regard to advisory opinions issued by the Codes of Conduct Committee, the following opinions are of special interest to federal clerks:

- No. 51: Propriety of a Law Clerk to a Judge Working on a Case in Which a Party Is Represented by the Spouse's Law Firm
- No. 64: Employing a Judge's Child as Law Clerk
- No. 73: Requests for Letters of Recommendation and Similar Endorsements
- No. 74: Law Clerk's Future Employer
- No. 81: When Law Clerk's Future Employer Is the United States Attorney
- No. 83: Law Clerks' Bonuses and Reimbursement for Relocation and Bar-Related Expenses
- No. 92: Political Activities for Judicial Employees[2]

When determining whether certain behavior is permissible, you should keep in mind that the pertinent code of conduct for the court is not all-inclusive — it does not contain all applicable ethical restrictions. You must remember to review all relevant canons, statutes, regulations, and advisory opinions. An activity that may be permissible under a general section of a canon may not be permissible under one of the more specific provisions. Additionally, if you still have questions after examining the governing canons and statutes, the clerk should seek guidance from the judge.

◈ STATE COURT ALERT!

A judicial clerk in state court should determine whether the court has a code of conduct or statutes governing a clerk's ethical responsibilities. If so, obtain a copy of those canons or statutes and read them.

◈ HELPFUL HINT

A judicial clerk at either the federal or state court should also determine whether the employing judge has ethical guidelines that may be more restrictive than the governing canons or statutes and that may not permit conduct that is acceptable under the authorities.

---

2. Federal Judicial Center, *Maintaining the Public Trust: Ethics for Federal Judicial Law Clerks* 6 (Fed. Jud. Ctr. 2002).

II. Ethics

A. Common Ethical Problems

Just as federal judges' conduct must comport with the rules and guidelines set forth by the *Code of Judicial Conduct*, federal judicial clerks are bound by the ethical rules set forth in the Code of Conduct for Judicial Employees. While no code may apply to the conduct of judicial clerks in state courts, clerks are bound by the rules of professional responsibility that are generally applicable to all attorneys licensed by the bar to practice in that state. The ethical duties of clerks are the same as, or very similar to, those of judges.

While most ethics questions can be resolved using common sense, to avoid embarrassing the judge it is important that judicial clerks understand their ethical obligations. Ethical issues faced by judicial clerks most often arise in the following areas: (1) confidentiality; (2) conflicts of interest; (3) outside legal activities; (4) outside professional, social, and community activities; (5) political activity; and (6) receipt of honoraria or gifts.

1. Confidentiality: What Goes on in Chambers Stays in Chambers

Canon 3D of the Code of Conduct for Judicial Employees prohibits a judicial clerk from disclosing confidential information received in the course of the clerk's official duties, employing confidential information learned in the course of the clerk's duties for personal gain, and commenting on the merits of an action currently pending before the judge. To those ends, judicial clerks owe the judge complete confidentiality. A judicial clerk must keep the judge's confidences and protect the integrity of the court. Clerks should never reveal confidential information to the public. "Confidential information . . . includes any information . . . receive[d] in chambers that is not filed in the public docket" or that is not a matter of public record.[3] The judge's instructions or assessments of the case are confidential. Clerks should never comment on the judge's views or offer a personal appraisal of the judge's opinions. The judge is the only one who can or should communicate his or her personal views.

When dealing with attorneys, litigants, judicial clerks in other chambers, family or friends, or the press, judicial clerks may never discuss the substance of a case. Clerks may, however, refer members of the public to the public record. Additionally, if permitted to do so by the judge, clerks may also comment on technical and administrative matters, how the court works, and rules and procedures. Thus, court rules, court procedures, how the court operates, court records, and information disclosed in public

3. *Id.*

court proceedings are not confidential. However, the following information is always confidential and cannot be disclosed by a judicial clerk:

- Statements, or even hints, about the judge's likely actions in a case;
- Disclosure of the timing of a judge's decision or order, or any other
  judicial action, without the judge's authorization;
- The content of case-related discussions with a judge;
- Observations about the judge's decision-making process in specific
  cases;
- Documents or other information related to a sealed case; and
- Information obtained in the course of a law clerk's work that is not
  available to the general public.[4]

Attorneys will often telephone to speak with the judge's clerk. The
attorneys will wish to know how their cases are progressing or ask advice of
the clerk regarding a substantive or procedural matter. A clerk should
never engage in a substantive discussion of the case with counsel. If the
attorney attempts to find out what the judge is thinking, the clerk should
simply tell the attorney, "I'm sorry, but you will just have to wait until the
judge issues the opinion." With regard to procedural matters, a clerk may
refer counsel to the appropriate rule but should never, ever offer legal
advice.

Occasionally, a clerk will work on a case that interests the media.
Canon 3D of the Code of Conduct for Judicial Employees requires that
judicial clerks refrain from public comment on pending actions. Because
speaking to the press may reflect poorly on the court, even with regard to
the disclosure of information that is a matter of the public record, most
judges strongly oppose clerks speaking with the media.

Furthermore, judicial clerks should not gossip about the judge or the
court. A clerk should never reveal any off-bench remarks or behavior of
judges or comment on the collegiality of the judge. Any information to
which the clerk is privy due to the special relationship with the judge
should be kept confidential. Revealing such information "is incompatible
with the clerk's role as confidant and sounding board."[5] If the judge
cannot speak freely to the clerk, without fear that the judge's questions,
half-formed ideas, preliminary thoughts, or personal opinions would be
made public, the decision-making process would be seriously impaired.

Finally, a judicial clerk's obligation of confidentiality does not end
when the clerkship ends. The maxim "what goes on in chambers stays
in chambers"[6] operates even when the clerk leaves the court. Former clerks
are bound by the same restrictions on confidentiality that apply to current

---

4. *Id.*
5. Jones, *supra* note 1, at 776.
6. *See* Gerald Lebovits, *Judges' Clerks Play Varied Roles in the Opinion Drafting Process,* 76
N.Y. St. B.J. 34, 34 (July/Aug. 2004); Jones, *supra* note 1, at 775.

employees.[7] In fact, "[t]he conventional wisdom is that law clerks must take confidences to the grave."[8] "Confidential relationships simply would not be confidential if confidences could be breached as soon as the relationship ended."[9]

The need to keep the court's confidence raises some problems for a judicial extern who is required to submit a writing sample or to keep a journal or share his or her experiences with a faculty supervisor. When the judicial clerk begins the externship, if he or she is required to submit a writing sample to complete the externship class, the clerk must ask the judge whether a writing sample may be submitted to the faculty supervisor and ask what information may be included in a journal or shared with a faculty supervisor. The judge may allow the clerk to submit a writing sample as is, or the judge may require the clerk to redact all names of litigants and places to maintain confidentiality. With regard to a journal or sharing information with a faculty supervisor, the court may permit the clerk to discuss the cases in a general matter, omitting reference to the names of parties. However, the judge may forbid the submission of a writing sample from the court or the disclosure of any information in a journal. If this is the case, the clerk should speak immediately with his or her faculty supervisor and determine how to handle the writing requirement and the journal or reporting requirement.

2. CONFLICTS OF INTEREST: AVOIDING THE APPEARANCE OF IMPROPRIETY

Canon 3F(1) of the Code of Conduct for Judicial Employees requires judicial clerks to avoid conflicts of interest and the appearance of impropriety or partiality. Conflicts of interest arise when the clerk (or the clerk's spouse or other close relative) is so personally or financially affected by the matter before the court that a reasonable person would question the clerk's ability to remain impartial when performing his or her official duties. Conflicts arise out of financial interests and familial or employment relationships. Canon 3F(2) prohibits a clerk from performing his or her official duties with regard to a case currently pending before the judge when the clerk, or the clerk's spouse or resident minor child, has a financial interest in the subject matter or is a party to a case. Additionally, Canon 3F(2) prohibits a clerk from performing his or her official duties with regard to a case currently pending before the judge when the clerk, or a close relative, is a party, lawyer, or material witness, or has an interest that could be substantially affected by the outcome of a case. Furthermore, if the clerk has a personal bias or prejudice concerning a party to a case, or if the clerk served, or a lawyer with whom the clerk practiced serves, as

---

7. Federal Judicial Center, *supra* note 2, at 6-7.
8. Lebovits, *supra* note 6, at 34.
9. Richard W. Painter, *Clerks Honor Bound to Keep Confidences*, Wall St. J., May 8, 1998, at A15.

counsel in a case, Canon 3(F)(2) also prohibits the clerk from helping the judge.

Because an appellate court may disqualify the judge due to a clerk's continued participation in a matter where the clerk has a conflict of interest, when the clerk discovers that a conflict of interest exists, the clerk should immediately bring it to the judge's attention. As with most other decisions in the judge's court, "the decision about what to do about an apparent conflict of interest . . . belongs to the judge, not the clerk."[10]

a. Conflicts Arising out of Financial Interests

Judicial clerks, like judges, may not perform official duties in matters where they have a financial interest in either the subject matter of the litigation or in a party to a case. Financial interests that create a conflict of interest include ownership of stocks and other ownership interests. While ownership of just one share of stock in a party creates a conflict of interest, ownership of bonds or mutual funds generally do not create a conflict. Thus, it is imperative that a judicial clerk be aware of the clerk's financial interests so as to avoid working on matters that pose a financial conflict of interest. Additionally, as soon as the clerk is aware that such a conflict exists or may exist, the clerk should inform the judge of the conflict so that the judge can assign the case to another law clerk.

b. Conflicts Arising out of Professional and Familial Relationships

i. Professional Relationships

Because of the brief tenure of most judicial clerkships, conflicts of interest often arise out of the clerk's professional relationships. Conflicts resulting from professional relationships generally arise with paid judicial clerkships rather than unpaid externships. Often, when a clerk begins working with the judge, the clerk has already secured employment following the clerkship. A clerk who begins a term in chambers and is already assured of employment with a particular law firm or government agency must not work on cases before the court where the clerk's future employer serves as counsel. The judge will be able to avoid conflicts of interest with a "Chinese wall" — by isolating the clerk from the future employer's litigation.[11] This same rule applies to clerks who are in the job market seeking employment once their clerkship ends. Not only should a clerk inform the employing judge of any employment interviews or offers, but also "[w]hen a clerk has accepted a position with an attorney

---

10. Jones, *supra* note 1, at 778.
11. Rebecca A. Cochran, *Judicial Externships: The Clinic Inside the Courthouse* 33 (2d ed., Anderson 1999).

or with a firm, that clerk should cease further involvement in those cases in which the future employer has an interest."[12]

During the interview process, benefits provided by prospective employers in connection with the interview process, such as transportation and lodging, meals, and entertainment, may be accepted by a clerk.[13] Additional benefits may be offered following the clerk's acceptance of an offer of employment, including payment of bar-related expenses or signing and clerkship bonuses. While a clerk may not accept a bonus while employed by the judge, the clerk may be able to accept reimbursement of bar expenses if the employing judge agrees.

ii. Familial Relationships

Conflicts of interest can arise from a clerk's familial relationships. A conflict can arise when a clerk has a familial relationship with an individual who is a party or witness in a case pending before the judge. A conflict also arises when the clerk's spouse is an attorney working on a case pending before the judge. The same is true when the clerk's spouse is not involved in a case pending before the judge, but is simply a partner or associate at a firm handling the matter. Just as with professional relationships, judicial clerks owe the judge prompt notice of a familial relationship that affects a case in the judge's court.

c. Conflicts After the Clerkship

Even following a clerk's tenure with the court, conflicts of interest may remain. A clerk appearing before the judge as counsel in cases on which the clerk worked for the judge is not appropriate. Clerks should not work on any matter pending before the judge while the clerk was in chambers.

In addition to avoiding involvement on cases pending before the judge during the clerk's tenure with the court, some judges require that a specific amount of time pass before a former clerk can appear before the judge on any matter. The employing judge must be consulted about his or her policy on this matter.

d. Examples of Actual and Potential Conflicts of Interest

In *Maintaining the Public Trust: Ethics for Federal Judicial Law Clerks*, the Federal Judicial Center identifies several situations in which actual conflicts of interest would arise. These situations include the following:

- In a previous legal job, you worked on a lawsuit that is now assigned to your judge.
- A law firm that has hired you to work after your clerkship serves as counsel in a matter before your judge.

---

12. Jones, *supra* note 1, at 778.
13. Judicial Conference Gift Regulations §5(i).

- You witnessed a crime, and the alleged perpetrator's case is now before your judge.
- You or your spouse or minor resident child own stock in a company that is a party before your judge.
- Your sister or brother is a plaintiff in a class action lawsuit pending before your judge.[14]

If any of these situations arise, the clerk must immediately notify the judge.

The Federal Judicial Center also identifies some situations in which a conflict of interest *could* arise. These situations include the following:

- A neighbor's name appears on a witness list in a case your judge is handling.
- An attorney you meet at a social function, and with whom you engage in a long discussion, appears the next day to argue a motion before your judge.[15]

While these situations do not necessarily disqualify a clerk from working on a case, the clerk should immediately alert the judge to the potential conflict.

3. ACTIVITIES

For the most part, judicial clerks may engage in many of the same activities as any other member of the public. However, some activities by clerks are limited if participation in those activities could interfere with the clerk's duties or otherwise give the appearance of impropriety. The types of activities that are restricted include political activities, the private practice of law, and the receipt of gifts or honoraria.

a. Political Activities

A judicial clerk's ability to participate in political activities is limited. A clerk may engage in certain political activities that many Americans consider fundamental to participating in the democratic process. For instance, a clerk may belong to a political party and vote in primary and general elections. A clerk may also express a personal opinion about a candidate or political party, as long as it is clear that he or she is doing so as a private individual and not in his or her official capacity.

Clerks may not, however, engage in other political activities. Clerks may not serve as an officer of a political organization or organize political meetings. Nor may clerks publicly endorse a political candidate. Thus, a clerk may not work on political campaigns, solicit campaign contributions, or make campaign speeches. Clerks may not even contribute to a political campaign or wear candidates' buttons.

---

14. Federal Judicial Center, *supra* note 2, at 10.
15. *Id.*

b. Private Practice of Law

Generally, judicial clerks are not permitted to engage in the private practice of law. Several rationales justify this restriction. First, it would be extremely difficult for a clerk to satisfy his or her responsibilities to the court and to find the time necessary to competently practice law. Second, a conflict of interest may arise as the clerk owes a duty to both the court and clients. Third, even if no actual conflict arises, the clerk's behavior may give rise to the appearance of impropriety.

While clerks generally may not engage in the private practice of law, they may provide routine legal work for family members, such as drafting a will, and other pro bono services. However, clerks may not render such services if they interfere with the clerk's ability to perform his or her official duties, create the appearance of impropriety, or rely on information gleaned from the clerk's position with the court or otherwise exploit that position. If you intend to engage in outside legal activities, be sure to check with the judge. What is and is not appropriate is within the discretion of the judge.

c. Receipt of Gifts or Honoraria

The restrictions on the receipt of gifts and honoraria primarily apply to paid judicial clerks. Externs, who are generally law students, are not typically affected by these restrictions. With regard to gifts, clerks are limited to receiving gifts from family and friends on holidays or for other special occasions, gifts arising from a spouse's business or professional activities, and social hospitality. Clerks may not receive gifts intended to influence them in the performance of their official duties.

An honorarium is "a payment of money or anything of value for an appearance, speech, or article."[16] A clerk may receive compensation for teaching and for a writing that is more extensive than an article, such as a book. The Judicial Conference has concluded that such compensation is not an honorarium. A clerk may also accept a memento or token of no commercial value that is given in connection with the clerk's participation in an event, such as a bar-related function or symposium, or for drafting an article.

B. Exercises

Imagine that you are clerking for Judge Onest, either as an unpaid extern or as a paid law clerk. Read the following hypotheticals and decide whether they present an ethical dilemma. If they do, explain why. What action should you take? If you find no ethical problem exists, explain why it does not.

---

16. 5 U.S.C., appx. 7 §505(3).

1. Your spouse is an attorney representing a party in a case before the judge.

2. An attorney who works for your spouse's law firm represents a party in a case before the judge.

3. In law school, you were on law review and wrote a case note expressing your opinion on the merits of a case now on appeal before the judge.

4. An environmental hazard in a case before the judge borders your parents' property.

5. An attorney from a law firm at which you interviewed for a job following your clerkship represents a party in a case before the judge.

6. Your aunt is a plaintiff in a class action suit pending before the judge.

7. Three months after your clerkship with Judge Onest ended, a case in which you are counsel is assigned to the judge.

8. You are in open court and witness a humorous exchange between Judge Onest and an attorney. You decide to share this funny story by publishing it as a cartoon in the state bar journal.

9. You clerked for Judge Onest three years ago. During your clerkship, the judge presided over a prisoner litigation case in which the plaintiff claimed that he was Rastafarian and his First Amendment rights were being violated because the prison required him to cut his hair. In a previous lawsuit, this same prisoner raised the same First Amendment violations but claimed to be a Native American. You are at a cocktail party and want to tell this funny story and share the judge's views of the plaintiff.

10. You clerked for Judge Onest in federal district court. Later, Judge Onest is nominated to be a justice on the U.S. Supreme Court. A journalist approaches you and wants to interview you about the judge. The journalist inquires about several things, including the process used by the judge to make decisions and the judge's personal views on controversial issues like gun control and abortion.

11. You are clerking for Judge Onest in federal district court. Bud Howard, a longtime political hero of yours, is running for the U.S. Senate. You want to volunteer on Bud Howard's political campaign. Can you?

12. You are clerking for Judge Onest in federal district court. Bud Howard, a longtime political hero of your spouse, is running for the U.S. Senate. Your spouse wants to make a financial contribution to Howard's political campaign. Can he or she?

13. Following your clerkship, you went to work for a firm. One day, a coworker walks into your office and asks you what Judge Onest's views are on filing a motion requesting permission to file a sur-reply and what arguments might convince the judge to grant such a request. Can you answer this question? Why or why not?

Additional Resources

◆ Rebecca A. Cochran, *Judicial Externships: The Clinic Inside the Courthouse* (2d ed., Anderson 1999).

◆ Federal Judicial Center, *Chambers Handbook for Judges' Law Clerks and Secretaries* (West 1994).

◆ Federal Judicial Center, Code of Conduct for Judicial Employees (Fed. Jud. Ctr. 1996).

◆ Federal Judicial Center, *Maintaining the Public Trust: Ethics for Federal Judicial Law Clerks* (Fed. Jud. Ctr. 2002).

◆ John Paul Jones, *Some Ethical Considerations for Judicial Clerks*, 4 Geo. J. Legal Ethics 771 (1990-1991).

◆ Gerald Lebovits, *Judges' Clerks Play Varied Roles in the Opinion Drafting Process*, 76 N.Y. St. B.J. 34 (July/Aug. 2004).

CHAPTER 5 | Research Process

I. Research Tips

Judges are extremely busy because of the caseload facing the courts and do not have the time necessary to read the authorities governing all of the legal principles at issue in each case. Therefore, judges will often assign cases to their judicial clerks and request that the clerk not only research the issues in the briefs but also prepare a draft of a court document, often a judicial opinion or bench memorandum. Because "[a] well-crafted judicial decision can be made only in the context of precedent[,] the law clerk's role is to make sure the judge has the materials with which to understand the jurisprudence related to the case."[1] Thus, legal research is the most important task you will be asked to perform.

When researching the issues presented in counsels' briefs, you should check the authorities that counsel for the litigants relied on. You should review these authorities to determine whether they were accurately interpreted and cited by counsel. You should also update those authorities to ensure that they remain good law and that no other applicable authorities have been issued since the briefs were filed.

However, you must not rely solely on the authorities presented in the litigants' briefs. While you must check each of the listed authorities presented in counsels' briefs for relevance and accuracy, you must also conduct independent research. You must determine whether counsel for the

---

1. Federal Judicial Center, *Chambers Handbook for Judges' Law Clerks and Secretaries* 139 (West 1994).

litigants have overlooked controlling precedent or any other authorities that may be helpful to the court.

A. Getting Started

Whenever given an assignment, you should ask some preliminary questions to ensure its successful completion. First, you should always ask if there is a deadline for the assignment. If so, you must determine how much time to devote to research and when to begin the writing process. You must also be sure to complete the assignment by that deadline. Second, you should determine what type of work product the judge wants you to produce. Does the judge want you to draft an opinion and order? A bench memorandum? Or does the judge simply want you to report orally on what you found? Establishing what type of work product to complete is important. You do not want to produce the wrong document for the judge. Additionally, the research necessary to produce a satisfactory judicial opinion is much greater and goes into much more depth than that required for a bench memorandum or an oral report. You do not want to perform too much or too little research.

Third, you should ask the judge or the staff attorney whether a specific legal resource is commonly recognized as authoritative with regard to the legal area you are researching. Judges often rely on such resources when resolving issues and sometimes even cite to these resources in their opinions. Therefore, you should be aware of and consult these resources when appropriate. For instance, federal courts often cite to *Moore's Federal Practice*[2] or Wright and Miller's *Federal Practice and Procedure*[3] when dealing with issues of civil and criminal procedure. With evidentiary matters, the courts rely on *Weinstein's Federal Evidence.*[4] With regard to drafting jury instructions, most of the federal courts of appeal have pattern jury instructions, which are found on the court's website.

Fourth, ask the judge or the staff attorney if they have any research pointers regarding the issues in the case. For instance, the judge or staff attorney may mention a particular legal term or term of art that you could use as a search term. A term of art is a "short expression that . . . conveys a fairly well-agreed meaning, and . . . saves the many words that would otherwise be needed to convey that meaning."[5]

After obtaining answers to the preliminary questions listed above, you should take a couple of additional preparatory steps. First, you should make certain that you understand the specific legal issue that is before the court. This can most successfully be accomplished by recording the

---

2. James William Moore, Daniel R. Coquillette, Gregory P. Joseph, Sol Schrieber, Jerold Solovy & Georgene Viaro, *Moore's Federal Practice* (3d ed., Matthew Bender 1997).
3. Charles Alan Wright et al., *Federal Practice and Procedure* (West 2010).
4. Joseph M. McLaughlin, *Weinstein's Federal Evidence* (2d ed., Matthew Bender 1997).
5. Robert W. Benson, *The End of Legalese: The Game Is Over*, 13 N.Y.U. Rev. L. & Soc. Change 519, 561 (1984-1985).

issue in writing. Articulating the issue in writing helps you to clarify the issue and indicates whether your understanding of the issue is accurate and precise. Misunderstanding the issue may cause you to waste precious time researching the wrong issue.

The next step you should take before starting the research process is to review the facts of the case before the court. The facts of the case are important in the research process because the trial judge will apply the law to those facts. When the facts of the precedents are distinguishable from the case currently before the court, those cases may have little relevance. The only relevant information from those authorities may be the general legal principle that governs the issue.

Once you have obtained answers to the preliminary questions regarding the time frame for the assignment, the type of document that is to be produced, whether specific legal resources exist that apply to the area at issue and which the court holds in high regard, and whether certain terms of art exist, and you have identified the issues before the court and the facts of the case, you are ready to begin the research process.

B. The Research Process

The research process includes creating search terms, determining which sources to consult, conducting the research itself, examining the authorities discovered, and updating those authorities. If you have difficulty at any stage of the research process, you can seek assistance from the court's reference librarian. While the presence of librarians in state courts may vary from court to court, in the federal court system all circuit courts have a court librarian, as do many of the district courts. Librarians can assist you in many tasks, including recommending what area of law to research, devising search terms, identifying the available resources, determining what is faulty in the researcher's research strategy when it is not successful, and obtaining a resource on loan from another library.

1. CREATING SEARCH TERMS

The first step you should take when researching in print or online is to prepare a list of search terms. When devising those search terms, you should ask certain questions that resemble the questions asked by reporters — who, what, when, where, and why? The answer to those questions will be the search terms that you use to begin your research.

Who: You should determine who the parties are in terms of their legal relationship. Are the parties a landlord and tenant? An employer and employee? A physician and patient? An educator and student?

What: You should determine what area of law, including claims and affirmative defenses, is involved in the litigation. For instance, when filing the complaint, did the plaintiff file a negligence action or a breach of contract claim against the defendant? In answering the claim, did the defendant assert an affirmative defense, such as self-defense or battered woman syndrome? In addition to the claims and defenses asserted by the parties, you should determine what relief the plaintiff is seeking. Does the plaintiff seek an injunction? Or does the plaintiff seek monetary damages, including compensatory and/or punitive damages?

When: You should determine when the events in controversy occurred. Generally, the specific date on which the events took place will not be important. However, if the question before the court is governed by a statute or is a question that rests on the date of the events, such as a statute of limitations question, then the date may well matter.

Where: You should determine where the events took place. The location of the events is important both jurisdictionally and substantively. The location of the events determines which court(s) will have jurisdiction over the litigation and what law governs the dispute. Additionally, the law governing the dispute may also be affected by the location where the action occurred. For instance, if the events occurred in or near a public school, hospital, confessional, or on federal property, a different rule of law may be applicable than if it did not occur in those places.

Why: You should identify why the parties acted as they did. This concerns their motives and intentions. Was the conduct of a party negligent? Reckless? Intentional?

2. DETERMINING WHICH SOURCES TO CONSULT

The second step in the research process is to determine which sources you will consult. Two general types of authorities exist — secondary sources and primary sources of law. Secondary sources are not law; they simply review an area of law and are often written by experts in the field, law professors, or law students. Primary sources of authority, on the other hand, are the law. You will find both secondary and primary sources of law helpful in different ways.

You have likely been introduced to legal research at this stage in your legal education. Therefore, this section will not provide a detailed review of the sources of law but will offer advice on when to search in secondary sources as well as helpful tips regarding specific primary sources of law.

a. Secondary Sources

When determining which resources to consult, you should evaluate your level of knowledge about the areas of law being researched. If you know little to nothing about an area of law, then you should begin by reviewing secondary sources, including legal encyclopedias, annotations from the *American Law Reports*, law review articles, and specialized treatises. Although secondary sources are not law, they can help you gain a rudimentary understanding of an area of law. Secondary sources may help you refine some search terms or identify relevant terms of art with which you may not be familiar. Additionally, secondary sources may identify primary authorities, which are "the law," for you to review.

If you are researching secondary sources electronically, you must decide whether to search on Westlaw or LexisNexis. The type of research you are conducting is the key to determining whether to conduct secondary research in Westlaw or LexisNexis. Generally, if conducting legal research, Westlaw and LexisNexis are equally good. You could search in either Westlaw's "Topical Practice Areas" database or LexisNexis's "Areas of Law by Topic" database. These databases, much like the table of contents in print resources, are organized by subject and cover a wide range of topics. However, Westlaw has a slight edge with regard to legal research in secondary sources since *American Law Reports* is no longer located on LexisNexis. That source is now unique to Westlaw. On the other hand, LexisNexis has an edge if you are researching nonlegal matters, such as a news event. LexisNexis carries far more nonlegal newspapers and magazines than Westlaw.[6]

Specialized treatises are good research tools because they provide a scholarly analysis of a particular area of law. The author will provide a critical analysis of the area of law, which includes an extensive interpretation of doctrines and significant cases. Additionally, the author will often express an opinion about the current state of the law and suggest how the law ought to develop. Some treatises include the text of relevant legislation, legislative histories, and regulations. Because of the depth of coverage offered by a treatise and the expertise of the author, some treatises are extremely influential and have helped to shape the development of the law. Both Westlaw and LexisNexis include treatises. LexisNexis carries treatises published by Matthew Bender, which are well respected by the legal community. Westlaw includes most of the Thompson West treatises, including many state-specific treatises.

Furthermore, if researching a particular state's law, you should determine whether a legal encyclopedia focusing on that state's law exists. If so, state encyclopedias often include annotations to references not mentioned in more global encyclopedias like *American Jurisprudence Second* or *Corpus Juris Secundum*. However, you should remember that lawyers almost never cite secondary sources. You must cite to primary authorities for any legal propositions. Furthermore, you must verify all statements of law found in a secondary source to distinguish the author's opinions from what the court's decision actually stated.

b. Primary Authorities

As stated previously, primary authorities are the law. Primary authorities include statutes, administration regulations, and case law. While primary authorities include both mandatory and persuasive authorities, you should focus the search on finding mandatory authorities that are

6. The contents and scope of the databases in Westlaw and LexisNexis change constantly. Be sure to contact customer support for assistance if you cannot locate a particular source.

binding in your jurisdiction. Throughout the research process, you should
carefully distinguish between binding and persuasive authorities, devoting
the majority of your effort to locating and reviewing mandatory authority.
Persuasive authorities, or authorities that are law in another jurisdiction,
can be helpful when dealing with an issue of first impression in your jurisdiction or when there is a gap in the law governing the issue in your
jurisdiction.

i. Statutes

The next step is to determine whether a statute governs the area of law
in question. When using print resources to conduct statutory research,
whether in a federal or state jurisdiction, you should use an annotated
version of the code. Regardless of whether you are researching in a
print code or on Westlaw or LexisNexis, if you discover a controlling
statute, you should check the annotations following the text of the statute
to identify other relevant sources of authority. Furthermore, to decide
whether the current version of the statute is relevant to the litigation
before the court, you should check the history of any amendments to
the statute to determine the manner in which the statute was amended
and the date the amendment went into effect.

Additionally, you should not only review the statute that you discovered while researching, but you should also examine the greater statutory
scheme into which that statute fits. You can gain an understanding of the
statutory scheme by examining the table of contents that sets forth the
organization of the relevant code sections and by reviewing the statutes
that precede and follow the statute. The surrounding statutes will often
provide useful information, such as a purpose statement or definitions of
terms found in the statute. Serendipity will sometimes allow a researcher to
locate other statutes that may affect the issue that were not identified when
conducting the initial search.

Westlaw and LexisNexis each contain annotated codes that can be
searched through keyword searches or browsed using a table of contents
feature. The table of contents feature allows you to review statutes that
precede and follow the relevant statute by clicking on buttons labeled
"previous" and "next." While the statutory research features on Westlaw
and LexisNexis are similar, conducting statutory research on Westlaw is
somewhat more efficient than on LexisNexis. When you are viewing a
statute on the screen, Westlaw automatically updates the statute using
KeyCite. When looking at the screen, you will see the text of the statute
on the right side of the screen and the KeyCite references for that statute
on the left. KeyCite also uses flags to alert the researcher of any action that
affected that statute or if such action is pending. KeyCite flags denote that
pending legislation may affect the statute, that there is an amendment to
the statute, or that a court has determined the constitutionality or uncon-
stitutionality of the statute.

An important tip to remember is that statutory research is often easier to conduct in print resources than online. First, when conducting electronic statutory research, a word search will retrieve only the terms specified. If the search terms do not include the statutory language, the search will not be fruitful. On the other hand, an index to a code in print is organized by subject and includes cross-references to direct the researcher to the correct terms or concepts. Second, while online resources allow you to browse using a table of contents and to review surrounding statutes, the process is somewhat difficult to navigate and may cause you to get lost or overwhelmed. Print resources, however, allow you to easily flip back and forth between the table of contents and various statutes to determine if other statutes may be relevant to the issue and to understand the overall statutory scheme.

ii. Regulations

When a statute governs an area of law, an important tip to remember is that references to regulations are often found in the annotations following a statute in annotated codes. The print U.S. Code Service (U.S.C.S.) contains more references to regulations than does the print U.S. Code Annotated (U.S.C.A.). However, there is no distinction in this regard between the electronic versions of the U.S.C.S. and the U.S.C.A.

On the other hand, if you do not locate a reference to regulations from an annotated code or secondary sources, you must determine whether regulations exist that affect how the law operates. Federal agencies create regulations to implement legislation enacted by Congress. Proposed regulations and newly adopted regulations are published in the *Federal Register*. Regulations are then codified in the *Code of Federal Regulations* (C.F.R.). The print C.F.R. is updated annually. Westlaw and LexisNexis carry the C.F.R. and incorporate amendments and new regulations more frequently than the print C.F.R. An electronic version of the C.F.R., called the "e-CFR," is also located on the Government Printing Office's website. The Government Printing Office updates the e-CFR daily.

iii. Cases

In addition to statutory and regulatory research, you must conduct case law research. When determining which digest to consult or which online database to select, remember that the narrower the source, the more efficient your search will be. For instance, if searching Westlaw for cases that are mandatory precedent in the U.S. Court of Appeals for the Sixth Circuit, one would not select the ALLFEDS database, which compiles cases decided by all federal courts, but rather a database limited to cases decided by the Sixth Circuit and the U.S. Supreme Court. Additionally, if searching with the print digests, it would be wise to search the *Federal Practice Digest*, which will direct you to decisions issued only by federal courts. This will make the research more efficient and far less overwhelming.

When conducting case law research, remember to identify the relevant West topic and key numbers and examine the pertinent headnotes. You can search topic and key numbers in print digests or electronically on Westlaw by conducting a key number search. Once you have identified a relevant topic and key number, you must review surrounding key numbers to determine whether they are relevant and to determine whether there are additional cases that may be on point. Some tips for shortcutting the search for the proper topic and key numbers include reviewing the headnotes identified by some secondary sources, by the cases relied on in the briefs by counsel for the litigants, and by the key number outlines found in the West Digest System.

When researching cases electronically on Westlaw, some researchers choose to begin with a natural language search or a Boolean search rather than a topic and key number search. When you know little about the area of law, you can start with a natural language search. This type of search will often produce sufficient information to assist you in forming a more specific Boolean search. However, you must remember that a natural language search will not retrieve all relevant authorities. Thus, you must supplement a natural language search with a Boolean search or a topic and key number search.

c. Internet Resources

There are many helpful online resources in addition to Westlaw and LexisNexis. These online resources include federal government resources, private resources that are free to use, and private resources that charge a fee.

Several federal government websites provide helpful information. FirstGov (*http://www.firstgov.gov*) is the U.S. government's official portal to many government resources, including statutes and regulations. FDsys (*http://www.gpoaccess.gov/fdsys*) is a service offered by the Government Printing Office. FDsys contains the *Federal Register*, the *Code of Federal Regulations*, and the *United States Code*, as well as congressional bills, hearings, and reports. FDsys was formerly GPO Access; this database is somewhat easier to use than FirstGov. Thomas (*http://thomas.loc.gov*) is the Library of Congress's website containing legislative information, including the *Congressional Record*, committee reports, and other legislative history documents. Additionally, each federal court has a website that provides helpful information for that jurisdiction. State courts have such websites as well.

There are some free legal research websites that operate somewhat like Westlaw and LexisNexis. Two of the better websites include FindLaw (*http://www.findlaw.com*) and the American Bar Association's Lawlink Legal Research Jumpstation (*http://www.abanet.org/lawlink/home.html*). Furthermore, many state bar associations are in the Casemaker consortium, which is another free legal research system. Google Scholar (*http://scholar.google.com*) includes a free search engine for researching legal opinions for federal and state trial courts, intermediate appellate courts, and courts of last resort. Once you access Google Scholar, click the "Legal opinions and journals" radio button, and type your query in the search box. You can search for cases by case name (e.g., *Gideon v. Wainright*) or by topic (e.g., student free speech). Justia (*http://www.justia.com*) is another free online source for researching the law and secondary sources.

Other fee-based legal research websites in addition to Westlaw and LexisNexis provide helpful legal materials. These websites contain a wide variety of information. Two such websites are Loislaw (*http://loislaw.com*) and VersusLaw (*http://www.versuslaw.com*).

If you are conducting online research and discover a website that seems helpful, you must evaluate the source of the information. Anyone can publish information on the Internet. Sometimes that information is accurate and unbiased; sometimes it is not. If it is a government website, it is generally safe to rely on it. However, if the website is hosted by an organization or a private individual, some investigation may be necessary to determine if the organization or individual is likely to present skewed information. If so, do not rely on the website.

3. Examining and Updating the Authorities

Once your research has yielded seemingly relevant authorities, you must review those authorities to determine whether they are applicable to the litigation before the court. With regard to pertinent cases, you should also review the cases cited by those authorities. The authorities relied on by the initial cases will often be more on point than the initial cases.

Once you have discovered the relevant statutes, regulations, and cases, you must update those authorities by cite checking, which is often referred to as "shepardizing." Cite checking is done to ensure that the authorities found while researching remain good law, to discover more recent decisions, and to find more authoritative or better-reasoned decisions. Electronic cite checking can be conducted using Shepard's, which is located on LexisNexis, or KeyCite, which is found on Westlaw.

Although it is analytically useful to view updating as the final step in the research process, with finding and reading the law as the first two steps in the process, it is important to remember that the research process is not linear. The research process is more like a wheel, which has no beginning and ending point. The researcher is continuously looping through the stages of research. For example, you may find and read a case that is on point and update that case to make certain that it remains good law. However, that case may have mentioned another case that the researcher has not already discovered while researching. You will then need to locate this new case, read it, and if it is on point, update this new case.

II. Taking Research Notes

As a researcher, you may spend a considerable amount of time working on a research problem and reading a large number of sources. Often, the research process is interrupted, either by a more pressing assignment or the end of the workday. To avoid memory lapses and duplication of effort, you must have an organized, concise method for taking notes on your findings.

Given the number of sources that need to be read, you cannot remember everything. When you work without notes, you will often have to duplicate earlier steps in the research process. For example, when you find a case, you will read it initially to determine whether it is relevant to the research issue. Then you will read it again if you come across the citation further along in the research process and cannot recall whether you have already read the source. Then you will read it a third time when preparing a document for the court. Another example of duplicated effort that could be avoided by good note taking arises when you come across a source while researching but initially determine that the source is not relevant and discard it without noting how the source was located. Later, if you discover that the source was useful for a given purpose and cannot remember the citation to the source or which research tool lead to the source, you will have to repeat steps in an effort to relocate the source. Both of these scenarios result in a tremendous waste of time. Effective note taking is the only way to avoid needlessly wasting time. While taking notes takes time, it saves considerably more time then it uses.

"Because lawyers' livelihoods depend so heavily on doing research and doing it efficiently,"[7] an effective note-taking process is a tool that furthers that purpose. This chapter provides a four-step approach to note taking that a novice researcher can use in whole or in part, and it summarizes some of the note-taking tips that effective legal researchers have discovered. Because each researcher will develop a unique note-taking style, a researcher may modify the recommended approach in any manner that makes the approach more useful to that researcher. However, "by incorporating some of the following time-tested fundamentals, each researcher [will not] have to reinvent the wheel."[8]

---

7. Christopher G. Wren & Jill Robinson Wren, *The Legal Research Manual: A Game Plan for Legal Research and Analysis* 124 (2d ed., Legal Educ. 1986).
    8. *Id.*

A. The Four-Step Approach to Note Taking[9]

1. STEP ONE: THE PLAN

List your search terms at the top of a page. Beneath these search terms, list all the primary and secondary sources of law that will be consulted. For instance, if researching forgery, you would consult, among other things, a statutory code and the case digests. These generic sources would appear listed on the page. Under each generic entry would be listed the specific source to be searched, such as the West Virginia Code Index or the *South Eastern Digest*. The search terms are listed under each specific source, so that you can keep track of which term has been examined in which source. If a term is examined in a source and no information is located, you should indicate this by striking a line through that search term. If the research source refers you to an authority, you should note the citation to that authority under the search term.

Finally, the information recorded during this step in the note-taking process will serve as the research trail. It will record every source that has been consulted and the date it was consulted, every search term that was researched in a particular source, and every authority referenced by that source. By tracking this information, you can flow smoothly in and out of the research process. You will not need to remember where you stopped researching when last interrupted — the information will be recorded in the research notes. Thus, you can pick up the trail where you left off, without fear of repetition or of overlooking vital information.

If researching electronically, a researcher's activity is recorded by Westlaw's "research trail" and Lexis's "history" function. These online services record not just the searches ran, but also the number of results from each search and the amount of time the researcher spent on each search. While these websites save the research activity for a period of time, you should still print out your research activity.

RESEARCH HYPOTHETICAL

You are a judicial extern for Judge Gracious Wigal in the 17th Judicial Circuit in Monongalia County, West Virginia. The case the judge asked you to research concerns a defendant, John Hood, who was charged with forgery and check kiting. The charges arose from an incident in which Hood paid for a used car with a bad check and then paid for the tags and title with a stolen check that belonged to another man who shared the same name as Hood.

---

continues on next page

9. This four-step note-taking process is adapted from materials produced by Professor Grace Wigal at West Virginia University College of Law.

You have partially completed the research needed for this assignment. When you devised your research strategy, you decided to begin by looking for relevant primary authorities, such as statutes and case law. You also decided to search some secondary sources to help you gain an understanding of the general area of law and to help you differentiate between the crimes of forgery and check kiting.

Your next step was to create search terms. The terms that you decided on were forgery, impersonation, check, and draft. When you searched the West Virginia Code, your searches under forgery hit pay dirt (you discovered three statutes that seemed to be on point), although the search under impersonation was a dead end. Rather than searching under check or draft, you decided to continue following the forgery/impersonation line of research and moved on to search for cases. When you ran searches in the digests (or searched the West key number system) for forgery and impersonation, you found some topics and key numbers that seemed to be on point. Your search under check, however, was another dead end.

See Figure 5-1 at the end of the chapter for a sample page of the information recorded at this step in the note-taking process.

2. STEP TWO: ACTIONS TAKEN WITH REGARD TO EACH AUTHORITY

Step two allows you to track several things. First, list all the authorities to which the sources you consulted directed you. Thus, in a column down the left side of the page, you would list any statutes, topic and key numbers, or specific secondary sources that seemed relevant. When reading through those authorities, you will see references to other authorities that look helpful. Rather than running to get that authority at that moment, you should note the citation and examine the new authority at a later, more convenient point in the research process. Thus, in a column down the middle of the page, list the citations to any cases that you discovered when reading the annotations to a statute or searching the headnotes under a particular topic and key number.

Next, note the actions that you have taken with regard to each of the authorities listed. It will be extremely helpful to use a code to help track your actions and to prevent you from rereading, overlooking, or failing to update authorities. For instance, if an authority has been printed, place a check mark beside the citation. Draw a line through a citation to show that you have read the authority and found it irrelevant. Place an asterisk beside an authority that you believe to be especially important. For those authorities that are relevant, note whether they have been updated or "shepardized." If the authorities have been updated, the date on which they were updated should be noted. If the authorities remain good law, use a symbol to note that information. If they have received negative treatment, note the type of negative treatment the authority has received and whether it can still be used for some purpose.

RESEARCH HYPOTHETICAL (CONTINUED)

When you searched the topics and key numbers that you located, you wrote down the citations to the cases that appeared relevant. You then located those cases, skimmed them, determined which cases were on point and which were not, and wrote down any citations to sources that the relevant authorities directed you to. For those authorities that were helpful, you updated them to be sure that they were still good law.

See Figure 5-2 at the end of the chapter for a sample page of the information recorded at this step in the note-taking process.

---

3. STEP THREE: NOTES ON INDIVIDUAL AUTHORITIES

At this stage in the note-taking process, you should take notes on specific authorities that are relevant to the issue before the court. Notes on the authorities should be taken separately; devote a page to each individual authority. The full citation to an authority should be placed at the top of the page. Follow the citation with a brief description of the facts and the outcome of the case. The notes following the facts should include any relevant information that you may rely on when drafting a legal document, including governing rules of law, reasoning, or quotable passages. If an authority contains a quotable passage, note that it contains a "good quote," include the page on which the passage is located, and paraphrase the passage. Also, include the actual holding of the case and the page on which it is located.

When taking notes on individual authorities, you should also record any tentative conclusions you may reach regarding how those authorities affect the litigation before the court. While your opinions may change as you discover new principles or learn more about how they apply to the facts before the court, recording those opinions throughout the process will help you avoid returning to an opinion that you later conclude is inaccurate. Additionally, recording tentative conclusions allows you to subject those views to closer scrutiny, thus enabling you to detect errors in reasoning and to develop new avenues of research.

> **RESEARCH HYPOTHETICAL (CONTINUED)**
>
> After locating pertinent cases and recording the new sources to which they direct you, you took detailed notes on the cases that seem useful. Your notes on these cases are essentially a brief of each case, recording all the relevant information that might be helpful to you later in drafting a memorandum for the judge. You note the citation to the case, identify the facts and procedural history, the issue, the court's reasoning, and its holding.
>
> See Figure 5-3 at the end of the chapter for a sample page of the information recorded at this step in the note-taking process.

4. STEP FOUR: THE RESEARCH OUTLINE

The final step in the note-taking process is to assimilate the notes from the authorities into a research outline. The research outline will not necessarily be used to aid in organizing the document that you are drafting for the court; rather, the outline will be used to aid your understanding of the areas of law at issue. The research outline will trace the analysis of an issue from the beginning to the end and allow you to identify any gaps in the research that may exist. For instance, if the issue before the court is one of negligence, the prima facie test consists of the elements duty, breach, causation, and harm. If your research outline reveals that information regarding the elements of duty, breach, and harm has been located, but no information has been located with regard to causation, you will have to complete additional research regarding that element.

The creation of a research outline should be completed simultaneously with step three of the note-taking process. When beginning the outline, list the issues that are before the court for resolution. As you read relevant authorities and identify rules of law governing the different issues before the court, record the legal principles and any relevant reasoning under the proper issue, and note which authority or authorities stand for that particular principle or proposition. Thus, a research outline allows you to determine where a particular authority fits (or does not fit) into the analysis of an issue.

Finally, the research outline will be of great help when you sit down to begin the writing process. Although the issues may not be discussed in the written work product in the same order that they appear in the research outline, the research outline will serve as a good starting point when determining how to organize the written document. You should also annotate the research outline by circling or underlining the points that you want to mention in the final work product. You may even wish to number the points to indicate the order in which those points should be discussed. This will allow you to easily convert your research outline and notes into a working outline for the final written work product.

RESEARCH HYPOTHETICAL (CONTINUED)

After reading the authorities that you have located, you begin to draft a research outline. The outline notes which statute governs the crime, the penalty for the crime, the elements of the prima facie case, any relevant defenses (and the citations to where information regarding those defenses is located), and which party bears the burden of proof. Please keep in mind that the outline will evolve and become more detailed as you complete more research.

See Figure 5-4 at the end of the chapter for a sample page of the information recorded at this step in the note-taking process.

B. Summary

The four-step note-taking approach will provide a written record of your research and will help to ensure that your research is complete and organized. As you gain experience as a legal researcher, less note taking will be necessary and your note taking will become more streamlined. However, the principles identified above will continue to be helpful.

III. When to Stop Researching: The Circular Theory of Research

The suggestions in this chapter will help you become an efficient researcher. In addition to helping you gain speed, these suggestions will help you be thorough. However, given that the research process is like a wheel that will not stop until the researcher stops its rotation (see Figure 5-5), a researcher will always ask herself when it is time to stop researching. There is no easy answer to that question. A good rule of thumb is to continue researching if you suspect that you might benefit from additional research. Unfortunately, novice researchers such as judicial externs generally lack confidence in their research skills and feel that they are missing something. Remember that the perfect authority seldom exists — if it did, the answer to the problem would be clear and there likely would be no need to research the issue. Thus, if you feel that you might benefit from additional research, just remember that at some point, "the benefit of continuing to research will be too small to justify the additional effort."[10] When you feel that the research is going in circles, with each new source referring to the same authorities that have already been located and to no new authorities, you can conclude that you have likely discovered all worthwhile authorities bearing on the research problem. The research can be safely concluded at this point, because continuing efforts will not yield new leads or authorities.

Figure 5-5.   THE CIRCULAR THEORY OF RESEARCH

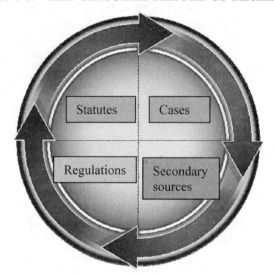

Additional Resources

- Robert W. Benson, *The End of Legalese: The Game Is Over*, 13 N.Y.U. Rev. L. & Soc. Change 519 (1984-1985).
- Federal Judicial Center, *Chambers Handbook for Judges' Law Clerks and Secretaries* (West 1994).
- Amy E. Sloan, *Basic Legal Research: Tools and Strategies* (4th ed., Aspen 2009).
- Christopher G. Wren & Jill Robinson Wren, *The Legal Research Manual: A Game Plan for Legal Research and Analysis* (2d ed., Legal Educ. 1986).

10. Amy E. Sloan, *Basic Legal Research: Tools and Strategies* 318 (4th ed., Aspen 2009).

Figure 5-1.   STEP ONE: THE PLAN

Descriptive Words: forgery, impersonation, check, draft

PRIMARY SOURCES

Statutory Codes
   W. Va. Code Index
      √ Forgery   √ ~~Impersonation~~
         61-4-5
         61-4-6
         65-2-1
      Check   Draft

Digests w/Topics and Key Numbers
   S.E. Digest Index
      √ Forgery   √ ~~Check~~
         False Pretenses #26
         False Pretenses #27
         Forgery #3

      √ Impersonation   Draft
         False Pretenses #29

SECONDARY SOURCES

Law Reviews
      Forgery   Impersonation
      Check   Draft

Treatises
      Forgery   Impersonation
      Check   Draft

Figure 5-2.   STEP TWO: ACTIONS TAKEN

Source	Citations (found in sources listed in column 1)	Updated?
False Pretenses #26 (Va.-W. Va. Digest)	X 618 S.E.2d 765	NA
	X 623 S.E.2d 324 (evidence)	NA
	X 593 S.E.2d 324	NA
False Pretenses #26 (Va.-W. Va. Digest 2002 Pocket)	√ 645 S.E.2d 461*	Yes — good
	√ 721 S.E.2d 438*	Yes — criticized
	√ 575 F.2d 394	Yes — good*
645 S.W.2d 461	√ 523 S.E.2d 681	
	75 ALR 3d 327	
75 ALR 3d 327	267 S.E.2d 619	

Figure 5-3. STEP THREE: NOTES

Watts v. State, 645 S.E.2d 461 (W. Va. 1983).

Facts and Procedure

D paid for auto repairs w/credit card issued to someone else. D pleaded guilty to credit card abuse charge. Sentence suspended; D put on probation. Probation revoked and sentence went into effect.

Issue

D appealed—charge underlying conviction defective b/c the "knowingly" language in indictment related only to card not being issued to D, but did not relate to his use of it w/o cardholder's consent.

Reasoning

Indictment alleged that D "w/intent to fraudulently obtain automobile repair service from A.I. Graves, did present a Montgomery Ward credit card w/ knowledge that the card had not been issued to [D], and that card was not used w/the effective consent of the cardholder, Carol Ann Blennert . . . ."

In similar case, indictment alleged that D "intentionally and knowingly, w/intent to fraudulently obtain . . . automobile rental service from Dianne Kessler, present a Master Charge Credit Card, w/knowledge that the card had not been issued to him the D, and that said card was not used with the effective consent of the cardholder, Ceclia E. Poerier . . . ."

In that case, ct. concluded held that allegations in indictment were sufficient b/c the allegation "w/knowledge" related to allegation that card had not been issued to D and also related to allegation that card was not used w/the effective consent of the cardholder.

Holding

The indictment is sufficient because the allegation "with knowledge" relates not only to the card not being issued in the D's name but also to the allegation that the card "was not used with the effective consent of the cardholder."

Figure 5-4. STEP FOUR: RESEARCH OUTLINE

I.   Statutory Rule
         W. Va. Code §61-4-5 pertains to forging checks.
II. Penalty
         W. Va. Code §61-4-6 says this is a felony, one to ten years or one
         year plus fine.
III. Elements
         W. Va. Code §61-4-5 requires
             (1) creation of draft,
                 American Express, 523 S.E.2d 681
             (2) with intent to defraud, and
             (3) no authority to charge the other's account or the draft
                 exceeds the authorized amount.
IV. Defenses
         Unforeseen events doctrine
             Smith v. Jones, 618 S.E.2d 765 (copied)
             Smith v. Smyth, 614 S.E.2d 645
             Law review article, *Unforeseen Events* (copied)
V.   Burden of Proof
         Plaintiff bears burden of proof—preponderance of the evi-
         dence
             Smith v. Jones (copied)

6 Standards of Review

The term "standard of review" means something slightly different at the trial level than it does at the appellate level. At the trial level, the standard of review refers to the standard that is used to decide motions. *Review* is somewhat of a misnomer—at this stage in the litigation, the trial court is not reviewing the motion; it is viewing it for the first time. Think of the standard of review as the standard, or *test*, that the court uses to decide a motion. On the other hand, at the appellate level, the standard of review is a principle used to divide decision-making power between the trial court and the appellate court. Our judicial system gives the authority to make some decisions to juries, some to trial judges, and others to appellate judges. The standard of review governs the level of deference the appellate court gives to another decision maker's decisions. The standard of review governs how closely the appellate court will scrutinize the trial judge's or the jury's decisions and the extent to which its own independent judgment should control the outcome. Thus, the standard of review serves as the appellate court's "measuring stick"[1] for determining "how 'wrong' the lower court has to be before it will be reversed."[2]

Regardless of which court you are in, the applicable standard of review significantly affects the outcome of the case. Using different standards can lead to vastly different results. An "error that may be a ground for reversal

---

1. Teresa J. Reid Rambo & Leanne J. Pflaum, *Legal Writing by Design: Writing Great Briefs and Memos* §22.2, at 375 (Carolina Acad. Press 2001).
2. Mary Beth Beazley, *A Practical Guide to Appellate Advocacy* §2.3, at 12 (2d ed., Aspen 2006).

under one standard of review may be insignificant under another."[3] For example, the result under the same set of facts could well be different depending on whether the appellate court reviewed the decision of a lower court using the de novo standard of review, which affords no deference to the lower court, rather than the clearly erroneous or abuse of discretion standards, which are extremely deferential to the lower court.

Judge Harry Pregerson of the U.S. Court of Appeals for the Ninth Circuit has called standards of review "the keystone of appellate decision-making."[4] Because the standard of review can significantly affect the outcome of a case, it is essential that judicial clerks have a basic understanding of those standards and how they operate. Unfortunately, judges commonly complain that their clerks, as well as lawyers appearing before the court, have little understanding of standards of review and how they affect judicial decision making.

This chapter will provide you with a general overview of the standards as they are used by the federal courts. This overview is designed to familiarize you with the different standards of review, the appropriate circumstances in which you should use each standard, and the language used by the courts with regard to each standard of review. Please keep in mind that this chapter is an oversimplification of the standards of review. Many considerations come into play with regard to the standards, including the deciding court, the reviewing court, the subject matter of the case, and so on. In light of the fact that each case is a puzzle in which the different pieces form a unique picture with regard to the standards of review, this chapter could not hope to be a comprehensive review. Instead, this chapter provides only a rudimentary education on the various standards. Furthermore, if you are clerking in state court, you should not assume that the articulations of the individual standards presented in this chapter are the same as in your jurisdiction. Some states define the standards in a similar manner as the federal courts; others treat them somewhat differently.

I. Appellate Standards of Review

Trial and appellate courts play by different rules. When an appellate court agrees to hear an appeal, it is not agreeing to retry the case. It is not agreeing to rehear the evidence; the court is simply agreeing to *review* the particular decision that is being appealed for error. Thus, the question on appeal is not whether the appellant should have won at trial, but rather whether the particular ruling that is being appealed satisfies the relevant standard of review.

---

3. Ruggiero J. Aldisert, *Winning on Appeal: Better Briefs and Oral Argument* §5.2, at 57 (Rev. 1st ed., Nita 1996).
4. Rambo & Pflaum, *supra* note 1, at 373.

Think of standards of review as akin to burdens of proof, with which you are likely somewhat more familiar.

> At *trial*, one party bears the burden of proving his or her case by a *preponderance of the evidence*; by *clear and convincing evidence*; or by evidence *beyond a reasonable doubt*. [However, o]n *appeal*, the appellant has the burden of showing that the jury's findings of fact are not supported by *substantial evidence*; that the trial court's factual findings are *clearly erroneous*; that the trial court *abused its discretion*; or that the trial court erred *as a matter of law*.[5]

Thus, the standard of review serves as a hurdle that the appellant must overcome to win the appeal. The more deference the appellate court gives the trial court, the higher the hurdle.

When determining what standard of review applies to a given case, you will need to conduct research in your jurisdiction. Standards of review vary from state to state and between the states and the federal government. While you can conduct general research on standards of review, often the best place to start when trying to determine what standard applies in any given situation is to research the law regarding the substantive issues in the case. Often, case law regarding the substantive issues identifies the applicable standard and explains what the standard means and how it operates. In a decision, the court usually sets forth the standard of review immediately before beginning the legal analysis.

At the start of your research regarding the appropriate standard of review, ask two questions. First, determine what type of decision was made. The standard of review that applies in a particular case depends on the type of decision being appealed. The standard of review is different with regard to decisions concerning findings of fact, conclusions of law, and discretionary matters. Second, if the matter is a question of fact, ask who decided the matter being appealed. The standard may vary depending on whether the decision maker was a judge, jury, or administrative agency.

A. Questions of Fact and the Clearly Erroneous and Substantial Evidence Standards

1. QUESTIONS OF FACT

A *question of fact* must be answered by referring to the basic facts of the case or from the inferences drawn from those facts. Basic facts are the historical facts and the narrative accounts of events that are discerned from the evidence. Such facts "are the who, what, when, where, and how of every legal dispute."[6] Basic facts also include an individual's subjective mental state (what the individual knew or intended). Inferences

---

5. *Id.* at 376.
6. Randall H. Warner, *All Mixed Up About Mixed Questions*, 7 J. App. Prac. & Process 101, 115 (2005).

of fact are inferred from the basic facts. Rather than being decided based on direct evidence presented at trial, as are basic facts, inferences of fact are based on circumstantial evidence. Such inferences "are permitted only when . . . logic and human experience indicate a probability that certain consequences can and do follow from the basic events or conditions."[7] Questions of fact are decided based on the evidence. They are decided without reference to the law; the law is irrelevant.

The following are examples of questions of fact:

- Did the yellow truck run the red light?
- Did Mr. and Mrs. Jones leave their ten-year-old child home alone with their baby for four days?
- Did Mr. Smith drive his vehicle at 110 miles per hour while traveling with a child?
- Whose signature is on the contract?
- Did Ms. Smith act in good faith when she purchased the drill press?

The answer to a question of fact, known as a *finding of fact*, depends on the particular circumstances or factual situations arising in the case before the court. A *trier of fact* resolves questions of fact. A trier of fact can be a jury, trial judge, hearing officer, administrative law judge, or board from an administrative agency.

Appellate courts apply a different standard of review to factual findings made by trial judges, juries, and administrative agencies. The nature of the fact finder determines the level of deference the appellate court gives to its findings of fact. While these standards may seem quite similar to each other, they are not the same. The level of deference granted to juries and administrative agencies is even greater than that applicable to trial judges.

2. TRIAL JUDGE: THE CLEARLY ERRONEOUS STANDARD

Under Rule 52(a) of the Federal Rules of Civil Procedure, an appellate court cannot set aside findings of fact made by a trial judge unless those findings are clearly erroneous. "Clearly erroneous" means "more than maybe or probably wrong": It means so wrong that it strikes the court "with the force of five-week-old, unrefrigerated dead fish."[8] Thus, even when some evidence supports a trial court's findings of fact, an appellate court can reverse the finding if it has "the definite and firm conviction that a mistake has been committed."[9] As long as the trial court's account of the evidence is plausible in light of the entire record, the appellate court may not reverse it even if the appellate court would have weighed the evidence differently had it been acting as the trier of fact. Consequently, "where the

---

7. Ruggiero J. Aldisert, *Opinion Writing* 55 (AuthorHouse 2009).
8. *Parts & Elec. Motors, Inc. v. Sterling Elec. Inc.*, 866 F.2d 228, 233 (7th Cir. 1988).
9. *United States v. United States Gypsum Co.*, 333 U.S. 364, 395 (1948).

evidence will support either of two permissible conclusions, a trial judge's choice between the two cannot be clear error."[10]

Thus, when an appeal concerns findings of fact, the appellate court cannot substitute its judgment for that of the trial court. Rather, the appellate court gives the trial court's decisions great, but not complete, deference. The appellate court defers to the trial judge's factual decisions because the trial judge was in the best position to understand the evidence. The appellate court is reviewing the case based on the bare record, which tells an incomplete story of what occurred at trial. Furthermore, given that the appellate court's review is based solely on the record, it is difficult for it to judge the credibility of witnesses. The trial judge, on the other hand, is in a better position to judge the credibility of the witnesses — that judge has observed the entire trial, including the witnesses' demeanor, tone of voice, and body language.

◆ HELPFUL HINT

When drafting a decision for the appellate court in a matter where the clearly erroneous standard is applicable, the standard will have a significant impact on your analysis of the matter. Not only must you identify and describe the standard at the beginning of the "Discussion of the Issues" section before the start of legal analysis, but you must also incorporate the standard of review into the analysis of the issue. For example, if you conclude that the trial court's finding of fact was clearly erroneous, you must identify the erroneous finding and show how the evidence demonstrates that the finding was clearly erroneous. Finally, you must demonstrate how the clearly erroneous finding of fact altered the outcome of the case.

Example A: Trial Court's Findings Were Clearly Erroneous

[W]e cannot accept the District Court's findings as adequate for reasons which we shall spell out in detail and which we can summarize as follows:

First, the primary evidence upon which the District Court relied for its "race, not politics," conclusion is evidence of voting registration, not voting behavior; and that is precisely the kind of evidence that we said was inadequate the last time this case was before us. Second, the additional evidence to which appellees' expert, Dr. Weber, pointed, and the statements made by Senator Cooper and Gerry Cohen, simply do not provide significant additional support for the District Court's conclusion. Third, the District Court, while not accepting the contrary conclusion of appellants' expert, Dr. Peterson, did not (and as far as the record reveals, could not) reject much of the significant supporting information he provided. Fourth, in any event, appellees themselves have provided us with charts summarizing evidence of voting behavior and those charts tend to refute the court's "race, not politics," conclusion.

* * *

continues on next page

---

10. Martha S. Davis, *A Basic Guide to Standards of Review*, 33 S.D. L. Rev. 469, 476 (1988).

We concede the record contains a modicum of evidence offering support for the District Court's conclusion. That evidence includes the Cohen e-mail, Senator Cooper's reference to "racial balance," and to a minor degree, some aspects of Dr. Weber's testimony. The evidence taken together, however, does not show that racial considerations predominated in the drawing of District 12's boundaries. That is because race in this case correlates closely with political behavior. The basic question is whether the legislature drew District 12's boundaries because of race rather than because of political behavior (coupled with traditional, nonracial districting considerations). It is not, as the dissent contends, whether a legislature may defend its districting decisions based on a "stereotype" about African-American voting behavior. And given the fact that the party attacking the legislature's decision bears the burden of proving that racial considerations are "dominant and controlling," *Miller*, 515 U.S. at 913, 115 S. Ct. 2475, given the "demanding" nature of that burden of proof, *id.*, at 929, 115 S. Ct. 2475 (O'Connor, J., concurring), and given the sensitivity, the "extraordinary caution," that district courts must show to avoid treading upon legislative prerogatives, *id.*, at 916, 115 S. Ct. 2475 (majority opinion), the attacking party has not successfully shown that race, rather than politics, predominantly accounts for the result. The record leaves us with the "definite and firm conviction," *United States v. Gypsum Co.*, 333 U.S. at 395, 68 S. Ct. 525, that the District Court erred in finding to the contrary. And we do not believe that providing appellees a further opportunity to make their "precinct swapping" arguments in the District Court could change this result.

We can put the matter more generally as follows: In a case such as this one where majority-minority districts (or the approximate equivalent) are at issue and where racial identification correlates highly with political affiliation, the party attacking the party attacking the legislatively drawn boundaries must show at the least that the legislature could have achieved its legitimate political objectives in alternative ways that are comparably consistent with traditional districting principles. That party must also show that those districting alternatives would have brought about significantly greater racial balance. Appellees failed to make any such showing here. We conclude that the District Court's contrary findings are clearly erroneous. . . . [11]

Example B: Trial Court's Findings Were Not Clearly Erroneous

Application of the foregoing principles to the facts of the case lays bare the errors committed by the Fourth Circuit in its employment of the clearly erroneous standard. In detecting clear error in the District Court's findings that petitioner was better qualified than Mr. Kincaid, the Fourth Circuit improperly conducted what amounted to a de novo weighing of the evidence in the record. The District Court's finding was based on essentially undisputed evidence regarding the respective backgrounds of petitioner and Mr. Kincaid and the duties that went with the position of Recreation Director. The District Court, after considering the evidence, concluded that the position of Recreation Director in Bessemer City carried with it broad responsibilities for creating and managing a recreation program involving not only athletics, but also other activities for citizens of all ages and interests. The court determined that petitioner's more varied educational and employment background and her extensive involvement in a variety of civic activities left her better qualified to

---

11. *Easley v. Cromartie*, 532 U.S. 234, 244, 257-258 (2001) (internal references omitted).

implement such a rounded program than Mr. Kincaid, whose background was more narrowly focused on athletics.

The Fourth Circuit, reading the same record, concluded that the basic duty of the Recreational Director was to implement an athletic program, and that the essential qualification for a successful applicant would be either education or experience specifically related to athletics. Accordingly, it seemed evident to the Court of Appeals that Mr. Kincaid was in fact better qualified than petitioner.

Based on our own reading of the record, we cannot say that either interpretation of the facts is illogical or implausible. Each has support in inferences that may be drawn from the facts in the record; and if either interpretation had been drawn by a district court on the record before us, we would not be inclined to find it clearly erroneous. The question we must answer, however, is not whether the Fourth Circuit's interpretation of the facts was clearly erroneous, but whether the District Court's finding was clearly erroneous. See *McAllister v. United States*, 348 U.S. 19, 20-21, 75 S. Ct. 6, 7-8, 99 L. Ed 20 (1954). The District Court determined that petitioner was better qualified, and, as we have stated above, such a finding is entitled to deference. . . . When the record is examined in light of the appropriately deferential standard, it is apparent that it contains nothing that mandates a finding that the District Court's conclusion was clearly erroneous.

* * *

Our determination that the findings of the District Court regarding petitioner's qualifications, the conduct of her interview, and the bias of the male committee members were not clearly erroneous leads us to conclude that the court's finding that petitioner was discriminated against on account of her sex was also not clearly erroneous. The District Court's findings regarding petitioner's superior qualifications and the bias of the selection committee are sufficient to support the inference that petitioner was denied the position of Recreational Director on account of her sex. Accordingly, we hold that the Fourth Circuit erred in denying petitioner relief under Title VII.[12]

3. JURIES AND AGENCIES: SUBSTANTIAL EVIDENCE STANDARD

The substantial evidence standard of review is used with regard to findings of fact made by both juries and administrative agencies. With regard to administrative agencies, the fact finder may be a hearing examiner, an administrative law judge, or the board to which the administrative law judge reports. This standard, which is one of reasonableness, is a more deferential standard than the clearly erroneous standard. The substantial evidence standard requires only that reasonable minds could find the evidence sufficient to support the jury's or the administrative agency's factual finding. Furthermore, it is not the amount of the evidence that is important, but the overall believability of the evidence. Thus, the substantial evidence standard is an extremely deferentially standard.

---

12. *Anderson v. City of Bessemer*, 470 U.S. 564, 576-577, 580 (1985) (footnotes omitted).

a. Agencies

The Administrative Procedures Act, 5 U.S.C. §706(2)(E), provides that an appellate court, or a district court acting in an appellate function, may not set aside findings by administrative agencies engaged in formal agency adjudication or rule making unless they are "unsupported by substantial evidence."[13] Substantial evidence means something "more than a mere scintilla" of evidence.[14] However, substantial evidence "does not mean a large or considerable amount of evidence, but rather 'such relevant evidence as a reasonable mind might accept as adequate to support a conclusion.'"[15] Thus, substantial evidence affords "a substantial basis of fact from which the fact in question can be reasonably inferred."[16] Substantial evidence is evidence that is sufficient to "justify, if the trial were to a jury, a refusal to direct a verdict when the conclusion sought to be drawn from it is one of fact for the jury."[17]

Again, as with findings of fact by trial judges, appellate courts are extremely deferential to findings by administrative agencies because such agencies are considered experts in their area. Further, the appellate court cannot weigh the evidence or determine the credibility of witnesses as well as can the administrative decision maker. Therefore, an appellate court will not substitute its judgment for that of the administrative agency.

b. Juries

Just as appellate judges are prohibited from second-guessing the factual findings of a trial judge sitting without a jury under Rule 52(a), the Seventh Amendment of the U.S. Constitution prevents appellate judges from second-guessing the factual findings of a jury. In fact, appellate review of a jury's factual findings and verdict is *more* limited than review of a trial judge's factual findings. "The [S]eventh [A]mendment prevents the appellate judge from jumping over the jury rail to become the thirteenth juror."[18] Most state constitutions also have provisions that prohibit appellate judges from substituting their factual finding for those of the jury.

The substantial evidence standard also applies to verdicts rendered by juries. A jury verdict must be sustained if substantial evidence exists to support it. If some evidence exists on which the jury could have based its factual finding, then the finding will not be disturbed. When determining whether substantial evidence exists to support a jury verdict, the appellate court considers the evidence in the light most favorable to the verdict and

---

13. Informal agency actions, on the other hand, receive less deference under the arbitrary and capricious standard of review.

14. *Consolidated Edison Co. v. NLRB*, 305 U.S. 197, 229 (1938).

15. *Pierce v. Underwood*, 487 U.S. 553, 564-565 (1988).

16. *NLRB v. Columbian Enameling & Stamping Co.*, 306 U.S. 292, 299-300 (1939).

17. *Id.* at 300.

18. Ruggero J. Aldisert, *The Appellate Bar: Professional Responsibility and Professional Competence—A View from the Jaundiced Eye of One Appellate Judge*, 11 Cap. Univ. L. Rev. 445, 468 (1982).

with all reasonable inferences from the evidence drawn in support of the verdict. Thus, the testimony of a single credible witness that is contradicted by the testimony of multiple witnesses may constitute substantial evidence sufficient to affirm a jury's findings of fact. Hence, appellate courts are extremely reluctant to find that there is insubstantial evidence to support a jury's finding.

4. CRIMINAL CASES

Review of factual findings for criminal cases is somewhat different from civil cases. In criminal cases, appellate courts recognize two types of factual findings — guilt-related findings of fact and non-guilt-related findings of fact. Guilt-related findings of fact include the same factual findings that a jury would have to make when determining whether a defendant was guilty or not guilty of a crime. For instance, whether a defendant entered a premises without permission or made efforts to withdraw from a conspiracy are guilt-related findings of fact. Non-guilt-related findings of fact include such matters as whether the police read the defendant his *Miranda* rights or whether the defendant's guilty plea was knowingly and voluntarily made after being advised by the court of the effect of such a plea.

Jury decisions on both guilt- and non-guilt-related findings of fact and the application of law to those facts are reviewed under the same standard of review. A jury's findings are reviewed under the substantial evidence standard; although, in a criminal case, this standard is often referred to as the sufficiency of the evidence. On the other hand, the trial judge's findings of fact reviewed under different standards. Appellate courts review a trial judge's non-guilt-related factual finding under the clearly erroneous standard. Guilt-related factual findings, however, are reviewed under the substantial evidence standard, the same standard that the court would have used if a jury had decided the case. The use of a different standard for guilt-related and non-guilt-related factual findings is likely attributable to a desire to avoid penalizing or impeding a defendant's choice to a trial by jury or by the court. A defendant would be ill advised to choose trial by jury if the appellate court gave more deference to guilt-related findings by a jury than it did to such findings by a court.

Review of factual findings in criminal cases is also somewhat different than in civil cases due to the difference in the evidentiary burdens. When reviewing a criminal case, the appellate court must consider whether the evidence "is sufficient fairly to support a conclusion that every element of the crime has been established beyond a reasonable doubt."[19] On the other hand, when reviewing factual findings for most civil cases, the appellate court must determine whether every element of the prima facie case was proven by a preponderance of the evidence. Given that the

19. *Jackson v. Virginia*, 443 U.S. 307, 313-314 (1979).

preponderance of the evidence burden is a less demanding burden than beyond a reasonable doubt, an appellate court's conclusion that the factual findings in a civil case were not clearly erroneous could be found to be clearly erroneous in a criminal case. This is true as well for the review of facts in civil cases that require proof by clear and convincing evidence.

◈ HELPFUL HINT

When an appellate court reviews an appeal of a criminal case, it must not only consider the standard of review but also take into account the burden of proof. Consequently, an appellate court must consider whether the evidence presented at trial is sufficient to support a conclusion that every element of the crime has been established beyond a reasonable doubt.

Example A: Jury Decision

This is an appeal from a judgment of sentence for receiving stolen property. Appellant argues that the evidence was insufficient and that trial counsel was ineffective. Finding these arguments without merit, we affirm.

The test of sufficiency is whether, after viewing the evidence in the light most favorable to the Commonwealth, and then drawing all reasonable inferences favorable to the Commonwealth, the trier of fact would find that every element of the crime charged had been proved beyond a reasonable doubt.[20]

Example B: Trial Court Decision

After a non-jury trial, the appellant . . . was convicted of criminal conspiracy . . . and unlawful delivery of a controlled substance. . . . On June 1, 1981, a sentence of 3 to 10 years imprisonment was entered for each offense and ordered to be served concurrently. This appeal followed.

On appeal, appellant assails the sufficiency of the evidence and claims that the trial court erred in allowing opinion testimony to be admitted into evidence regarding the typical modus operandi of drug sellers and erred in refusing to grant a mistrial. We affirm the judgment of sentence.

The test to be used in evaluating an appellant's sufficiency of evidence argument is whether, viewing the entire record in the light most favorable to the Commonwealth, a finder of fact could reasonably have found that all elements of the crime charged had been proved beyond a reasonable doubt.[21]

---

5. SUMMARY

Thus, it is important to remember that when findings of fact are being appealed, regardless of whether the decision maker was a judge, jury, or administrative body, the appellant bears a heavy burden. Appellate courts are very reluctant to overturn findings of fact. This reluctance is particularly strong when the fact finder is a jury or administrative agency. In fact, an appellate court gives extreme deference to findings of fact made by a

---

20. Aldisert, *Opinion Writing*, *supra* note 7, at §5.14(a).
21. *Id.*

jury or an administrative agency under the substantial evidence standard. On the other hand, an appellate court generally gives somewhat less deference to a trial judge's factual findings. A trial judge's factual findings receive deference only under the clearly erroneous standard.

B. Discretionary Matters and the Abuse of Discretion Standard

1. DISCRETIONARY QUESTIONS

Trial judges are given discretion to decide a wide variety of issues. Discretion is essentially the power of a trial judge to decide certain matters without being bound by strict rules established by statutes or precedent. Instead, a judge's discretion is constrained by the rules of equity, the circumstances of the particular case before the court, and factors or guidelines provided by the law. These factors or guidelines do not tell the judge what to decide, but simply provide some guidance to the judge regarding how to make the decision. Discretion allows a trial judge to exercise his or her reason and judgment when resolving a question.

Trial judges have great discretion on matters concerning the management of the litigation process, including discovery and the progress of trial. More specifically, trial judges have discretion with regard to decisions on nondispositive motions, which require the judge to rule on incidental questions that arise during litigation.[22] Such incidental questions might regard objections or the admissibility of evidence. Furthermore, the trial judge has discretion on procedural matters, such as granting continuances, permitting a party to exceed the page limit, amending the pleadings, and so on. In addition to these procedural matters, trial judges have broad discretion on how to instruct the jury and on equitable matters. While discretionary matters cover a wide range of issues, two characteristics will help you identify them. First, discretionary matters often require the trial judge to balance efficiency and fairness concerns. Second, although a legal standard may apply to a discretionary issue, this standard will often simply serve as a guideline to aid the judge in the decision-making process rather than as a bright-line rule.

2. THE ABUSE OF DISCRETION STANDARD OF REVIEW

With regard to matters entrusted to the trial court's discretion, the trial judge's only duty is to refrain from acting unreasonably or arbitrarily. An appellate court will only reverse such decisions when the trial court has *abused* its discretion. In this context, abuse of discretion is the equivalent of *misuse* of discretion. Under the abuse of discretion standard, appellate

---

22. Nondispositive motions do not dispose of claims, but simply resolve more routine procedural matters. Dispositive motions, on the other hand, are not within the trial judge's discretion. Dispositive motions include those motions where a party requests that the court dispose of some or all of the claims asserted in a complaint, petition, counterclaim, or cross-claim.

courts give great deference to trial court decisions on discretionary matters. The appellate court defers to the trial judge's decisions on discretionary matters because the trial judge is "in a better position to evaluate the factors relevant to the decision" and "is more familiar with the dynamics of trials" than are appellate judges.[23] Presiding over the trial provides the trial judge with information that is necessary to resolve discretionary matters. For instance, when deciding an evidentiary matter, the trial judge often balances the probative value of the proffered evidence against any prejudicial effect that the evidence is likely to have on the trier of fact. The trial judge's evidentiary ruling will depend on his observations of the parties, witnesses, and jurors as well as the context in which the evidence will be considered. Appellate judges, on the other hand, review the case based on the bare record, which tells an incomplete story of what occurred at trial.

The abuse of discretion standard is somewhat more expansive than those standards applied to findings of fact. Consequently, an appellate court generally will not substitute its judgment for that of the trial court. Rather, an appellate court will interfere with a trial court's exercise of discretion only when the trial court exceeded its discretion by committing a clear error in judgment.

But what constitutes an abuse of discretion? What is a clear error in judgment? Discretion is abused only where no reasonable person would adopt the view taken by the trial court. In other words, only where the judge's discretion is exercised in a manner not justified by the evidence will the appellate court conclude that a trial judge has exceeded his or her discretion. A trial judge abuses his or her discretion by failing to consider a relevant factor that should have been given significant weight or considering and giving significant weight to an irrelevant or improper factor. Furthermore, a trial judge may abuse his or her discretion if he or she commits a clear error of judgment when weighing proper factors.

Given that a trial judge may abuse his or her discretion only in limited circumstances, appellate courts rarely reverse trial judges' decisions on discretionary matters. Hence, just as when appealing a finding of fact, an appellant challenging a discretionary ruling bears a heavy burden.

3. Working with the Abuse of Discretion Standard

When drafting a decision for the appellate court in a matter where the abuse of discretion standard is applicable, the standard will have a significant impact on your analysis of the matter. You must not only identify and describe the standard in the "Standard of Review" section or at the

---

23. Alan D. Hornstein, *Appellate Advocacy in a Nutshell* §3-2 (West 1984). Additional reasons justifying deference to the trial judge on questions on the exercise of his or her discretion include: (1) the need for flexibility in case management, (2) the need for flexible legal standards to address all possible circumstances, (3) the need to support the trial judge's control over the courtroom, and (4) judicial comity (respect for the decisions of other judges). Linda H. Edwards, *Legal Writing: Process, Analysis, and Organization* 297 (5th ed. 2010).

beginning of the "Discussion of the Issues" section before the start of the legal analysis but also incorporate the standard of review into the analysis of the issue. You can reason through an abuse of discretion analysis in two ways. First, you may explore the record, closely examine the trial court's decision, and scrutinize the reasonableness of the court's action. Another way of reasoning through an abuse of discretion analysis is to essentially place the case before the court on a spectrum with regard to the relevant authority. This requires you to compare the facts of the case before the court to the relevant precedent.

◆ HELPFUL HINT

An appellate opinion applying the abuse of discretion standard must, at a minimum, state the standard of review and whether it has been satisfied. The litigants, however, will not be satisfied if the analysis stops there without offering an explanation for the decision. Thus, if you conclude that the trial court abused its discretion, you must identify the specific decision the judge made in error, use appropriate authorities to explain why that decision was incorrect, and specify why and how that error altered the outcome of the case.

Example A: Abuse of Discretion Occurred

In this appeal by the government, brought pursuant to 18 U.S.C. §3731, we are asked to decide whether the district court abused its discretion when it precluded a key government witness from testifying at trial in a criminal case as a sanction for the government's failure to turn over to the defendant certain exculpatory evidence prior to trial. We hold that although the government withheld materially exculpatory evidence in direct violation of a valid district court order, it was an abuse of discretion for the district court to issue a preclusion order based on a violation of *Brady v. Maryland*, 373 U.S. 83, 83 S. Ct. 1194, 10 L. Ed. 2d 215 (1963), because the defendant was not prejudiced by the government's nondisclosure.[24]

Example B: No Abuse of Discretion Occurred

Appellants claim that the trial court erred in not permitting rebuttal testimony by an expert witness. . . . Appellee's expert has testified that a prior accident on the same motorcycle was not causally related to the accident in question. Appellants wished to have their expert rebut this with testimony about undetectable damage. The trial court and the *en banc* court held that this was inadmissible, as the proffered rebuttal testimony had not been revealed in discovery. . . .

The admission of rebuttal evidence is normally within the discretion of the trial judge. . . . Even if the trial court erred in this matter — and we do not hold that it did — the excluded testimony was not so critical as to warrant a new trial. The grant or refusal of a new trial by the lower court will not be reversed by this Court in the absence of a clear abuse of discretion or an error of law which controlled the outcome of the case. . . .[25]

---

24. Aldisert, *Opinion Writing*, *supra* note 7, at 65-66.
25. *Id*. at 65.

C. Questions of Law and the De Novo Standard

1. QUESTIONS OF LAW

A *question of law*, on the other hand, concerns the selection or creation of law governing a legal issue or the interpretation of a legal principle. When a court considers whether a legal standard applies in a given case, it is deciding a question of law. When a court interprets a legal standard, it defines that standard in a manner that will apply to all similar cases. Questions of law are decided without reference to the facts. They are not dependent on particular circumstances or factual situations, but rather are capable of being applied to many situations. A question is one of law only if it requires the court "to make, revoke, interpret, or change legal rules in a manner that will apply to other cases."[26] The answer to a question of law is referred to as a *conclusion of law*. The answer to a question of law is generally expressed as a broad legal principle. Questions of law are always resolved by a judge or an individual acting in a similar capacity as a judge, such as a magistrate judge.

The following are examples of questions of law:

- Is an individual negligent when that individual runs a red light?
- Does leaving a baby with a ten-year-old child for four days satisfy the legal definition of child neglect?
- Does driving a vehicle at 110 miles per hour with a child in it satisfy the legal definition of reckless endangerment of a child?
- What statute of limitations applies to a particular tort?

2. THE DE NOVO STANDARD OF REVIEW

The de novo standard of review applies to questions of law, including all constitutional issues and questions of statutory interpretation. Appellate courts also review de novo the trial judge's decisions with regard to dismissal of pleadings, summary judgments, directed verdicts, jury instructions, and judgments notwithstanding the verdict. With the exception of decisions concerning jury instructions, all the previously mentions decisions are on dispositive motions. Dispositive motions include those motions where a party requests that the trial court dispose of some or all of the claims asserted in a complaint, petition, counterclaim, or cross-claim.

When an appellate court uses the de novo standard, it independently reviews the matter and substitutes its judgment for that of the trial court. Thus, the appellate court gives no deference to the trial court's decisions; in fact, the legal findings of the court below have no weight whatsoever. This is not to say that appellate review under the de novo standard is completely new with regard to the evidence. Rather, the appellate court's

---

26. Warner, *supra* note 6, at 115.

review is limited to those parts of the record that are relevant to the legal issues. Furthermore, the appellate court's review is "guided by a general presumption of regularity, by comity, and by an implicit tendency to affirm" that arises from trust in the decision maker below.[27]

An appellate court is willing to substitute its judgment for that of the trial court with regard to questions of law because appellate courts view their role as interpreting law and assuring that the lower courts consistently apply the law. Furthermore, while the trial court might be in a better position than the appellate court to determine factual matters, it is not in a better position to determine how the law applies to those facts. The appellate court is in a better position to determine questions of law. The resolution of questions of law "does not require . . . intimate knowledge of trial dynamics nor any special sensitivity to the events or context of the particular trial."[28] Rather, the resolution of questions of law requires knowledge and understanding of the law. It requires the ability to select, interpret, and apply the law. Appellate judges are experts on the law; they were trained to know and understand the law. As for selecting, interpreting, and applying the law? That is what appellate judges *do* day after day. Further, the fact that they have more time to research and reflect on important legal issues than do their trial court brethren, who often work under great time pressures, puts them in a better position to resolve those matters.

◆ HELPFUL HINT

When drafting a decision for the appellate court in a case where the de novo standard is applicable, the standard will have almost no impact on your analysis of the matter. Although you must identify and describe the standard at the beginning of the "Discussion of the Issues" section before the start of the legal analysis, you will draft the legal analysis as though the matter is being heard for the first time. Reference need only be made to the trial court's decision when discussing the procedural history of the case on appeal and at the end of document, where the appellate court either affirms or reverses the decision below.

Example A

The standard is familiar. Summary judgment may be granted only if no genuine issue of material fact exists. Rule 56(c), Fed. R. Civ. P.; *Goodman v. Mead Johnson & Co.*, 534 F.2d 566, 573 (3d Cir. 1976), *cert. denied*, 429 U.S. 1038, 97 S. Ct. 732, 50 L. Ed. 2d 748 (1977). An issue is "genuine" only if the evidence is such that a reasonable jury could find for the nonmoving party. *Anderson v. Liberty Lobby, Inc.*, 477 U.S. 242, 106 S. Ct. 2505, 2509, 91 L. Ed. 2d 202 (1986). At the summary judgment stage, "the judge's function is not himself to weigh the

continues on next page

---

27. Davis, *supra* note 10, at 476.
28. Alan D. Hornstein, *Appellate Advocacy in a Nutshell* §3-2 (West 1984).

> evidence and determine the truth of the matter, but to determine whether
> there is a genuine issue for trial." *Id.*, 106 S. Ct. at 2510. On review, this court
> applies the same test that the district court should have adopted. *Dunn v.*
> *Gannett New York Newspapers, Inc.*, 833 F. 2d 446, 449 (3d Cir. 1987).[29]
>
> **Example B**
>
> The [appellants] argue that the district court misapplied the law of personal
> jurisdiction and New Jersey's conflict of laws rules. Because these issues involve the
> selection, interpretation, and application of legal precepts, review is plenary.[30]

D. Mixed Questions of Law and Fact

A *mixed question of law and fact* is not as easily defined as its question of
fact and question of law counterparts. Rather, the mixed question category
has become a "catchall" for any question that "cannot neatly be labeled
law or fact."[31] Generally, mixed questions refer to (1) evaluative determinations, (2) questions of definition application, or (3) compound questions.[32] Because mixed questions of law and fact include so many different
types of questions, courts have been unable to decide on one standard of
review to apply to all mixed questions. Some courts apply the de novo
standard to mixed questions; others apply a more deferential standard. No
real consistency exists. Many courts have described their approach to
selecting the standard of review in a mixed question case as depending
on whether the question is "primarily" or "essentially" factual or legal.[33]
The problem with such an approach is that it allows the standard of review
for an issue to change from case to case. While the standard may vary from
issue to issue, it should be the same for one issue from case to case. This
lack of consistency makes it appear that courts can apply whatever standard
of review will lead to the outcome they wish to achieve.

This section examines each of these types of mixed questions. It also
identifies the standard of review that courts have applied to the different
types of questions and explains the rationale for applying that standard.
When courts apply a different standard of review to mixed questions in the
same category, this section attempts to explain the rationale for treating
the questions differently.

1. EVALUATIVE DETERMINATIONS

a. Definition

An *evaluative determination* requires a decision maker to exercise its
judgment as to whether an individual's conduct or belief or a set of

---

29. Aldisert, *Opinion Writing, supra* note 7, at 67.
30. *Id.* at 68.
31. Warner, *supra* note 6, at 102.
32. *Id.* at 128.
33. *Id.* at 107.

circumstances satisfies a community standard. An evaluative determination is not asking the decision maker to decide *what happened*, though it will have to resolve that question to move on to the evaluative determination. Instead, an evaluative determination asks the decision maker to determine whether the individual's conduct or belief, or the set of circumstances that occurred, was fair or reasonable.

Evaluative determinations are somewhat easy to identify. Often, a question articulated in terms of "reasonableness" or "fairness" requires an evaluative determination. The fact that the law cannot be refined into a precise set of legal principles is another telltale sign of an evaluative determination.[34] While rules can be created to address recurring circumstances, evaluative determinations must be made on a case-by-case basis due to the countless number of circumstances that may arise.

The law requires a decision maker to exercise its judgment in a variety of cases. Some questions that require a decision maker to make an evaluative determination include the following:

- Reasonable care in negligence cases
- Proximate causation in tort cases
- Comparative fault in tort cases
- Probable cause in Fourth Amendment cases
- Reasonable suspicion in Fourth Amendment cases
- Reliance on a defendant's misrepresentation in fraud cases
- Materiality in securities fraud cases
- Reasonable accommodation under the Americans with Disabilities Act
- Fair use in copyright cases[35]

b. Standard of Review

When deciding whether to apply de novo review or a more deferential standard of review to an evaluative determination, the U.S. Supreme Court uses a policy approach. This policy approach requires the court to determine which judicial actor is better situated to decide a particular issue. However, once a court has established the standard for a particular issue, it will not be required to go through the policy analysis again. It will not be required to undertake this process each time the issue arises. Rather, the standard of review is determined on an issue-by-issue basis.

i. Deferential Standards of Review

Some examples of questions to which the courts apply a deferential standard of review include the following:

- Reasonable care in a negligence action
- Award of attorney's fees under the Equal Access to Justice Act

34. *Id.* at 120.
35. *Id.* at 119-120.

With regard to the question of reasonable care in a negligence action, the courts apply the clearly erroneous standard of review. With regard to the award of attorney's fees under the Equal Access to Justice Act, the legal standard requires that fees be awarded "unless the court finds that the position of the United States was substantially justified."[36] This question essentially asks the trial court to determine whether the government's position was a reasonable one. Consequently, the courts have concluded that the issue of attorney's fees is reviewed under the abuse of discretion standard of review.

ii. De Novo Review

Courts have applied a de novo standard of review to several types of evaluative determinations. Some examples include the following:

- Probable cause in Fourth Amendment cases
- Reasonable suspicion in Fourth Amendment cases
- Fair use under the Copyright Act

With regard to these questions, courts have simply decided that judges are in a better position than juries to decide these issues. This is particularly true with regard to constitutional issues, such as probable cause and reasonable suspicion. Because probable cause and reasonable suspicion are terms that define the scope of a suspect's Fourth Amendment rights, appellate courts must exercise an "independent review" to maintain uniformity of the law itself and consistency with regard to the application of that law. An individual's constitutional rights should not vary because of the whims of a group of jurors.

2. QUESTIONS OF DEFINITION APPLICATION

a. Definition

A *question of definition application* requires a decision maker to determine whether specific circumstances satisfy a previously established legal definition. Definition application takes a previously defined legal standard and applies it to the facts of the case before the court. This legal standard, though previously defined, cannot be further refined. It cannot be refined to the point where the consequence follows automatically from the facts. Definition application is *not* interpretation of a legal standard. Legal interpretation requires a decision maker to refine a legal definition so that it applies to all similar cases. A question of definition application, on the other hand, occurs when a legal standard includes a term or phrase that the decision maker is incapable of mechanically applying to the basic facts.

---

36. 28 U.S.C. §2412(d)(1)(A) (2006).

To illustrate when a term or phrase cannot be mechanically applied, let's examine two elements of a claim of negligent infliction of emotional distress — "closely related person" and "zone of danger."

> In some jurisdictions, negligent infliction only applies where one person witnesses death or injury to a closely related person and is also within the "zone of danger" such that he might himself have been injured. The definition of "closely related person" can be refined to the point where there is no ambiguity: Courts could hold, for example, that a sibling is a closely related person, but a friend is not. As to this issue, there is no need for definition application. Once the jury determines that the plaintiff was not a sibling of the injured person, a question of historical fact, the legal consequence follows automatically. The same cannot be said of "zone of danger." No matter how many cases attempt to define "zone of danger," there will always be a need to apply that definition to a set of facts unless a court was so obsessed with bright line rules that it required the plaintiff to be within, say, ten feet of the injured person to be deemed within the zone of danger.[37]

Courts can easily draw bright-line rules with regard to whether an individual is related to the injured person — parents, siblings, spouses, and children are closely related; friends and boyfriends or girlfriends are not. Thus, whether an individual is closely related to the injured person is not a question of definition application. On the other hand, despite the fact that courts have refined the definition of "zone of danger" as much as possible, a jury must decide close calls. The determination of whether an individual was within the zone of danger depends on the facts of the particular case before the court. Therefore, the "zone of danger" question is a question of definition application.

Before a decision maker can engage in definition application, it will generally be required to determine the basic facts of the case. Consequently, fact finding and definition application often go hand-in-hand. They are not, however, one process. If the facts are undisputed, the decision maker must still determine whether those facts satisfy a legal definition. That question is one of pure definition application.

The number of questions that require definition application is infinite. Some examples of questions of definition application include the following:

- Whether a plaintiff was within the "zone of danger" for purposes of negligent infliction of emotional distress
- Whether a suspect was "in custody" for purposes of *Miranda* warnings
- Whether a person was "domiciled" in a particular state for purposes of diversity jurisdiction

---

37. Warner, *supra* note 6, at 123 (footnotes omitted).

- Whether a convicted criminal "physically restrained" the victim for purposes of determining whether the defendant's sentence should be enhanced
- Whether an employer's conduct amounts to an "abusive work environment" under Title VII
- Whether a particular candidate qualifies as an "independent candidate" under the Hatch Act
- Whether a company performed services "in connection with" rail transportation for tax purposes[38]

b. Standard of Review

After determining that the question is one of definition application rather than a pure question of law that requires interpretation of a legal rule, the court must determine whether to apply a deferential or plenary standard of review. Like with evaluative determinations, courts use a policy approach when deciding which standard of review to apply to a question of definition application. The policy approach requires the court to consider which judicial actor is better situated to decide the question.

i. Deferential Standard of Review

Several courts have applied a deferential standard of review to questions of definition application. There are a few reasons why the trial court is in a better position than the appellate court to decide such questions. First, "the court that finds the facts will know them better than the reviewing court will, and so its application of the law to the facts is likely to be more accurate."[39] Second, because questions of definition application are case specific and thus unlikely to recur, the appellate court's duty to maintain consistency with regard to the law is not triggered.

ii. De Novo Review

Although courts generally apply a deferential standard of review to questions of definition application, occasionally, courts will review such questions de novo. Courts apply de novo review rarely and only when "strong countervailing policy considerations exist."[40] For instance, the de novo standard tends to be used by courts when reviewing constitutional issues. Appellate courts must independently review constitutional issues to maintain uniformity of the law and consistency in the application of that law. As with evaluative determinations, an individual's constitutional rights should not vary because of the whims of a group of jurors.

---

38. *See id.* at 121-123, 132-134.
39. *Thomas v. Gen. Motors Acceptance Corp.*, 288 F.3d 305, 307-308 (7th Cir. 2002).
40. Warner, *supra* note 6, at 135.

3. COMPOUND QUESTIONS

a. Definition

A *compound question* jumbles two or more issues together, some of which are factual and some of which are legal. Thus, to resolve the question, the decision maker must determine two things. It is first required to determine what happened (the basic facts). Next, the decision maker is required to either evaluate the conduct of the defendant by community standards (an evaluative determination) or to apply the law to those basic facts (definition application). For example, when evaluating whether an officer had probable cause to arrest an individual, the decision maker is required to not only determine the underlying facts, but also whether "the known facts and circumstances are sufficient to warrant a man of reasonable prudence in the belief that contraband or evidence of a crime will be found."[41]

b. Standard of Review

When selecting the appropriate standard of review for a compound question, the court should not treat a compound question as one question, but rather should parse the larger issue into its component parts. It is important to distinguish between the evaluative determination or definition application and the underlying facts. First, the court must identify the type of question presented by each subissue. Are they questions of fact? Law? Mixed questions? If one of the subissues is a mixed question, what type of mixed question is it? Is it an evaluative determination? A question of definition application? Once the court has parsed the issue and determined the type of question presented by each subissue, it must then identify the proper standard of review for each subissue. Remember that questions of fact are reviewed deferentially. The standard of review for evaluative determinations and definition application vary depending on the issue. With regard to probable cause, the example from above, the underlying factual question is reviewed deferentially. The reasonableness issue, on the other hand, is reviewed de novo.

E. Summary of Appellate Standards of Review

In summary, the applicable standard of review determines the level of deference that appellate judges grant to the trial court's findings. When reviewing findings of fact, the scope of that review is exceedingly narrow. Decisions made by a jury or an administrative agency are given great deference, almost to the extent that the review is nonexistent. Appellate courts give decisions made by a trial judge nearly the same level of respect that they accord to jury findings. The scope of an appellate court's review

---

41. *Ornelas v. U.S.*, 517 U.S. 690, 696 (1996).

of discretionary matters, while somewhat broader than that for factual findings, is still greatly limited. The broadest review is given to questions of law. If you were to visualize the standards of review as a ladder, with the lowest rung being no deference and the highest rung being the greatest amount of deference, it would look something like Figure 6-1.

Figure 6-1. STANDARDS OF REVIEW LADDER

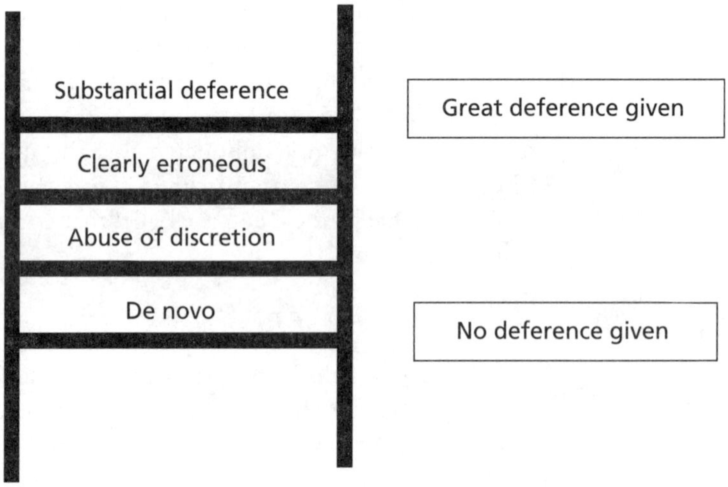

II. Standards of Review in the Trial Court: Motions

Trial courts use motion standards of review to resolve dispositive motions, such as motions to dismiss for failure to state a claim and motions for summary judgment. Motion standards of review are also used to resolve some other nondispositive motions, such as motions for injunction. The use of the term "standard of review" when used in the context of deciding a motion is a somewhat inaccurate classification. Unlike appellate standards of review, a motion standard of review does not require the deciding court to give a particular level of deference to another decision maker when reviewing its decision. Rather, a motion standard of review provides the test that a trial judge must use when deciding whether to grant or deny a motion currently before the court.

Given that motion standards of review are specific to a particular motion, when trying to determine what standard applies, be certain to research the relevant rules and authorities in your jurisdiction. Generally, if your motion is mentioned in either the civil or criminal rules of procedure, start your research with the governing rule. Then, research cases in which the courts have applied the standard. The courts in those cases may have opined on the meaning of the standard, and those elaborations on the standard's meaning may become part of the standard of review.

A. Motion to Dismiss

As stated previously, in the chapter concerning the civil litigation process, a motion to dismiss for failure to state a claim on which relief can be granted is often filed before filing an answer to the complaint. The plaintiff, the party making the allegations in the complaint, must allege facts that, if true, would constitute a cognizable cause of action. With a motion to dismiss for failure to state a claim for which relief may be granted, the defendant challenges the sufficiency of the allegations in the pleading. Rule 12(b)(6) provides the standard of review for this type of motion: The court can dismiss a complaint only if the plaintiff can establish no legal remedy that will entitle him or her to relief. Thus, the court should not dismiss a complaint for failure to state a claim unless it appears beyond a doubt that the plaintiff can prove no set of facts that would entitle them to relief. Further, the court is limited to evaluating whether a plaintiff's complaint sets forth sufficient allegations to satisfy the elements of a cause of action rather than whether the plaintiff has submitted sufficient evidence to prove his or her claim.

It is important to remember that a motion to dismiss for failure to state a claim challenges the other party's *allegations* of fact, not actual facts. The standard of review requires the court to take the allegations in the complaint as true and view them in the light most favorable to the nonmoving party. Hence, the plaintiff's allegations must be assumed to be true, and further, must be construed in plaintiff's favor. The court is to assume that the factual allegations in the complaint can be proven and then decide whether, if proven, those allegations would amount to a cause of action. If not, the court must grant the motion to dismiss.

In its opinion resolving a motion to dismiss for failure to state a claim, when discussing what happened in the complaint, the court will refer to the plaintiff's allegations or to alleged facts, not to actual facts. However, if a defendant admits to a fact or allegation in the memorandum in support of the motion, that allegation is as good as proven. The court can refer to it as a fact or a conceded fact.

B. Motion for Summary Judgment

The purpose of a trial is to determine what the facts are in a case when the evidence is contradictory. If the evidence isn't contradictory, there is no need for trial. The court, which decides matters of law, can resolve the matter without the need for further fact finding. A motion for summary judgment accomplishes this outcome when the facts are not in dispute. Unlike a motion to dismiss for failure to state a claim for which relief can be granted, which challenges the *allegations* in the complaint, a motion for summary judgment challenges the undisputed *evidence* in the case as insufficient to result in a legal remedy. The party requesting summary judgment is asking the court to decide the case on its merits.

Rule 56(c) of the Federal Rules of Civil Procedure provides the standard of review for a motion for summary judgment. Rule 56(c) allows a trial court to grant a motion for summary judgment only when the evidence shows that there is no genuine issue of material fact and the moving party, or the party requesting summary judgment, is entitled to judgment as a matter of law. Furthermore, many jurisdictions require the nonmoving party (the party opposing the motion) to produce substantial evidence on matters for which that party bears the burden of production at trial.[42] Thus, when researching the standard of review for summary judgment, be sure to research not only how your jurisdiction articulates the standard, but also which party carries the burden of proof for the underlying causes of action.

When considering the standard of review for a motion for summary judgment, what is meant by "no genuine issue of material fact"? A material fact is a determinative fact, one that is capable of altering the outcome of the case. It is the nonmoving party who usually has to demonstrate that there is a dispute about a material fact, but not in all jurisdictions. A genuine issue exists only if the evidence with regard to a material fact would support a decision in favor of either the moving or nonmoving party. If rational jurors could disagree on how to interpret the evidence, the court cannot grant the motion for summary judgment, and the case goes to trial. Thus, the appellate standard for a jury finding is the trial court's benchmark when determining whether to grant a motion for summary judgment.

When determining whether the party requesting summary judgment is entitled to judgment as a matter of law, the court looks to rules governing the substantive issues in the case. In deciding a motion for summary judgment, the court views the evidence in the light most favorable to the party opposing the motion. The court will examine the evidence presented by the parties and determine whether the plaintiff can satisfy the prima facie case governing the claim. The court may also consider whether the evidence demonstrates that the defendant is entitled to an affirmative defense. If the evidence presented by the parties, even when viewed in the light most favorable to the nonmoving party, fails to satisfy the prima facie case or satisfies a defense, and no reasonable juror could conclude otherwise, the court must grant the motion for summary judgment.

When dealing with a motion for summary judgment, the parties may rely on various types of discovery, including deposition testimony, answers to interrogatories, admissions, affidavits, documents, and other exhibits. However, it is crucial that any evidence relied on by the parties in the memoranda in support of, or in opposition to, the motion be attached to the memoranda. This is crucial because the evidence produced through the discovery process is generally not presented to the court until needed to support a motion or at trial. If the evidence has not been presented to the court, the court cannot rely on it when resolving the motion. For the court, that evidence does not exist.

---

42. *Celotex v. Catrett*, 477 U.S. 317, 322-323 (1986).

III. Exercises

1. Which standard or standards of review favor an appellant? Favor an appellee? Why?

2. For each of the following issues on appeal, determine whether the issue is a question of fact, a question of law, a mixed question of law and fact, or a question of the trial court's exercise of discretion. Then determine what standard of review the appellate court would likely use when reviewing the appeal.

   You represent Amelia House in a constructive eviction claim against Gold Acre Realty, her landlord and owner of the apartment building. To prevail on a claim of constructive eviction, a plaintiff must prove that the property was unsuitable for occupancy for the purposes for which the occupancy is intended.

   a. There was a bench trial. The trial judge ruled in favor of Gold Acre Realty and against House. The trial judge decided that the building does not contain rats. House has appealed the trial judge's decision that the building does not contain rats.

   b. There was a bench trial. The trial court decided that the apartment was suitable for occupancy as a residence. House has appealed the court's decision that the apartment was suitable for occupancy as a residence.

   c. There was a jury trial. The trial court ruled in favor of Gold Acre Realty and against House. The trial court decided that to prevail on a claim for constructive eviction, the landlord must have intended to force the tenant to move. House appeals the trial court's decision that intent is an element of a claim for constructive eviction.

   d. When Gold Acre Realty filed its answer to House's complaint, it added a series of allegation detailing House's rental payment history and showing that House had sometimes paid her rent late. House filed a motion to strike these allegations from Gold Acre Realty's answer, arguing that this information is irrelevant to a claim for constructive eviction. Rule 12(f) of the Federal Rules of Civil Procedure provides that a court "may" order any immaterial allegations stricken. The trial court denied House's motion to strike the allegations. House appealed.

   e. There was a jury trial. The trial court admitted into evidence some hearsay statements of House. House appeals the trial court's decision to admit the statements.

3. Why should an appellate court be required to give greater deference to the decision maker below when reviewing findings of fact than it is required to give when reviewing conclusions of law? Should this rule affect the types of issues an appellant should raise on appeal?

4. The clearly erroneous and abuse of discretion standards of review are deferential standards. What action does the appellate court take when it is required to apply a deferential standard but is unable to discern how the trial court reached its decision? Does it go ahead and determine whether the trial court decision was in error? Or should the court take some other course of action? If so, what action should the court take and why?

5. Federal Rule of Civil Procedure 52(a)(6) provides that "[f]indings of fact, whether based on oral or other evidence, must not be set aside unless clearly erroneous, and the reviewing court must give due regard to the trial court's opportunity to judge the witnesses' credibility." Some appellate courts have given less deference to findings of fact based on documentary evidence or undisputed facts than they give to findings of fact based on credibility determinations. Based on Rule 52(a)(6), is it appropriate for these courts to give less deference to findings of fact based on documentary evidence or undisputed facts? Or should they be applying the same level of review as is applied to credibility determinations? Why?

6. What standard of review does an appellate court apply when reviewing a trial court's grant of summary judgment? Why?

Additional Resources

- Ruggiero J. Aldisert, *Opinion Writing* (AuthorHouse 2009).
- Ruggero J. Aldisert, *The Appellate Bar: Professional Responsibility and Professional Competence — A View from the Jaundiced Eye of One Appellate Judge*, 11 Cap. Univ. L. Rev. 445 (1982).
- Ruggiero J. Aldisert, *Winning on Appeal: Better Briefs and Oral Argument* (Rev. 1st ed., Nita 1996).
- Mary Beth Beazley, *A Practical Guide to Appellate Advocacy* (2d ed., Aspen 2006).
- Martha S. Davis, *A Basic Guide to Standards of Review*, 33 S.D. L. Rev. 469, 476 (1988).
- Linda H. Edwards, *Legal Writing: Process, Analysis, and Organization* (5th ed., Aspen 2010).
- Alan D. Hornstein, *Appellate Advocacy in a Nutshell* (West 1984).
- Richard K. Neumann, Jr., *Legal Reasoning and Legal Writing: Structure, Strategy, and Style* (6th ed., Aspen 2010).
- Teresa J. Reid Rambo & Leanne J. Pflaum, *Legal Writing by Design: Writing Great Briefs and Memos* (Carolina Acad. Press 2001).
- Randall H. Warner, *All Mixed Up About Mixed Questions*, 7 J. App. Prac. & Process 101 (2005).

7

Writing Techniques to Use When Drafting Documents for the Court

There are various types of documents that a judge could ask you to draft as a judicial clerk. The most common documents that judges typically ask clerks and externs to draft include judicial opinions, bench memoranda, jury instructions, and orders. Before examining specific documents, however, this chapter discusses several techniques that good writers use. These techniques should be followed when drafting any document for the court—not just when drafting the four documents examined in this chapter.

I. General Tips

Sloppy writing suggests the writer put insufficient time into drafting the document. The quality of a court document, particularly a judicial opinion, is determined by its "tone, organization, style, method, and reasoning."[1] Court documents must be thorough, accurate, logical, grammatical, professional, and timely. They should contain no misspellings or misstatements of fact or law. Nor should they contain any ambiguous language or awkward phrases. They should read easily and flow smoothly from one section of the document to another. The following tips will help you produce documents that satisfy most of these criteria.

---

1. Gerald Lebovits, Alifya V. Curtin & Lisa Solomon, *Ethical Judicial Opinion Writing*, *http://law.bepress.com/expresso/eps/1743*, at 1 (2006).

First, when drafting a court document, do not forget what you previously learned about writing just because you've moved into a genre with which you have little experience. Remember to use those paragraphing rules and to write strong sentences. If you are a little rusty on good writing techniques, you can consult any number of resources designed to aid a writer in improving his or her writing. Two good resources for legal writers to consult are *Just Writing*[2] and *Plain English for Lawyers.*[3]

Second, you should generally use active voice rather than passive voice. With active voice, the subject of the sentence is engaged in action. With passive voice, the subject of the sentence is being acted on. Examples of each are set forth below:

Active voice: Cody hit the ball.
Passive voice: The ball was hit by Cody.

Sentences that are written in active voice are often clearer and shorter than sentences written in passive voice. Active voice is also easier for readers to process mentally. Readers can visualize Cody (the subject of the sentence) hitting (the verb) the ball (the object) as soon as they read the words. In contrast, with passive voice, readers must read the entire sentence before they can process it or visualize it in their minds. Because the actor is not mentioned until the end of the sentence, readers are unable to visualize who is doing the action until they have read the entire sentence.

However, while the active voice is often preferable to the passive voice, passive voice is appropriate in some instances. When the actor is unknown or unimportant, passive voice can be used. Passive voice is also appropriate when the writer wants to downplay or obscure the identity of the actor. However, the court will not use this technique, which counsel can use effectively for a litigant, when fulfilling its fact-finding mission.

Third, avoid using nominalizations because they weaken the sentence and make it verbose. Nominalizations turn verbs into nouns by adding a suffix to the verb. The following suffixes are often added to verbs to create nominalizations: -al, -ment, -ent, -ant, -ence, -ance, -ency, -ancy, -ion, -ity. While not all words with these suffixes are nominalizations, when editing your documents, you can search for nominalizations by looking for these suffixes. Examples of nominalizations include "reached an agreement" rather than "agreed," "made a statement" rather than "stated," and "conducted a review" rather than "reviewed."[4]

Using a nominalization dilutes the impact of the sentence by moving the main action from the verb to the noun. "Because the real action in the sentence is somewhere other than the verb, the writer must find a substitute to fill the verb slot in the sentence."[5] This substitute verb is

---

2. Anne Enquist & Laurel Currie Oates, *Just Writing* (2d ed., Aspen 2005).
3. Richard Wydick, *Plain English for Lawyers* (5th ed. 2005).
4. Enquist & Oates, *supra* note 2, at 124; Nancy A. Wanderer, *Writing Better Opinions: Communicating with Candor, Clarity, and Style*, 54 Me. L. Rev. 47, 63 (2002).
5. Enquist & Oates, *supra* note 2, at §6.2.4.

often "a form of the verb *to be* or some other filler verb that expresses no real action."[6] Because these substitute verbs express no action and are generally bland, using a nominalization tends to sap the energy from the writing.

Using nominalizations leads to verbosity because, in addition to requiring a substitute verb, an article (e.g., a, an, the) and a preposition (e.g., of, on, at) are often needed to form a proper sentence. These extra words can be eliminated by rewriting the sentence so that the verb, not the noun, is doing the work.

Fourth, avoid using "elegant variation" when writing court documents.[7] Elegant variation is using synonyms interchangeably to avoid using the same word. Do not be afraid to repeat the same word or phrase, especially when it is a term of art and has particular legal significance. Legal writers refrain from using elegant variation because lawyers are trained to see changes in words as changes in meaning. Therefore, you should not use a different word unless you mean something different. Thus, elegant variation is avoided with regard to terms of art because "they have distinct meanings a synonym cannot replace."[8] An example of elegant variation includes using "suit," "action," "litigation," and "case" interchangeably.

Fifth, be concise. You should omit unnecessary words or phrases like "at this point in time" and "in the process of." You can also avoid needless repetition by omitting redundant words. For example, in "past history," "past" may be omitted without affecting the clarity of the sentence. Omit "throat-clearing expressions" that add little or nothing to the meaning of the sentence. Such expressions include "it is significant that," "it is generally recognized that," and "it should be noted that."

II. Word Choice

A court document must convey information to the reader in a manner that he or she will understand. Because word choice will have the greatest effect on the reader's ability to comprehend a document, you must select words carefully. Refrain from using words that make the document more difficult to read and understand.

Thus, when drafting documents for the court, you should avoid using "fancy" words when simple words will suffice. In fact, you should select the simplest word that adequately communicates the idea. Use simple words so that the reader need not constantly run to the dictionary to understand what is being said in the document. Understanding the law is difficult enough. Do not add to the lay reader's struggle by using challenging words.

---

6. *Id.*
7. Wanderer, *supra* note 4, at 63.
8. Lebovits, Curtin & Solomon, *supra* note 1, at 23.

When selecting a word, consider how many of your readers are likely to know its meaning. If that number is low, consider whether there is another word that expresses the same concept with which your readers will be more familiar. If so, use the word that would be more readily understood by a larger audience. For example, do not use "abecedarian," which few readers will understand, when "elementary" has essentially the same meaning and far more readers will be familiar with it.

Also, avoid the use of legalese. "Legalese is the language of lawyers, containing words that do not often appear outside the legal profession."[9] It is a word or phrase that a lawyer might use in drafting a legal document but would not use in everyday situations, such as when speaking with her grandparents or spouse. Examples of legalese include "said" or "aforesaid," the use of "same" and "such" as a pronoun, "hereinafter," and "inter alia." While most legalese is avoidable, legal language is sometimes critical. For example, "negligence" is a term of art. To use ordinary language to convey the same information conveyed by the term "negligence" would take up at least a paragraph of space.[10] Thus, "negligence" should be used. In contrast, many legal writers use the word "said" to mean "the." For example, "said plaintiff then slipped on the ice." "Said" is not a term of art; rather, it is useless legalese.

The use of legalese detracts from the effectiveness of a document just as the use of unfamiliar or arcane words does. The use of legalese creates a needlessly stilted tone and makes the document one that cannot easily be understood by the public. Therefore, when selecting a word, remember that you should write decisions so that a variety of audiences can understand them. Consequently, a judge, and thus a judicial clerk, must translate legalese into language that those not trained in the law can understand.

III. Editing and Proofreading

Every document issued by a court must be accurate in every way. The quality of a court document is determined by its organization, reasoning, style, and tone. A document should read easily and flow smoothly from one section to another. Furthermore, a document that contains misspelled words or inaccurate citations shows a lack of care in the document's preparation and brings the accuracy of the substance of the document into question. Because sloppy writing suggests that the writer put insufficient time into drafting the document, a writer must edit and proofread a document to ensure that it is error free and professional in appearance before submitting it to the judge. When editing, you will correct large-scale

---

9. *Id.*
10. Terms of art "have distinct meanings a synonym cannot replace." *Id.*

problems with the document's organization, reasoning, and readability. When proofreading, on the other hand, you will focus on minutia such as typographical, grammatical, and formatting errors. Both editing and proofreading are of the utmost importance.

The primary goals of editing are to improve the organization of the document and the manner in which the law or facts have been presented, eliminate verbosity and ambiguities in the text, improve writing style, correct grammar and punctuation errors, and ensure that citations are included where necessary. While editing, you must also confirm that the cases cited in the draft stand for the proposition of law for which the cases are cited. When editing your own work, it is best to set the completed draft aside for at least a day before starting the editing process. Time away from the draft will provide you with a fresh view of the document. A fresh view will allow you to identify larger issues, such as poor organization or faulty reasoning, as well as smaller issues, such as a missing citation or a poorly written sentence.

There are several other techniques that may aid you when editing a draft. One technique is to read the document out loud, which may reveal problems with the structure of a particular sentence or paragraph. Another technique is editing in stages, with the focus at each stage being on a different issue. For example, during the first stage, the clerk could review the draft, looking only for grammar and punctuation problems. Once these problems have been corrected, you could then review the document to ensure that the style is consistent throughout the document. Next, you could review the document with an eye toward missing citations. Finally, after you have edited the document using some combination of the above-mentioned techniques, you should ask another person — for instance, a co-clerk — to review the draft and make suggestions for improvement.

Once you have made any improvements suggested by the individual who reviewed your draft, and you are satisfied with the substance of the document, you are finished with the editing stage. Your final task is proofreading the document to eliminate sloppiness, such as typographical, grammatical, and formatting errors. Additionally, compare the case title to the docket sheet to ensure that the names of the parties are correct and that the case number is accurate. Proofreading demands meticulous attention to detail and painstaking care. You may have to scour the document again and again to ensure maximum accuracy. Do not be tempted to skip this step to save time — proofreading is a necessary step in the writing process. The judge will evaluate your writing, and if your work looks sloppy, the judge will conclude that the substance of the document is sloppy as well.

Just as with editing, you should put the document aside for at least a day before starting the proofreading process. Time away from the document will allow you to see small problems such as citation errors, repetition of words, superfluous words, missing letters or words, and missing punctuation marks. For example, a fresh view of the draft will allow you to see that you typed the word "statue" when you really intended to type "statute."[11] With regard to missing words, articles (e.g., a, an, the) are frequently omitted from sentences. In addition to searching for citation errors and superfluous or missing words or punctuation marks, you must ensure that any quotations are carefully and accurately quoted. If the quoted material has been altered or any text has been omitted, you should make certain that brackets and ellipses are used appropriately. Furthermore, you should make certain that any quotations of 50 or more words, or spanning at least four lines of text, are block quoted.

Another helpful technique that you may employ is reading the document backwards. Skimming the draft from the end to the beginning prevents the writer's mind from filling in what the writer expects to see by taking the text out of context. Employing this technique will allow you to notice if a word or punctuation mark is out of place or missing. For example, when reading the document backwards, you may notice that a quotation is missing an opening or closing quotation mark.

When proofreading citations, you must ensure that the format of the citations is proper and complies with that used by the court. The citations format is likely to comply with that set forth in either the local court rules or a common citation system used by either *The Bluebook: A Uniform System of Citation*[12] or the *ALWD Citation Manual: A Professional System of Citation*.[13] For cases cited in the document, you must make certain that the parties' names are spelled correctly and that the volume, court, page number, and year of the decision are accurate.

Once you have finished editing and proofreading the opinion, it should be free of large-scale problems with organization and reasoning as well as small-scale problems such as typographical, grammatical, and citation errors. When you are satisfied with the substance of the document and are sure that the document is professional in appearance, you should submit the draft to the judge. The judge will review the document and make some alterations and suggestions.[14] The judge may electronically change the document, or you may be expected to do so. If the latter, you should make the changes in a timely fashion and return both the original, marked-up copy of the draft and the amended draft to the judge for further review. This cycle may continue many times before the document is final. You should, however, be prepared for the judge to scrap the draft and tell you to start over with a different focus. If this occurs, you should not take this constructive criticism as a personal affront but should use the situation as a learning experience.

---

11. As another example, legal writers sometimes type the word "pubic" when they really mean "public."

12. *The Bluebook: A Uniform System of Citation* (Columbia L. Rev. et al. eds., 19th ed., Harv. L. Rev. Assn. 2010).

13. Association of Legal Writing Directors & Darby Dickerson, *ALWD Citation Manual: A Professional System of Citation* (4th ed., Aspen Law & Bus. 2010).

14. The judge may not go through this process with regard to bench memoranda.

Additional Resources

- Erik Paul Belt, *Readers v. Opinion Writers*, 23 U. Mich. J.L. Reform 463 (1990).
- Calvert G. Chipchase, *Federal District Court Law Clerk Handbook* (ABA 2007).
- Federal Judicial Center, *Chambers Handbook for Judges' Law Clerks and Secretaries* (West 1994).
- Anne Enquist & Laurel Currie Oates, *Just Writing* (2d ed., Aspen 2005).
- Richard B. Klein, *Opinion Writing Assistance Involving Law Clerks: What I Tell Them*, 34 No. 3 Judges' J. 33 (1995).
- Gerald Lebovits, Alifya V. Curtin & Lisa Solomon, *Ethical Judicial Opinion Writing*, *http://law.bepress.com/expresso/eps/1743* (2006).
- Joseph L. Lemon, Jr., *Federal Appellate Court Law Clerk Handbook* (ABA 2007).
- Nancy A. Wanderer, *Writing Better Opinions: Communicating with Candor, Clarity, and Style*, 54 Me. L. Rev. 47, 63 (2002).
- Eugene A. Wright, *Observations of an Appellate Judge: The Use of Law Clerks*, 26 Vand. L. Rev. 1179 (1973).
- Richard Wydick, *Plain English for Lawyers* (5th ed. 2005).

8
Drafting a Judicial Opinion

I. Introduction

One of the most common documents that a judicial clerk may be asked to draft is a judicial opinion. Trial court clerks draft opinions and orders resolving the motions before the court; appellate clerks draft opinions resolving issues raised on appeal. An opinion informs the litigants, particularly the losing party, why the court reached the decision that it reached with regard to the issues before it. Thus, an opinion "tell[s] the parties why the winner won and the loser lost"[1] and provides legal support for the decision. In addition to justifying the decision to the losing party, an opinion also justifies the court's position to the public. Further, an opinion provides guidance to future litigants and to the courts, which are bound by stare decisis.

"[O]pinions are simply explanations for judgments—essays written by judges explaining why they recorded the judgment they did."[2] However, opinions written at the trial and appellate stages have slightly different purposes. At the trial stage, the purpose of an opinion is to justify the judge's decision on a motion or the outcome of the case at a bench trial. At the appellate stage, on the other hand, judges write opinions to resolve controversies in their jurisdiction or to correct an erroneous trial court opinion.

---

1. Gerald Lebovits, Alifya V. Curtin & Lisa Solomon, *Ethical Judicial Opinion Writing*, *http://law.bepress.com/expresso/eps/1743*, at 8 (2006).
2. Thomas W. Merrill, *Judicial Opinions as Binding Law and as Explanations for Judgments*, 15 Cardozo L. Rev. 43, 62 (1993).

A. Preparing to Draft the Opinion

When a judge assigns you a case, the judge may require you to draft a memorandum for the judge to use in drafting an opinion, or the judge may require you to produce a first draft of the opinion. Let's assume the judge asks you to produce a first draft of the opinion. When the judge assigns the case, the judge's instructions to you may be very broad. The judge may simply hand the case file and the briefs to you and instruct you to produce a first draft of the opinion. In this situation, you are expected to review the matter and work it out for yourself. Once you have reviewed the matter, you should draft the opinion.

On the other hand, at the time the judge assigns the case, the judge may meet with you to provide some guidance on the matters to be resolved. During this conference, the judge may identify the issues to be decided and emphasize salient points that he or she believes to be of particular importance. When this conference concludes, you ought to have some idea of how the issues are to be resolved, even if you are not certain how to justify those results. You must work out for yourself the problem of how to justify the results. If the judge discusses the case with you, this conference should be the basis for the opinion that you draft. However, if you discover that the judge was mistaken on either a factual issue or a legal point of law, it is imperative that you bring the matter to the judge's attention. While the judge has the final mandate on an issue, it is your duty to prevent the judge from making a mistake.

Regardless of the depth of the judge's instructions at the time the case is assigned, you must complete certain tasks when preparing an opinion. Remember that at the trial level, the court's reasoning is simply to justify its decision. However, before you can resolve the matter before the court, you must take some preliminary steps. First, you must determine whether the court has authority to adjudicate the dispute. Thus, at the trial level, you must review the pleadings to ascertain whether the court has personal and subject-matter jurisdiction. Second, you must ensure that service of process was proper in a civil litigation or that the indictment in a criminal matter was sufficient. Finally, you must determine whether any conflicts of interest exist. At the appellate level, on the other hand, the purpose of the opinion is to determine whether the trial court erred, and if errors were made, whether they were prejudicial. However, before determining whether errors were made, you must determine whether personal and subject-matter jurisdiction exist. You must also determine whether a final appealable order exists and, thus, whether the court has appellate jurisdiction over the matter. After determining that the court has jurisdiction over the appeal, you must then note which issues on appeal were preserved at the trial level. Once you have established jurisdiction and which issues were preserved for appeal, you must then determine the appropriate standard of review. Often, law establishes the standard of review. It serves as a guide as to the level of deference the appellate court must give to the trial court's determinations of law and fact. Finally, you must determine whether any conflicts of interest exist.

When addressing the substantive issues raised by the parties, you should begin by reviewing the briefs of the litigants and gaining a clear understanding of the issues. The first step in preparing to draft an opinion is to read the litigants' articulation of the issues. Once you have identified the issues as presented by the litigants, you must read the analysis section of the briefs and determine for yourself if the issues as articulated by the litigants are, in fact, the issues or if the issues are different. Sometimes the issues will be fairly close to those identified by the litigants. At other times, the issue will be completely different. It is important that you determine for yourself what the issues are. If your thinking is fuzzy regarding the issues, this will negatively affect the rest of the process.

Once you have a clear grasp of the issues, the second step when preparing to draft an opinion is to review the record to determine which facts are relevant. Parties may intentionally or unintentionally color the facts. Therefore, you should obtain the facts from the record itself, never from the litigants' briefs. While the adversary process often skews counsel's rendition of the facts in favor of his or her client, the court's opinion should show no trace of partisanship.

After the pertinent facts have been gathered from the record, the third step is reviewing the authorities relied on by counsel for the litigants to determine whether they were accurately interpreted by counsel. You should also update the authorities to ensure that they remain good law and that no other applicable authorities have been issued since the briefs were filed. Furthermore, you should conduct some additional legal research to determine that counsel for the litigants did not overlook any applicable authorities.

After reviewing the briefs, the issues, the facts, and the governing law, only one step remains before you are prepared to begin drafting the opinion: creating an outline. The best way to organize your thoughts and to ensure that nothing relevant is unintentionally omitted from the opinion is to draft an outline. The outline, which gives you a format for drafting the opinion itself, must be more than a skeletal outline that simply identifies the order in which the issues will be discussed. For the outline to be an effective tool, it must be fairly detailed. The outline should not only identify the issues, but also identify the pertinent authorities that relate to each issue, identify the relevant facts from the case currently before the court, and briefly state or summarize the reasoning that supports the conclusions reached with regard to the issues.

Do not make the mistake of skipping this step to save time. Drafting an outline forces you to organize the materials in a concrete manner. While transferring the information floating around in your head to paper or a word processor, any problems with organization will become clear. It will be much easier to adjust your thinking and organization at the outline stage than while revising the text of the opinion itself. Once a writer puts words in print, he or she often becomes wed to those words, even when they are problematic due to organization or substance. By dealing with this same problem at the outlining stage, rather than the revision stage, you will not only save yourself time, but also some grief.

B. Format of the Opinion

Once you have completed the necessary preparatory steps, you are ready to begin drafting the opinion. It is important to remember that the purpose and style of a judicial opinion is different from that of a memorandum, brief, law review article, or seminar paper for law school. An opinion is not an essay that covers the subject in minute detail or discusses the entire breadth of the legal issues involved. An opinion is merely intended to inform the litigants, and the general public, why the court acted in the manner that it did.

Before actually putting pen to paper (or fingers to keys), ask the judge or a co-clerk for a sample opinion written by the judge. A sample opinion will provide you with a template that the judge previously found acceptable. If the judge is unable to produce a sample opinion, do not panic. Generally, an opinion includes a caption, an introduction to the case, a statement of the facts, a statement of the issues in contention, a discussion and analysis of the law governing the matter, and a conclusion section. While the titles and arrangement of the sections may vary somewhat depending on the court or the case itself, the substance of the sections will remain the same.

1. CAPTION OF THE CASE

Begin the opinion with the full caption of the case. The caption provides information that allows the reader to identify the case before the court. This information includes the name of the court, the docket or case number, the names of the parties and their procedural designations, the name of the judge assigned to the case, and the title of the document ("Opinion"). Be sure to correctly identify the parties. Since the inception of the litigation, a party may have been added to or removed from the case. Furthermore, parties named in their official capacity may have changed since the complaint was initially filed with the court.

An appellate opinion will identify the judges on the panel as well as the judge who wrote the majority opinion and the author of any concurring or dissenting opinions. If the opinion is per curium, the caption will reflect this by stating "per curium" or "by the court." The caption may also include the names of the attorneys representing the parties.

2. INTRODUCTION

The introduction follows the caption of the case. The purpose of the introduction is to provide context for the reader by identifying who is involved in the case and what the case is about. By providing a context for the information that follows, the introduction allows the reader to better understand the opinion. Thus, the introduction should identify the parties, the claims filed by the parties, and the reason the case is presently before the court (on a specific motion or on appeal). This section generally is not more than one or two paragraphs. Despite its length, the introduction must provide the reader with enough information to understand the opinion as he or she reads through it.

The opening paragraph should begin by identifying the parties to the lawsuit by name and identifying who each party is in terms of the litigation (i.e., plaintiff or defendant, appellant or appellee). The introduction should also establish how the court will refer to the parties. Rather than using generic identifiers for the parties like plaintiff and defendant or appellant and appellee, use the names of the parties or functional designations (e.g., "Landlord" and "Tenant"). Identifying the parties by their names or functional designations lessens the burden on the reader to remember which party is which. Furthermore, less-specific references can cause confusion when there are many parties, including plaintiffs, defendants, cross-claimants, counterclaimants, and so on.

After identifying the parties, summarize the facts of the case in a sentence or two. The introduction should then set forth the procedural history of the case, explaining the nature of the action and how it came to be before the court and identifying the issue(s) that the court must decide. In an appellate opinion, the introduction should also identify what agency or court decisions are under review. Finally, the introduction should conclude with the actual ruling and state, if possible, the rule of law that the case reaffirms or establishes. The actual ruling at the trial level will be "granted," "denied," or "the court finds for the plaintiff/defendant." At the appellate level, the actual ruling will be, inter alia, "affirmed" or "reversed and remanded." Please note that not all judges include the holding in the introduction. You will have to determine the preference of the judge for whom you work.

3. STATEMENT OF THE FACTS

The statement of facts follows the introduction. The statement of facts is the story of the parties; therefore, it should be told in narrative form. This section should not include all the facts, but only those facts that are legally significant or necessary to establish the context of the events that occurred. Legally significant facts are those that are relevant to the issue before the court and will be relied on by the judge when deciding that issue. Thus, legally significant facts are determinative of the outcome of the case. For example, in a negligence action, any facts that the court would rely on to determine whether the defendant owed a duty to the plaintiff, whether the defendant breached that duty, whether the plaintiff suffered injury, and whether the defendant's breach of duty was the legal cause of that harm are legally significant facts that must be mentioned in the statement of the facts in an opinion. Do not omit facts that are significant to the losing party.

Always procure the facts directly from the record — not from the briefs of the parties — to ensure accuracy. However, while the facts should be obtained from the record, this does not mean that the statement of facts should simply reproduce the record or include verbatim quotations from deposition or trial transcripts or from the text of pleadings or motions. Rather, the statement of facts should be a brief summary of the facts, just a few paragraphs. While most cases will require only a few paragraphs, in a complicated case, the statement of facts may need to be longer for the reader to understand what happened.

Regardless, the facts should be limited to those necessary to understand the court's decision regarding the legal issue. Importantly, the statement of facts includes *facts*, not legal conclusions. A legal conclusion is just what it sounds like — a conclusion of law. When a writer includes a legal conclusion, he or she has examined what actually occurred (e.g., running a red light) and applied the law to that fact to reach a conclusion (e.g., that the defendant was negligent). Stating that the defendant was negligent is a legal conclusion because negligence is a concept defined by law, and you can only determine that a defendant was negligent by consulting one or more laws. Avoid legal conclusions. The statement of facts in a judicial opinion should present the facts in a neutral, objective manner.

While legal conclusions are not properly included in an opinion, you may include logical conclusions of fact, or inferences, in the statement of facts. Logical conclusions of fact are not facts but are conclusions that are reasonably inferred from the evidence presented by the litigants. The following is an example of an inference or conclusion of fact.

> Although the Hearing Officer did not make an explicit finding of unavailability, that finding must be inferred from the Hearing Officer's determination that Adams was entitled to benefits pursuant to subsection 55-B for 100% partial incapacity.[3]

Subsection 55-B requires a finding of unavailability in order to award benefits to a claimant. The fact that the Hearing Officer awarded benefits to Adams leads to the logical conclusion that the officer must have made a finding of unavailability. When including conclusions of fact in your statement of facts, be careful not to make inferences based on the law. Only include inferences that you have drawn from the facts themselves.

Furthermore, the absence of a fact may itself be a fact worth noting. Pointing out the absence of specific evidence or the absence of an allegation may be important depending on the matter before the court and the governing law.

---

3. *Id.* at 57.

Generally, present the facts in chronological order. Chronological order is ideal because it gives the statement of the facts a narrative flow by setting forth the chain of events that occurred. However, in rare instances, relating the facts in chronological order will be confusing to the reader. Confusion occurs when there are many different claims and many facts that relate only to specific claims. When relating the facts in chronological order is confusing, use a topical organization. For example, in a case where a plaintiff claimed that his employer had discriminated against him in violation of the ADA and claimed multiple disabilities, such as morbid obesity, diabetes, hypertension, and sleep apnea, it might be easier to group together the facts relating to individual disabilities rather than relating all the facts as they occurred in time. Thus, all the facts relating to the plaintiff's claim of discrimination based on his morbid obesity would be discussed; next, the facts relating to his claim of discrimination based on his diabetes would be discussed; and so on.

There are a few more things to note when drafting a statement of facts. First, discuss the facts in the past tense. Second, at the trial level, you may present the facts differently depending on the motion that is being decided. When dealing with a motion to dismiss, the court must assume that the plaintiff's factual assertions are true. Additionally, when resolving a motion for summary judgment, the court does not serve as a fact finder. Because summary judgment is not warranted if a material fact is in controversy, evidence that both supports and contests the motion must be set forth in the statement of the facts. Third, at the appellate level, state that the trial court "found" a particular fact to be true and "held" the conclusions of law.

Finally, when the opinion is complete, be sure to review the statement of the facts. Make certain that it includes all the facts relied on by the judge. Additionally, you must cite to the record for each fact mentioned in the statement of the facts. At the trial level, the record would include the pleadings and all the evidence, including depositions, documents, admissions, responses to interrogatories, affidavits, hearing or trial transcripts, and exhibits. At the appellate level, you would cite to the excerpts of record.

4. ISSUES IN CONTENTION

After the statement of facts, the opinion must clearly articulate the specific legal issues to be decided by the court. Although you may have briefly identified the issues in the introduction, it is important that you set forth the legal issues in more detail just before articulating the determination of those issues. Consolidating the issues in one paragraph, rather than scattering them throughout the opinion, is the better organizational strategy. The reader will be able to easily find the issues in contention and will not have to scour the entire opinion searching for them. Also, organize the issues in the same order that you will analyze them in the

Discussion. When there is only one legal issue, the issue in contention may be situated at the start of the discussion of the issue rather than set out in a separate section. Please note that some judges prefer to locate the issues in the contention section before the statement of facts section. You should determine the preference of the judge for whom you work.

In law school, you may have learned to articulate the issues using a "whether-when" or "under-does-when" formula. While such a formula may have been helpful when writing an office memorandum or a brief, judges tend to draft issues in a more sophisticated, less rote manner. When drafting the issues in contention, begin with language similar to the following: "The issue in this case is . . . ." Be sure to identify the legal question, and briefly include the legally significant facts. An issue has little meaning without the relevant facts.

Additionally, you must state the issues objectively. The reader should not be able to discern bias toward a party. Nor should the reader be able to discern, just from reading the issue statement, which party will be successful.

5. Discussion of the Issues

The discussion of the issues is the heart of the opinion. This section provides not only the court's resolution of the issues, but also the reasoning supporting its decision. This section sets forth the applicable legal principles, including the applicable standard of review, and applies them to the matters currently before the court. However, it is important to remember that a judicial opinion should resolve only the controversy before the court. The opinion should not discuss superfluous matters.

The standard of review is identified at the beginning of the discussion section and precedes the analysis of the substantive issues. When there is more than one issue, each with a different standard of review, the applicable standard should be discussed prior to the analysis of each substantive issue. Another option is to discuss all applicable standards of review in one paragraph, though this can be somewhat awkward. The standard of review precedes the analysis of the substantive issues because it mandates the level of deference that the appellate court gives to the lower court's findings and analysis. It creates the framework for how to view the facts and discuss the analysis. Consequently, the standard of review shapes the analysis of the issues and significantly affects the outcome of the case. Using different standards can lead to vastly different results. For more information regarding standards of review, see the discussion in Chapter 6.

After identifying the relevant standard of review, the opinion must then resolve the issues on appeal. The opinion should clearly explain the law governing the substantive areas in question and its application to the facts of the case to avoid any ambiguity. Ambiguity in an opinion, particularly an appellate decision, will likely lead to further litigation in an attempt by lawyers and litigants to determine the precise meaning of the opinion. In the opinion, to avoid ambiguity, you must be sure to set forth the facts that drive the outcome and to articulate why those facts, when considered in regard to the governing rule of law, lead to the result articulated by the judge. Additionally, clarifying the court's factual basis for the decision will provide future litigants and future courts with the information necessary to resolve future disputes.

Headings and an outline format, while not necessary if the opinion is short, help guide the reader through the opinion. If the opinion is long or involves several distinct issues, discuss each individual, unrelated issue before the court separately, and provide section headings that correspond to each issue. The section headings for these individual unrelated issues should be labeled with roman numerals (I, II, etc.). Then, when analyzing an issue, provide subheadings for any smaller categories within that subject that must be analyzed. The elements of the prima facie case or the factors to be considered when examining a claim are often good candidates for subsections. The subheadings for these sections are labeled with capital letters (A, B, etc.). Smaller categories within these subheadings are labeled with numerals (1, 2, etc.) and lowercase letters (a, b, etc.) as appropriate.

For example, let's assume that the case for which you are drafting an opinion on a motion for summary judgment involves a question of whether the defendant infringed on the plaintiff's copyright or whether the defendant's use of the copyrighted image was a fair use. The factors to be analyzed when determining whether an author or artist has violated an owner's copyright include the purpose and character of the use, the nature of the copyrighted work, the amount and substantiality of the portion used in relation to the work as a whole, and the effect of the use on the potential market or value of the copyrighted work.[4] The headings for such an opinion may look something like the following:

I. Copyright Infringement
   A. Violation of the Owner's Copyright
   B. Fair Use Defense
      1. Purpose and Character of the Use
      2. Nature of the Copyrighted Work
      3. Amount and Substantiality of the Portion Used
      4. Effect on the Market or Value of the Copyrighted Work

The section headings will serve as landmarks so that the reader does not get lost in the opinion. Additionally, breaking the opinion into shorter, more manageable chunks of information will make it less likely to overwhelm the reader and will aid the reader's understanding of the opinion.

When multiple issues are to be resolved, you must decide the order in which you will discuss those issues. The order in which you discuss the issues need not necessarily correspond with the order followed by counsel

---

4. 17 U.S.C. §107 (2000).

for the litigants in their briefs. Generally, you must discuss the most important issue first. However, if there is a preliminary procedural question that may affect the outcome of the matter, dispose of that issue first before discussing the substantive matters. Additionally, if there is a nonprocedural threshold issue, such as a statute of limitations question, resolve that issue before discussing the other substantive issues.

Following resolution of threshold issues, large claims or issues should be addressed before deciding less significant matters. However, if no one claim is larger than any other claim, first resolve the claim that most affects the litigation. For instance, if a defendant in a criminal appeal seeks a new trial, or in the alternative, a reduced jail sentence, the first issue you should address is whether to grant a new trial. If the court grants a new trial, there is no need to consider the defendant's request for a reduced sentence. However, everything else being equal, resolve the issues based on the hierarchy of authority: Resolve constitutional questions first, statutory questions second, common law questions third, and state law claims fourth. Regardless of the order in which the issues are discussed, the opinion should flow smoothly "from one point to the next, without repetition of facts already stated."[5]

Counsel for the litigants will likely present a plethora of issues in the briefs. The amount of discussion you should devote to a particular issue depends on the issue itself. When dealing with a point of law that is well settled, you can adequately resolve the issue with little discussion. Often, reference to one or two citations is sufficient. However, if the issue involves a novel question of law, or an area of law where the court's opinions seem to contradict each other, a longer, more detailed discussion will be required. Finally, issues with little merit require little discussion. While these issues do not merit detailed discussion, the opinion should not completely ignore such issues. To reassure counsel that the court took notice of the alleged errors, the opinion should mention these issues and note that they are without merit. The discussion of these meritless issues can be grouped together, rather than scattered throughout the opinion, and dispatched in a sentence or two at the end of the opinion. No additional discussion is necessary.

Organize the discussion of each individual issue using the IRAC (issue, rule, analysis, conclusion) structure. Begin the discussion of an individual issue by identifying that issue. This can be done with a descriptive section heading. Next, identify the governing rule of law and show how that rule operates. When discussing the law, do not trace the historical development of the law. A judicial opinion is not a law review article. Instead, identify the law as it currently exists. Thus, you would discuss the governing law in the present tense. You may deviate from this course of action only in a couple instances. First, you may trace the historical

---

5. George Rose Smith, *A Primer of Opinion Writing for Law Clerks*, 26 Vand. L. Rev. 1179, 1207 (1973).

development of the law when the court is dealing with an issue of first impression. Second, you may examine the law's history when the court is shedding light on or expanding its own law. When discussing law that is no longer in force, you must discuss it in the past tense.

Then, apply the governing rule to the facts of the case before the court. In the analysis of the issue, you should not only state the resolution of the issue, but also explain your reasoning as to why the court resolved the issue in the manner that it did and offer legal support for its reasoning. When discussing the issues, you must be sure to analyze all the serious issues in contention. When addressing a serious issue in contention, you must present the arguments of both parties and clearly state a conclusion as to which argument was more persuasive. You must also explain why that party's argument was more persuasive than the losing party's argument. Thus, when discussing serious issues in contention, you will analyze those issues with a fair amount of detail, clearly articulating your reasoning. You may, however, dispose of a meritless claim without offering an in-depth analysis of the issue. Such claims can often be disposed of in just a sentence of two. For example, at the trial level, a clerk might explain that "the Court has considered [insert the plaintiff's name] claim of [insert detail] and concludes that this claim is without merit. At the appellate level, a clerk would explain that "the Court has considered [insert the appellant's name] other assignments of error and concludes that they are without merit." The next sentence or two might provide a brief explanation as to why the claims or assignments of error are without merit.

6. CONCLUSION

The last paragraph of the opinion should contain the court's disposition of the case and its mandate. The disposition of the case is based on the sum of the conclusions for the individual issues on appeal. "If one of the individual conclusions is inconsistent with the final disposition, either that individual conclusion should be changed or the final disposition must be modified. The final disposition must be consistent with all of the individual conclusions."[6]

The disposition and mandate should not only set forth the decision that has been reached by the court but also identify the relief to be granted. At the trial level, the conclusion section must clearly articulate for whom judgment was rendered and identify what, if any, steps must be taken by the parties. At the appellate level, the judgment appealed may be affirmed, revised and rendered, or reversed and remanded. If the case is reversed and remanded, the opinion must include clear instructions for the trial court. These instructions should leave no doubt as to what is required of the trial court on remand. Don't just order the trial court to "enter judgment consistent with this opinion." Be more specific. For example, when a

---

6. Nancy A. Wanderer, *Writing Better Opinions: Communicating with Candor, Clarity, and Style*, 54 Me. L. Rev. 47, 60 (2002).

case is remanded for a new trial, you must clearly describe the scope of the new trial, including whether a completely new trial is warranted or if the new trial should be limited to certain issues. Similarly, if a case is remanded for resentencing, instruct the trial court on what the new sentence should be. Finally, the opinion will end with a signature line for the judge's signature.

For an example of an opinion, see the sample judicial opinion at the end of the chapter.

II. Drafting Tips

Armed with your outline and a template for the opinion, you are ready to begin drafting the opinion. Judicial opinions, as with other court documents, must be thorough, accurate, logical, grammatical, professional, and timely. The following tips will help you produce opinions that satisfy these criteria.

A. Miscellaneous Suggestions

Given the caseload that faces the court, it is important that you work efficiently and carefully manage your time. However, as inevitably happens when writing, you may suffer writer's block. If writer's block occurs, there is no need to flounder while waiting for the creative juices to flow. Instead, take more proactive measures. One measure that you can employ is to discuss the case with the judge so that you know exactly what he or she wants to say before writing. Another measure is to start writing where you feel comfortable. You need not begin writing the opinion at the beginning. The writing process is not a linear process for many people. Start with what you know. If you do not feel as though you know anything sufficiently well to begin writing, which often happens to novices, just begin drafting. What you write at this point is not nearly as important as the fact that you *are* writing. While your thoughts may be unorganized or ambiguous, later revision and editing can correct these problems. But if you do not begin to write, you will have nothing with which to work and will continue to stare at a blank computer screen or piece of paper. Referring to your outline should also help with writer's block because you have text on the page and a format for the discussion. If you failed to draft an outline at the preparation stage and you are suffering from writer's block, get started by outlining the discussion.

Another tip with regard to drafting an opinion is that footnotes are less appropriate in a judicial opinion than in a law review article and should be kept to a minimum. Any information that is necessary to understand the opinion, or is otherwise sufficiently important to mention, should be addressed in the body of the opinion rather than in a footnote. Tangential information, which is commonly discussed in footnotes, often does not deal directly with the case that is before the court and, therefore, is not subjected to the same close and careful scrutiny as the body of the opinion. Thus, a footnote may not accurately portray the court's view of the case, and worse still, may throw the rest of the opinion into doubt. Consequently, footnotes may undermine the goals of justifying the court's decision to the litigants and the public. Be aware that your judge may have a different preference; you must determine what the judge's preference is with regard to the use of footnotes.

B. Style

Furthermore, when drafting an opinion, you should mimic the judge's writing style. Because writing is connected to personality, each judge has his or her own individual writing style. While some judges prefer complex sentences and an extensive vocabulary, other judges prefer simple declarative sentences and plain English. Moreover, some judge use a very formal tone, while other judges use a somewhat less formal tone. Because the judge is the one consistent factor in the decision-making process, and not the numerous judicial clerks who come and go from the judge's chambers, you should attempt to emulate the judge's writing style to ensure continuity. To further that goal, you should read several of the judge's opinions to become familiar with his or her writing style and learn from the judge's edits to your drafts. However, while the judge is the boss, do not be afraid to make suggestions that would improve the clarity of the writing.

C. Tone

The tone of a judicial opinion should be professional. The opinion should be respectful of the parties and demonstrate that the court has carefully considered all the arguments that the parties have made. To that end, write the opinion so that a layperson with a high school education can understand it.

When drafting an opinion, word choice is crucial. Word choice is important because of its effect not only on the reader's ability to comprehend the opinion but also on the tone of the opinion. Thus, you should avoid use of arcane or unfamiliar words and legalese not only because such words make a judicial opinion difficult for the reader to understand but also because it makes the court appear pompous and condescending. If the court appears pompous and condescending, it will alienate lay readers, and they will be less likely to trust the court's reasoning. You might remember reading an arcane case in your first year of law school to identify with your audience. This result undermines the goals of a judicial opinion — justifying the outcome to the losing party and the public in general.

Additionally, avoid using humor in a judicial opinion. The use of humor interferes with the goals of justifying the outcome to the litigants and the public. First, it fails to show the litigants the proper respect by making light of their situation. Second, the use of humor may cause a reader to question whether the court has truly given careful thought to the decision. Finally, the use of humor may have a negative effect on the public's perception of the court system because it appears that the judge does not take his duties seriously.

III. Editing and Proofreading

You must edit and proofread the draft of the opinion to ensure that it is professional and error free. If, after reviewing the draft, the judge scraps the draft or has many suggestions for improvement, do not be disheartened. Although the opinion-drafting process relies on collaboration between the judge and the judicial clerk, it is imperative that you keep in mind that the responsibility for the decision-making process resides squarely with the judge. While the judge must agree with every word you have written in the opinion, the reverse is not true. You need not agree with the outcome desired by the judge. But even if you do not agree with the judge's decision and reasoning, you must do as the judge dictates. The judge is ultimately responsible for the opinion, not you.

IV. Checklist for Drafting a Judicial Opinion

When drafting the opinion, and before submitting it to the judge or the staff attorney, consider the following questions to determine whether the opinion does everything that it needs to do and that it is accurate.

____ Did you establish that the court has jurisdiction over the matters before it?

____ Did you include all the relevant information in the caption?

____ Did you correctly identify the parties, making certain of any added, removed, or substituted parties?

____ In the introduction, did you identify the parties by name and their procedural designations?

____ Did you identify the nature of the claims filed in the lawsuit?

____ Did you include all the legally significant facts in the statement of the facts?

____ Did you include the facts supporting the losing party?

____ Did you support all the factual statements in the opinion with references to the evidence, including depositions, documents, admissions, responses to interrogatories, affidavits, hearing or trial transcripts, and exhibits or to the excerpt of record?

____ Did you state the facts objectively and without bias?

____ Have you omitted legal conclusions and instead included the relevant facts on which those conclusions were based?

____ Are the issues to be decided clearly stated in one location rather than scattered throughout the opinion?

____ Did you articulate the issues objectively and without bias?

____ Did you organize the issues in the same order that they are discussed in the discussion section?

____ Did you begin the discussion by identifying and explaining the pertinent standard of review?

____ Did you address and resolve all issues?

____ Did you identify the losing party's arguments and adequately address each of them?

____ Did you verify that the cases cited by the parties stand for the propositions for which they are asserted?

____ Did you support the conclusions in the opinion with clear reasoning and legal authorities?

____ Did you rely on mandatory authority to support your conclusions where possible?

____ Did you minimize your reliance on persuasive authorities (unless the court is clarifying the law or addressing an issue of first impression)?

____ Did you clearly and succinctly state the court's disposition of the case?

____ Did you include clear instructions for the lower court?

____ Did you dispose of all the issues raised by the parties?

____ Did you indicate all omissions from quotations with ellipses?

____ Are all dates and numbers accurate?

____ Are all direct quotations from depositions, documents, admissions, responses to interrogatories, affidavits, hearing or trial transcripts, exhibits, and legal authority perfectly accurate?

____ Is the opinion free of grammar, punctuation, spelling, and citation errors?

____ Did you treat all parties with respect?[7]

Additional Resources

- Appellate Judges Conference, *Judicial Opinion Writing Manual* (West 1991).
- Ruggiero J. Aldisert, *Opinion Writing* (AuthorHouse 2009).

---

7. This checklist was adapted in part from checklists found in Wanderer, *supra* note 6, at 70, and Mary L. Dunnewold, Beth A. Honetschlager & Brenda L. Tofte, *Judicial Clerkships: A Practical Guide* 239-241 (Carolina Acad. Press 2010).

◆ Erik Paul Belt, *Readers v. Opinion Writers*, 23 U. Mich. J.L. Reform 463 (1990).

◆ Mary L. Dunnewold, Beth A. Honetschlager & Brenda L. Tofte, *Judicial Clerkships: A Practical Guide* (Carolina Acad. Press 2010).

◆ Federal Judicial Center, *Chambers Handbook for Judges' Law Clerks and Secretaries* (West 1994).

◆ Richard B. Klein, *Opinion Writing Assistance Involving Law Clerks: What I Tell Them*, 34 No. 3 Judges' J. 33 (1995).

◆ Gerald Lebovits, *Judges' Clerks Play Varied Roles in the Opinion Drafting Process*, 76 N.Y. St. B.J. 34 (July/Aug. 2004).

◆ Gerald Lebovits, Alifya V. Curtin & Lisa Solomon, *Ethical Judicial Opinion Writing*, *http://law.bepress.com/expresso/eps/1743* (2006).

◆ Joseph L. Lemon, Jr., *Federal Appellate Court Law Clerk Handbook* (ABA 2007).

◆ Thomas W. Merrill, *Judicial Opinions as Binding Law and as Explanations for Judgments*, 15 Cardozo L. Rev. 43 (1993).

◆ Richard K. Neumann, Jr., *Legal Reasoning and Legal Writing: Structure, Strategy, and Style* (6th ed., Aspen 2010).

◆ George Rose Smith, *A Primer of Opinion Writing for Four New Judges*, 21 Ark. L. Rev. 197 (1967-1968).

◆ George Rose Smith, *A Primer of Opinion Writing for Law Clerks*, 26 Vand. L. Rev. 1179 (1973).

◆ Nancy A. Wanderer, *Writing Better Opinions: Communicating with Candor, Clarity, and Style*, 54 Me. L. Rev. 47 (2002).

◆ Bernard E. Witkin, *Seminars for Circuit Court Judges*, 63 F.R.D. 453 (Fed. Jud. Ctr. 1974).

◆ Eugene A. Wright, *Observations of an Appellate Judge: The Use of Law Clerks*, 26 Vand. L. Rev. 1179 (1973).

SAMPLE JUDICIAL OPINION

**IN THE UNITED STATES DISTRICT COURT
FOR THE SOUTHERN DISTRICT OF OHIO
WESTERN DIVISION**

Caption of the case. This section identifies the case.

CALEB WINSLOW,
  Plaintiff,

  v.

  Case No. 2:99-CV-717

  Judge Aquilina

CITY OF CINCINNATI, et al.,
  Defendants.

Opinion and Order

Introduction.
Because this
section identifies
the legal issue in
contention, the
writer does not
include a section
later identifying
the issue.

Plaintiff Caleb Winslow brings this action under 42 U.S.C. §1983, seeking monetary damages from defendant Dominick Daniel, an officer of the Cincinnati Police Department ["CPD"].[8] Plaintiff alleges that defendant Daniel stopped plaintiff without legal justification and conducted an illegal pat-down search of him in violation of his rights under the Fourth Amendment. Defendant Daniel contends that he had reasonable suspicion to stop the vehicle in which plaintiff was a passenger and to perform a brief pat-down of plaintiff.[9] Trial to the Court was held on March 15, 2001. Pursuant to the provisions of Fed. R. Civ. P. 52(a), the Court now makes the following findings of fact and conclusions of law.

I. Findings of Fact

Statement of the
facts. In a trial
court opinion,
the findings of
fact serve as the
statement of the
facts.

Both plaintiff Caleb Winslow and Byron Hanson testified that on the evening of July 11, 1998, Winslow met Hanson at the latter's residence.[10] The two left for the area around the Xavier University in Cincinnati, Ohio, in Hanson's red Z-28 Camaro. They first went to The Magic Eight Ball, where they played pool and watched television. Later in the evening, the two walked to Libation's, a restaurant and bar, where they remained until about 2:30 a.m. They then walked back to Hanson's vehicle. Hanson was driving south on High Street when the men passed a Steak 'n Shake restaurant, decided to eat, and circled the block. Hanson turned north from Eighth Avenue onto High Street. As they waited in the left turn lane to enter the Steak 'n Shake premises, plaintiff noticed that a police cruiser was behind them.

Defendant Daniel testified that both he and Officer James Conroy[11] were on routine motor patrol in a marked police cruiser at approximately 2:45 a.m. on the morning of July 12, 1998. *Transcript*, at 8, 12. The officers were driving north on High Street, between Eighth and Euclid Avenues, when a group of five or six young men flagged them down. *Tr.*, at 14, 80; *Deposition of James Conroy*, at 14, 15. These young men, who were upset and very excited, informed the officers that a vehicle, possibly a Trans-Am, Camaro, or Thunderbird, had been following them and that the occupants of the

8. Plaintiff originally also named the City of Cincinnati as a defendant in this case. However, on July 19, 2000, the parties filed a stipulation of dismissal with prejudice with respect to the city. Accordingly, the City of Cincinnati is no longer a party to this lawsuit.

9. Other claims presented in the complaint were resolved adversely to plaintiff by earlier order of the Court. *Opinion and Order* (November 20, 2000).

10. A partial transcript consisting of defendant Daniel's testimony will be cited throughout the opinion; however, the testimony of other witnesses has not been transcribed.

11. Nicholas testified by deposition.

continues on next page

vehicle had been threatening to "kick their ass." *Tr.*, at 14-17; *Conroy Depo.*, at 14, 15. Although defendant initially testified on deposition that these men informed the officers that the vehicle following them was black, *Deposition of Dominick Daniel*, at 14, he testified at trial that the men did not indicate the color of the vehicle. *Tr.*, at 17.[12] The young men did not indicate that the occupants of the vehicle had weapons. *Tr.*, at 25-26; *Conroy Depo.*, at 45. One of the young men pointed a vehicle out as the one that had been following the group. *Tr.*, at 28; *Conroy Depo.*, at 15. Defendant testified that the vehicle, which was parked in a lot just south of the officers, and on the west side of High Street, sat in the lot for approximately 10 to 15 seconds before pulling north onto High Street. *Tr.*, at 28-29. Officer Conroy first observed the vehicle after it had pulled back onto High Street, apparently from either a side street or a parking lot. *Conroy Depo.*, at 20-21. When the vehicle passed the cruiser, the officers pulled onto High Street. *Id.* Although plaintiff disputes the incident with the group of young men, the Court finds that defendant's evidence concerning this group, i.e., the testimony of both defendant Daniel and Officer Conroy, is credible and that the group of young men did, in fact, approach the officers.

Although plaintiff testified that there was other traffic on High Street, defendant testified that no other vehicles were between the Hanson vehicle and the police cruiser. *Id.* at 35-36. According to defendant, the cruiser caught up to the Hanson vehicle when it slowed down to turn into Steak 'n Shake. *Id.* at 36. Plaintiff and Hanson testified, and defendant does not dispute, *Id.* at 45; *Conroy Depo.*, at 26, that the Hanson vehicle, followed by the police cruiser, pulled into the drive-through line at Steak 'n Shake. At the officers' directive, Hanson left the drive-through line and pulled into a parking space facing the neighboring 7-Eleven convenience store. *Tr.*, at 45. The parking lot was well lit. *Id.* at 47. Officer Conroy approached the driver's side of the vehicle and defendant approached plaintiff on the passenger side. *Id.* at 48; *Conroy Depo.*, at 26. Defendant did not specifically recall whether either of the occupants asked why they had been stopped. *Tr.*, at 49. However, defendant testified that he and Conroy informed the occupants of the vehicle why they had been stopped. *Id.* According to defendant, plaintiff objected that he and Hanson had done nothing wrong. *Id.* at 52. Defendant asked plaintiff for identification more than once, and plaintiff refused each request. *Id.* at 52-53; *Conroy Depo.*, at 28. Defendant also testified that plaintiff refused to even verbally provide his name and date of

---

12. Even on deposition, defendant later distanced himself from his earlier testimony about the color of the car. *Daniel Depo.*, at 29.

birth. *Tr.*, at 53. At that point, defendant ordered plaintiff out of the vehicle because "[h]e was going in the back of the cruiser . . . ." *Tr.*, at 63. *See also id.* at 57.

Plaintiff and Hanson testified that the officers did not inform them of the reason for the stop of the vehicle. In fact, both men testified that, when plaintiff asked the officers why he and Hanson had been stopped, the officers did not immediately answer. According to plaintiff, Officer Conroy eventually responded, "For harassing those people over there." Plaintiff then asked, "What people?" It was at this point that, according to plaintiff, defendant asked him if he "wanted to show him his i.d.?" Plaintiff responded in the negative. He again asked, "What people?" Defendant then asked him to step out of the vehicle. Plaintiff and Hanson both testified that, up to this point, neither officer questioned them about the alleged incident with the group of young men on High Street.

The Court finds that plaintiff was an extremely credible witness. His demeanor was forthcoming and his testimony was without evasiveness; he resisted exaggeration, even when testifying about his subjective response to the events of that night. The Court therefore accepts plaintiff's version of the events and his testimony that defendant requested identification only once before ordering plaintiff out of the vehicle.

The parties agree that plaintiff obeyed defendant's order to step out of the vehicle. *Id.* at 56. As plaintiff exited the vehicle, he made no furtive movements or threatening comments. Defendant saw no sign of weapons. *Id.* at 60-62. Once plaintiff exited the Hanson vehicle, defendant directed him to the back of the vehicle. *Id.* at 56. Defendant had plaintiff interlace his fingers behind his head, *id.*, and informed plaintiff that he would be patted down. *Id.* at 57. Defendant placed one hand on top of plaintiff's interlaced fingers and lightly patted down Winslow's outer clothing. *Id.* at 63.

Defendant testified that, prior to patting plaintiff down, he asked plaintiff "if there was anything that [defendant] should know about." *Id.* at 88. Although plaintiff responded in the negative, defendant felt a "hard . . . rectangular-shaped box," *id.* at 89, in plaintiff's front left pocket. Defendant asked plaintiff what the object was, and plaintiff responded that defendant did not "need to know what it is." *Id.* at 90.[13]

The parties agree that other police officers were in the Steak 'n Shake parking lot during some or all of these events. Plaintiff and

---

13. The object was apparently drug paraphernalia. Defendant detained plaintiff and issued him a misdemeanor summons for drug abuse and possession of drug paraphernalia. As noted *supra*, plaintiff's claim arising out of his arrest was previously resolved adversely to plaintiff. *Opinion and Order* (November 20, 2000).

continues on next page

Hanson testified that they did not observe either Officer Conroy or defendant speak with the other officers; defendant testified that, within minutes after stopping the Hanson vehicle, he and Officer Conroy sent another officer, whom defendant could neither identify nor describe at trial, *id*. at 59-60, down the street to locate the victims. *Id*. at 40, 59. *See also Conroy Depo*., at 36. The men were never located. *Id*. at 60; *Conroy Depo*., at 37.

As noted *supra*, Officer Conroy approached Hanson, who was driving his car that night. Conroy asked Hanson for identification, *Conroy Depo*., at 26, which Hanson provided. *Id*. at 46. Hanson was never directed to leave the car, nor was he patted down, searched, arrested or charged with any offense. Officer Conroy testified on deposition that he heard defendant ask plaintiff for identification and then direct plaintiff to get out of the vehicle. *Id*. at 28. Conroy "guess[ed]" that the order was issued because plaintiff did not provide identification. *Id*. at 29. At that point, Conroy moved to the other side of the car to assist his partner if necessary. *Id*. at 30. He focused his attention on plaintiff. *Id*. Conroy did not observe plaintiff do anything threatening toward either police officer. *Id*. Importantly, Officer Conroy did not fear for his personal safety. *Id*. at 31. Afterwards, defendant told Conroy that plaintiff "was being uncooperative, he wouldn't give him his ID and since we were investigating this, we had to get him out." *Id*. at 32. Defendant testified at trial that he had determined to place plaintiff in the cruiser in order to continue his investigation: "And he, being the passenger, was being uncooperative and we thought maybe he would be more cooperative if he didn't have his friend next to him." *Tr*., at 86.

Plaintiff testified that the pat-down was light and was completed within 15 to 30 seconds. The parties agree that there were other people in the Steak 'n Shake parking lot at the time of the pat-down. Plaintiff experienced "a little" embarrassment due to being searched in front of these people.[14]

Discussion of the issues.

II. Discussion

A. The Standard

The Fourth Amendment, which applies to the states by incorporation through the Fourteenth Amendment, protects "the right of the people to be secure in their persons, houses, papers, and effects, against unreasonable searches and seizures." U.S. Const. amend. IV. The Fourth Amendment protects citizens from unreasonable searches and seizures by providing that no arrest or search warrant "shall issue, but upon probable cause." *Id*. There are, however, certain

---

14. Plaintiff acknowledged that this was not his first arrest—or even pat-down.

"narrowly drawn exception[s] to the probable cause requirement of the Fourth Amendment." *United States v. Richardson*, 949 F.2d 851, 856 (6th Cir. 1991) (citations omitted). In *Terry v. Ohio*, 392 U.S. 1 (1968), the Supreme Court recognized that a police officer may conduct a limited stop for the purpose of "investigating possible criminal behavior even though there is no probable cause to make an arrest," as long as the officer can "point to specific and articulable facts" arousing reasonable suspicion of criminal activity. *Id*. at 21-22. In considering *Terry*'s concept of reasonable suspicion, the United States Court of Appeals for the Sixth Circuit has noted:

> Even if each specific fact relied upon by the authorities to make a *Terry* stop would not be a basis for suspicion when considered in isolation, the reasonable suspicion necessary to support an investigatory stop can still be found when it is "based upon an assessment of all circumstances surrounding the actions of a suspected wrongdoer," including those facts that would arouse suspicion only in someone experienced in law enforcement matters.

United States v. Garza, 10 F.3d 1241, 1245 (6th Cir. 1993) (citation omitted).

During a *Terry* stop, furthermore, a police officer may conduct a limited search for weapons if the officer believes that a suspect may be armed and dangerous. *Terry*, 392 U.S. at 27; *United States v. Walker*, 181 F.3d 774, 778 (6th Cir. 1999). "The officer need not be absolutely certain that the individual is armed; the issue is whether a reasonably prudent man in the circumstances would be warranted in the belief that his safety or that of others was in danger." *Terry*, 392 U.S. at 27. In this regard, the officer may not rely merely on a "hunch," but must be able to point to "the specific reasonable inferences which he is entitled to draw from the facts in light of his experience." *Id*.

The purpose of this limited search "is not to discover evidence of crime, but to allow the officer to pursue his investigation without fear of violence." *Adams v. Williams*, 407 U.S. 143, 146 (1972). Accordingly, a *Terry* pat-down "must be limited to that which is necessary for the discovery of weapons which might be used to harm the officer." *Walker*, 181 F.3d at 778.

B. Application

Plaintiff alleges, first, that defendant subjected him to a *Terry* stop without legal justification in violation of the Fourth Amendment. Defendant contends that he had reasonable suspicion to stop the vehicle in which Winslow was riding based on the allegations of the young men and their identification of the Hanson vehicle. The Court credits defendant's testimony in this regard and concludes that

continues on next page

defendant's initial stop of plaintiff did not violate plaintiff's Fourth Amendment rights. *See Florida v. J.L.*, 529 U.S. 266 (2000).

Next, plaintiff alleges that defendant conducted an illegal pat-down of him in violation of the Fourth Amendment. Defendant responds that the pat-down was justified and complied with the *Terry* standard. The fact that the Court has found in favor of the defendant on the issue of the initial stop is not necessarily determinative of the legality of the pat-down:

> Case law teaches that any search of the detainees must be limited to a protective frisk for weapons, and before such a pat down search can be conducted the police officer must have reason to believe that the suspect may be armed and dangerous.

United States v. Oates, 560 F.2d 45, 61 (2d Cir. 1977) (citations omitted).

The Court notes, first, that defendant's placement of plaintiff in the rear of his police cruiser constituted an arrest, for which probable cause was a necessary justification. The United States Court of Appeals for the Sixth Circuit has "long recognized that officers cross the line from an investigatory stop into an arrest when they place a suspect in a police vehicle for questioning." *See United States v. Butler*, 223 F.3d 368, 375 (6th Cir. 2000). *See also United States v. Mendenhall*, 446 U.S. 544, 554 (1980).

> When the agents placed [the defendant] in the back of the police car, they went beyond the bounds of *Terry*. Placing [the defendant] in the police cruiser not only constituted a seizure, as mentioned earlier, but also crossed the line into an arrest. [The defendant] was moved from his car to another location, and his freedom of movement was severely restricted.

Richardson, 949 F.2d at 857.

"Searches incident to a lawful arrest are justified without any level of suspicion." *United States v. Wall*, 807 F. Supp. 1271, 1275 (E.D. Mich. 1992). *See also Chimel v. California*, 395 U.S. 752, 762-63 (1969). "However, a warrantless search that provides probable cause to make a subsequent arrest may not be justified as a search incident to that arrest." *Wall*, 807 F. Supp. at 1275. *See also Smith v. Ohio*, 494 U.S. 541 (1990). Although defendant had no probable cause to arrest plaintiff at the point that he first decided to place plaintiff in the cruiser, defendant's subsequent discovery of drug paraphernalia on plaintiff's person provided the probable cause sufficient to justify plaintiff's actual arrest. *Opinion and Order*, at 13 (November 20, 2000). However, the issue remains whether the pat-down that lead to the discovery of the paraphernalia was justified under *Terry*.

Defendant argues that he had a reasonable articulable suspicion that plaintiff was armed and dangerous based on the totality of the circumstances: the victims' identification of the Hanson vehicle, *Tr.*, at 81, 97, the nature of the crime being investigated, i.e., misdemeanor menacing, the fact that only two individuals allegedly threatened a group of five or six, *id.* at 62, 85, 87, 97, and plaintiff's refusal to cooperate with defendant's investigation and request for identification. *Id.* at 58, 97. Defendant's testimony emphasized that it "crossed [his] mind" that weapons were involved in the alleged incident because the officer could not "think of any good reason why two people would threaten five people." *Id.* at 85. Defendant continued, "[I]f this was, indeed, the vehicle that was [threatening the group of young men] and there is [sic] two people making the threats, there was a possibility that there was a weapon. And that's what we believed." *Id.* at 88. However, defendant also repeatedly testified that he ordered plaintiff out of the Hanson vehicle with the intention of placing plaintiff in the cruiser to continue his investigation, *id.* at 57, 63, 86, and that he patted plaintiff down incident to that intention. *Id.* at 63. This, of course, is insufficient to meet the standard of *Terry*.

In determining the actual motivation for the pat-down of plaintiff, it is instructive to compare plaintiff's treatment on the night in question with that of Hanson. Defendant does not contend that plaintiff made any furtive or unusual movements to indicate that he was retrieving or hiding an object, and he concedes that plaintiff cooperated with defendant's orders to exit the vehicle and place his hands behind his head. The only fact that distinguishes plaintiff from Hanson was plaintiff's refusal to identify himself to defendant. The Court finds that it was this refusal that actually motivated defendant's pat-down of plaintiff. The Court must, therefore, determine whether a refusal to provide identification when asked during a *Terry* stop justifies a pat-down of the person.

The Supreme Court has stated that, upon making a *Terry* stop, the officer may ask the detainee a moderate number of questions to determine his identity and to try to obtain information confirming or dispelling the officer's suspicions. But the detainee is not obligated to respond. And, unless the detainee's answers provide the officer with probable cause to arrest him, he must then be released.[15]

15. In his concurrence in *Terry*, Justice White stated:

There is nothing in the Constitution which prevents a policeman from addressing questions to anyone on the streets. Absent special circumstances, the person approached may not be detained or frisked but may refuse to cooperate and go on his way. However, given the proper circumstances, such as those in this case, it seems to me the person may be briefly detained against his will while pertinent questions are directed to him. Of course, the person stopped is not obliged to answer, answers may

continues on next page

Berkemer v. McCarty, 468 U.S. 420, 439-40 (1984). *See also Butler*, 223 F.3d at 374. Just as the refusal to cooperate in a *Terry* stop cannot justify an arrest, this Court concludes that the mere refusal to identify oneself during the course of a *Terry* stop does not justify a pat-down for weapons. Moreover, the Court concludes that even the totality of the circumstances in the case at bar were insufficient to create a reasonable suspicion in defendant's mind that plaintiff was armed and dangerous. First, the Court notes that the alleged victims made no mention of weapons when informing the officers that they had been followed and harassed. *Tr.*, at 25-26. Second, defendant's partner, Officer Conroy, testified on deposition that he had no suspicion that plaintiff was armed and dangerous:

> Q: Did you see Caleb Winslow do anything threatening toward either of you officers before he was searched?
> A: No.
>
> * * *
>
> Q: And you did not see Mr. Winslow do anything that made you feel fearful for your personal safety; isn't that true?
> A: I did not, no.
>
> * * *
>
> Q: And you never saw Mr. Winslow do anything that would suggest he might become violent . . . ?
> A: Right.

Conroy Depo., at 30-32. Third, defendant testified at trial that he had not observed plaintiff make any threatening or furtive movements. *Tr.*, at 60, 61-62. Fourth, defendant testified in his deposition that he did not see anything about plaintiff's conduct that made him suspect that plaintiff might be armed and dangerous. *Daniel Depo.*, at 30. Fifth, although defendant testified at trial that plaintiff's refusal to provide identification created a suspicion in defendant's mind that plaintiff was armed and dangerous, defendant's only articulated basis for that suspicion was that he "saw no reason for [plaintiff] not to cooperate to get [the investigation] over with, so we could figure out what's going on and everybody could go on their own way." *Tr.*, at 98. While plaintiff's refusal to provide identification convinced defendant that more investigation was warranted, *see Tr.*, at 57, 85, the Court specifically finds that defendant's pat-down of plaintiff was not a consequence of the defendant's fear that plaintiff

---

not be compelled, and refusal to answer furnishes no basis for an arrest, although it may alert the officer to the need for continued observation.

Terry, 392 U.S. at 34 (White, J., concurring). "Although Justice White's concurrence was not part of the holding in *Terry*, it has been frequently cited or mentioned by the Court in subsequent opinions." *Risbridger v. Connelly*, 122 F. Supp. 2d 857, 864 (W.D. Mich. 2000).

was armed and dangerous. Under the circumstances, the Court concludes that "a reasonably prudent man in [defendant's] circumstances would [not have been] warranted in the belief that his safety or that of others was in danger." *See Terry*, 392 U.S. at 27.

C. Damages

Having found that plaintiff has established a violation of his Fourth Amendment rights, the Court must now consider the relief to which plaintiff is entitled by reason of that violation. "'The basic purpose' of §1983 is 'to compensate persons for injuries that are caused by the deprivation of constitutional rights.'" *Memphis Community Sch. Dist. v. Stachura*, 477 U.S. 299, 307 (1986) (quoting *Carey v. Piphus*, 435 U.S. 247, 254 (1978)). Even in the absence of proof of tangible loss, the victim of a constitutional violation is entitled to compensation for "humiliation, mental suffering and the intangible loss of civil rights . . . ." *Green v. Francis*, 705 F.2d 846, 850 (6th Cir. 1983).

Plaintiff testified that the unlawful pat-down was light and of short duration; he suffered "a little" embarrassment as a consequence. Under these circumstances, the Court finds that damages in the amount of $500.00 will reasonably compensate plaintiff for the "humiliation, mental suffering and the intangible loss" of his Fourth Amendment rights.[16]

III. Conclusions of Law

Conclusion. The conclusions of law serve as the conclusion section in a trial court opinion.

The Court has subject matter jurisdiction over this action pursuant to 28 U.S.C. §§1331 and 1343. The Court has personal jurisdiction over the parties.

The Court concludes that plaintiff's rights under the Fourth Amendment were not violated when defendant stopped the car in which plaintiff was a passenger, but that plaintiff's rights under the Fourth Amendment were violated when defendant conducted a pat-down of plaintiff.

The Court awards compensatory damages in favor of plaintiff and against the defendant in the amount of $500.00 (Five Hundred Dollars) in connection with the violation of plaintiff's Fourth Amendment rights.

The Clerk shall enter **FINAL JUDGMENT** accordingly.

Maria Aquilina

Maria Aquilina
United States District Judge

16. Although the complaint also contains a claim for punitive damages, plaintiff introduced no evidence at trial in support of this claim. The Court, therefore, assumes that plaintiff has abandoned any claim for punitive damages.

9 Drafting a Bench Memorandum

I. Introduction

Another document that a judicial clerk may be asked to draft is a bench memorandum. Unlike a judicial opinion, no one will read a bench memorandum except the trial judge or the panel of judges assigned in an appellate case. A bench memorandum aids the judge's preparation for oral argument during a motion hearing[1] or an appeal.[2] The document is generally just a few pages in length and is essentially a report that familiarizes the judge with the issues before the court on a motion or on appeal, summarizes the briefs of the parties prior to oral argument, objectively analyzes the issues, narrows the judge's focus to areas that may require more inquiry, and often recommends an outcome for the case. A bench memorandum must be not only impartial and critical but also thorough enough to summarize the issues in the case without being so thorough that the judge would have been better served by reading the briefs and the record.

---

1. The frequency with which a trial court clerk will be required to draft bench memoranda for motion hearings varies widely from judge to judge. Some judges require clerks to draft a bench memo for every motion hearing; others require clerks to draft bench memoranda only for hearings on particularly challenging motions. And some judges never have their clerks draft bench memoranda. These judges prefer their clerks to brief them orally on the case and then prepare a working draft of the opinion or order.

2. Appellate clerks will be required to draft bench memoranda for almost every case to which they are assigned.

A. Preparing to Draft the Bench Memorandum

The first few steps a clerk should take when preparing to draft a bench memorandum differ depending on the court hearing the case. If a trial judge is hearing the case, the clerk's first step is to make certain that the court has jurisdiction to hear the case. Whether the court has original jurisdiction to hear a case arises most often in federal district court. While this issue sometimes arises in state trial courts, it is not nearly as prevalent as in federal court.

Next, the clerk should review the procedural history of the case and determine which party carries the burden of proof for each issue. On the other hand, if the case is on appeal, the clerk should make certain that the appeal is authorized by the jurisdiction's rules of appellate procedure. Under the rules of appellate procedure, an appeal is generally authorized only when the trial court has issued a final judgment on the issue.[3] After determining that the appeal is authorized by the rule of appellate procedure, an appellate clerk should review the procedural history of the case and determine which standard of review controls the court's review of the appeal. While the parties will identify the applicable standards of review in their briefs, the clerk should conduct independent research to identify the appropriate standard of review for each issue. If the parties disagree as to the applicable standard of review, you will need to conduct additional research to resolve the question.

The remaining steps in preparing to draft a bench memorandum are essentially the same, regardless of the court hearing the case. The steps are as follows:

1. Read the record, including any trial transcripts and the briefs of the litigants.
2. Identify the issues before the court and determine which facts are relevant to the resolution of those issues. This isn't as easy as it seems. At the trial level, the parties often frame the issues differently. When this occurs, the clerk is responsible for determining what the issues are and framing them for the judge. Consequently, you may need to conduct independent research to determine what the issues are in the case. You will need to determine which party framed the issue properly. If neither party correctly articulated the issue, it is the clerk's job to do so. Furthermore, you may decide that the parties completely missed an issue or that the parties' briefs raise other peripheral issues. You will need to research any such issues. If you are required to reframe the issue or if you determine that the parties overlooked an issue, you must notify the judge.

---

3. Most jurisdictions' rules of appellate procedure allow an appeal to be taken from many other types of actions. *See* Fed. R. App. P. 4.

3. An appellate clerk must make certain that the issues raised by the parties are appealable. An issue is appealable if it was raised at trial and preserved for appeal. Once you have determined that an issue is appealable, you must determine whether the parties framed the issue correctly. To be correct, the parties must frame the issues in a manner that is consistent with the trial court decision and also with the issues argued in their trial briefs. If you disagree with the parties' articulation of the issues, or if there is inconsistency between the parties' articulation of the issues and that of the trial judge, you may modify the issues for the judge. You must then notify the panel of judges who will hear the case of the discrepancy. Unlike at the trial level, an appellate court clerk may not raise new issues. If the issue wasn't preserved for appeal at trial, it cannot be raised on appeal. Verify that the facts relied on by the parties support the propositions argued by the parties.

4. Examine the authorities relied on by the litigants in their briefs and update that research to ensure that no new authorities have been issued since the briefs were filed (a hearing may occur several years after the filing of the briefs). You should also conduct independent research to ensure that the parties did not miss any governing law. If you are unfamiliar with the area of law in question, begin your research by reviewing a secondary source such as a hornbook or legal encyclopedia. Once you've obtained a basic understanding of the law, review the cases cited by the parties and conduct your own research. When reading the cases, identify any policy considerations that seem to underlie the courts' decisions, any changes in the language or reasoning used by the courts, and if there are changes in the courts' language or reasoning, whether the state of the law is in flux.

5. Identify any issues that may require clarification or more research and devise a list of questions that the judge may need to ask during the hearing.

6. Draft a detailed outline of the bench memorandum.

The judge will give you deadlines for your bench memoranda. In a trial court, the turnaround time for the bench memo is typically fairly short, just a few days or so. In an appellate court, the deadline will generally be at least one week before the panel is scheduled to hear oral arguments in the case. If the memo is to be distributed to the other members of the panel, which is common, your deadline may be somewhat earlier. This will allow the judge to review your work prior to forwarding it to the other members of the panel. Meeting deadlines, though always important, is of particular import with regard to bench memoranda. Meeting the deadlines set by the judge will ensure that the documents needed to decide a case are available at the proper time in the decision-making process.

B. Drafting the Bench Memorandum

1. FORMAT

The typical format of a bench memorandum includes the following sections: (1) a caption, (2) an issue and short answer, (3) procedural history, (4) factual background, (5) standard of review, (6) analysis, and (7) recommendations. The names of the sections may vary based on the individual court. Some courts refer to the caption as the memorandum heading, the procedural history as the procedural statement and history, the factual background as simply facts, the analysis as the discussion, and the recommendations as conclusions. Furthermore, the general organization of the sections may vary based on the individual court. For instance, some courts follow the caption with the issue statement rather than the procedural history. Additionally, some judges do not desire a recommendation from the clerk. Moreover, some courts require additional sections, such as an overview section that serves a similar purpose as the introduction in a judicial opinion.

Thus, when drafting the memorandum itself, it is important to check with the judge regarding the desired format for the bench memorandum. The judge may or may not approve of the template set forth below. Ask the judge for a sample bench memorandum that has been prepared by a previous clerk. A sample bench memorandum will provide you with a template that the judge previously found acceptable. You may use the template set forth below to help you organize the information in a familiar scheme, but you should modify it to comply with the requirements of the judge.

a. Caption

Begin the bench memorandum with a caption that includes the usual information in a memo heading, as well as all the information needed to identify the case. More specifically, the caption should include (1) the title for the document (i.e., bench memorandum), (2) the name of the judge or judges for whom the memorandum is written, (3) the name of the person who prepared the memorandum (your name), (4) the date the memo was prepared, and (5) the case name, followed by the docket number. The judge may require that the memo heading contain additional information. This information may include the city where oral argument is to take place and the date on which it is scheduled; the name of the attorneys representing the parties; and the name of the court that decided the case below, with the name of the presiding judge listed in parentheses. The judge may also require that you include your recommendation regarding the disposition of the case in the information following the memorandum heading.

Most courts use a standard caption. If the court in which you work uses such a caption, you will simply complete the standard caption by plugging in the pertinent information.

b. Issue and Short Answer

This section summarizes the issues before the court and provides a brief answer to those legal questions. This section is similar to the "Question Presented" and "Brief Answer" sections that you likely drafted for an office memorandum in your legal writing class. Just as when drafting those sections in an office memorandum, in a bench memorandum, the issue and short answer must be stated objectively and with a fair amount of detail. In a bench memorandum, however, the brief answer must include the legal authority on which the recommended outcome rests and provide citations to that authority.

When drafting an issue in an appellate case, be sure to identify the pertinent standard of review. Just as the "Question Presented" in an office memorandum differs depending on the specific facts of the case, the issue in an appeal differs depending on the appropriate standard of review. Thus, when dealing with an abuse of discretion standard, the issue could be phrased in the following manner: "Did the district judge abuse her discretion when she awarded the plaintiff, Goliath Corporation, attorney's fees?" When dealing with a factual determination where the appellate court must apply the clearly erroneous standard, the issue could be phrased in the following manner: "Was the jury's verdict that Sean Thornton battered Will Danaher clearly erroneous when the two men engaged in a fist fight that lasted more than 40 minutes and was restarted at one point by Danaher punching Thornton in the face?"

For more information on standards of review, see the discussion of those standards in Chapter 6.

c. Procedural History

The procedural history should include information regarding how the case came to be before the court. Thus, in a trial court, the procedural history should detail the procedural process that preceded the motion that is before the court. In an appellate court, the procedural history should detail what procedurally happened in the trial court, articulate the trial court's ruling, and identify which party appealed the lower court's decision. The procedural history should include the specific dates on which the events occurred.

d. Factual Background

This section describes the events that led to the litigation and traces the procedural history of the case through the judicial system. This section should include a concise statement of facts that summarizes the legally relevant facts and includes any necessary contextual facts. These facts should be articulated in an objective fashion and must be supported by the record.

To obtain an overview of the facts, you must read the parties' briefs or motion memoranda, any appendices to those documents, and any findings of fact made by the trial judge. The decision of the lower court is a good place to find a concise and precise review of the facts. In a criminal case, the presentence report is a good place to find a summary of the facts.

Do not simply take the litigants' version of events as gospel. Verify the litigants' factual statements by reviewing the sources of fact in the case. At the trial level, the sources of fact include all the documents contained in the court file, including affidavits, exhibits from trial, and transcripts from prior hearings. At the appellate level, the sources of fact are found in the trial court record, which includes all the documents previously mentioned as well as the transcript of the trial. The appendices to the parties' briefs should supply the relevant excerpts of record. However, if the parties fail to provide the pertinent excerpt of the record for a fact on which one of them relies, you will need to comb through the record in an attempt to substantiate the existence of that fact and to determine that the fact means what the party says it means.

How do you verify that the facts actually support the propositions for which they are cited? To verify the facts as presented by the parties, you must compare the parties' characterizations of the facts against the sources of fact found in the record. For instance, when a party cites to a line from a deposition, you should not only verify that the line says what the party claims it says but also read a sufficient portion of the surrounding deposition to put the relevant fact into context. Sometimes, when a party takes a fact out of context, it will appear to support the party's argument, but when that fact is put into context, it does not support the party's position at all. This occurs much more frequently than one would imagine. If you discover any discrepancies when reviewing the record, you must bring them to the judge's attention. Thus, you will need to flag any disputed facts, any facts that were misstated or misrepresented by a party, or any facts that are contradicted by the record.

You must cite to the record for each fact included in the bench memorandum. Citing to the record informs the judge not only of the location of the fact in the record but also that your factual assertions are correct. If drafting a bench memorandum at the trial level, you will cite to the evidence, including depositions, documents, admissions, responses to interrogatories, affidavits, hearing or trial transcripts, and exhibits. At the appellate level, you will cite to the parties' briefs and the excerpts of record. When citing to the briefs and excerpts of record, clerks commonly use several abbreviations. Because the cover on the appellant's opening brief is blue, the abbreviation for this document is "Blue Br."[4] The same reasoning holds true for the appellee's response brief and the appellant's reply brief, which are referred to respectively as "Red Br." and "Gray Br."[5]

---

4. Joseph L. Lemon, Jr., *Federal Appellate Court Law Clerk Handbook* 22 (ABA 2007).
5. *Id.*

The excerpts of record are abbreviated "ER," and supplemental excerpts of record are abbreviated "SER."[6] The presentence report is abbreviated as "PSR," and the administrative record, if there is one, is abbreviated as "AR."[7] While appellate clerks commonly use these abbreviations, if you receive differing instructions from your judge regarding abbreviations, follow the judge's instructions.

Furthermore, when drafting the statement of the facts, distinguish between facts that are undisputed and those that remain unproven. A simple way to accomplish this is to inform the reader at the beginning of the statement of the facts that "[t]he following facts are undisputed unless otherwise indicated."[8] This statement informs the reader that any fact without a qualifier such as "alleges" or "asserts" is undisputed.[9] However, if the litigation is in the early stages, and discovery has yet to be completed, inform the reader that "the following facts are taken from the complaint" or that they "are presented in the light most favorable to the nonmoving party."[10]

Finally, when referring to the parties in an appeal, do not use generic procedural designations, such as "Appellant," "Plaintiff-Appellant," "Petitioner," or "Appellee."[11] Also, do not refer to the parties at the trial level by their procedural designation, such as "Plaintiff" or "Defendant." It is clearer to refer to the parties by name. When there are a number of defendants, however, it is often easier to refer to them as a single group by listing them once and then informing the reader that they will be referred to collectively as "Defendants."[12] When any governmental agency is a party, you should refer to that party as "the Government."[13]

e. Standard of Review

In a bench memorandum, the standard of review is usually included in a separate section and given a heading. However, if the case on which you are working has more than one issue with different standards of review, then the applicable standard of review should be included at the beginning of the discussion of each issue rather than in a separate section.

If the parties disagree as to the appropriate standard of review for an issue, you must make a note of this for the judge. You should then explain what standard you think is appropriate and support your conclusion with relevant law.

6. *Id.*
7. *Id.*
8. Calvert G. Chipchase, *Federal District Court Law Clerk Handbook* 38 (ABA 2007).
9. *Id.* at 39.
10. *Id.* at 38.
11. Lemon, *supra* note 4, at 25.
12. *Id.*
13. *Id.*

For more information on standards of review, see the discussion of those standards in Chapter 6.

f. Analysis

This section sets forth your independent analysis of the issues. This section should include the governing law, the parties' arguments, and your analysis of the issues. Your analysis should apply the pertinent law to the facts of the case in a manner that helps the judge resolve the issues in the case. Just as the discussion and analysis section is the heart of an office memorandum, so it is in a bench memorandum.

What structure should you use when analyzing an issue? The IRAC structure is a good method to use when organizing your analysis of an issue. Begin by identifying the issue before the court. Then, set forth the governing rule of law, whether it is a statute, regulation, or case law. Next, your analysis should summarize the arguments raised by the parties, particularly by the appellant (or, at the trial level, by the moving party). After summarizing the parties' arguments, apply the governing law to the facts of the case. Be sure to verify that the authorities relied on by the litigants in their briefs stand for the legal propositions that the litigants claim they do. Your analysis of the issue should also address the trial court's analysis and take into account the standard of review. You should also identify for the judge any matters that require clarification or further explanation during oral argument. Include a list of questions that inquiry at oral argument might resolve. If you are using the judge's voice when drafting the bench memorandum, you can convey questions or observations to the judge by using footnotes. Finally, conclude the analysis with a brief recommendation regarding how the case should be resolved.

When a case includes multiple issues, organize the analysis in subsections, with each issue being discussed under a separate heading. Organize each individual issue using the IRAC structure.

g. Recommendations

Finally, if desired by the judge, include your views on the merits of the case. You must support your recommendation with a few sentences of analysis and cite to the controlling authority. Finally, include any recommendations that you may have regarding disposition of the case. At the trial level, you will recommend that the judge either grant or deny the motion before the court. At the appellate level, you will recommend that the court either affirm the decision of the lower court or reverse and remand the case back to the trial court for further action. Additionally, you may need to include a recommendation on whether the court should decide the matter with a full, per curiam, or memorandum opinion. If you recommend either a per curium or memorandum opinion, the bench memorandum should include a draft of the recommended document.

When drafting the recommendation, if you disagree with the result that binding authority seems to compel, express this disagreement in the memorandum. If you are drafting the memorandum using the judge's voice, your disagreement and the basis for that disagreement can be brought to the judge's attention in a footnote. The judge may agree that justice requires a different outcome and may be able to distinguish the case before the court from the seemingly binding precedent. At the appellate level, the judge may even recommend that the issue be reviewed by the full court en banc so that the previous precedent could be overturned.

See the sample bench memorandum at the end of the chapter.

2. TONE

As with a judicial opinion, a bench memorandum has a formal, professional tone. However, unlike an opinion, which is always written in the judge's voice, bench memoranda can be written in either the clerk's voice or the judge's voice. The voice used when drafting a bench memorandum is completely within the judge's discretion.

The difference between the clerk's voice and that of the judge is essentially a difference in style. When writing with your voice, you are simply advising the court as to the proper outcome of a case. Thus, you will set forth the facts, the litigants' arguments, and the governing law in a neutral fashion. You will analyze the issues and offer a recommendation without writing "the court finds" or "the court holds."[14] You are not deciding the matter; you are simply advising the court on the facts and law and offering a recommendation. While you are offering a recommendation to the judge as to what the outcome of the case should be, your style should be more analytical than persuasive. The style you use should be similar to that which you used when drafting an office memorandum in your first year legal writing class. The judge will review all the materials and make the decision. The bench memorandum simply provides "an analytical framework in which the judge[] [has] access to the relevant issues, arguments, and controlling law."[15]

When you draft the memorandum in your voice, it is important to be diligent in the research and writing process. Remember that the bench memorandum will serve as the primary resource when drafting the opinion and disposition of the case following the oral argument. In fact, the bench memorandum itself can be converted into the opinion by rewriting the memorandum using the judge's voice. Assuming the judge agrees with your position on the case's outcome, your recommendation will become the disposition for the case.

In contrast, when using the judge's voice, you will write the memorandum as if speaking for the court. Instead of advising the judge, you will

---

14. Chipchase, *supra* note 8, at 26.
15. Lemon, *supra* note 4, at 18.

draft the memorandum as if you were deciding the matter as the judge. When using the judge's voice, you will set forth the facts, the litigants' arguments, and the governing law in a neutral fashion, but instead of advising the court and offering a recommendation, you will analyze the issues and reach a decision. "When using the court's voice, it is correct to say, 'The court holds,' and 'the court finds.'"[16] Further, you will draft the memorandum so that when complete, the judge can sign it and issue the disposition. Judges who prefer clerks to draft bench memoranda in the court's voice prefer this because it "avoid[s] unnecessary work when transforming the memo into the order."[17]

3. EDITING AND PROOFREADING

Finally, remember to edit and proofread the document before submitting it to the judge. Just as with an opinion or any other document that you submit to the judge, the bench memorandum should be free of errors and professional in appearance.[18] When editing a bench memorandum, pay particular attention to the voice you use when drafting. Do not shift back and forth between your voice and that of the judge.

C. The Bench Book

Once the bench memorandum is complete, incorporate it into a "bench packet" or "bench book" for the judge. This packet of information should contain not just the bench memorandum but also the docket sheet for the case; the opinion and disposition of the lower court (or the decision being appealed); the litigants' briefs; excerpts from the record; any relevant statutes, rules, and regulations; either the most important cases or summaries of those cases; and any other important documents from the case file.

Just as the bench memorandum helps the judge prepare *for* oral argument, the bench book assists the judge *during* oral argument. The bench book compiles pertinent information and documents that the judge may need to access quickly while on the bench hearing argument. Additionally, you can use the bench book when drafting the opinion following oral argument.

II. Checklist for Drafting a Bench Memorandum

When drafting the bench memorandum, and before submitting it to the judge or the staff attorney, consider the following questions to determine

---

16. Chipchase, *supra* note 8, at 27.
17. *Id.*
18. For information on editing and proofreading techniques, see Chapter 7.

whether the memorandum does everything that it needs to do and that it is accurate.

____ Did you establish that all the issues are properly before the court?

____ Did you state the burden of proof or standard of review?

____ Did you include all of the required identifying information in the caption?

____ Did you state the issues clearly and concisely?

____ If you had to reframe the issues, did you alert the judge of this fact?

____ If the parties missed an issue, did you alert the judge of this fact?

____ If in appellate court, did you articulate the issues in terms of the relevant standards of review?

____ Did you detail the procedural steps through which the case has passed, including specific dates?

____ Did you include all the legally significant facts?

____ Did you cite to the record for each fact included in the memorandum?

____ Did you verify that all the facts relied on by the parties existed and supported the proposition for which they were cited?

____ Did you identify and explain any discrepancies in the parties' versions of the facts?

____ Did you introduce each issue with a subheading?

____ Did you use the IRAC method to organize your analysis of each issue?

____ Did you state the governing rule for each issue and explain it?

____ Did you rely on mandatory authority when analyzing each issue?

____ Did you address each parties' arguments?

____ Did you make a recommendation to the court on the merits of the case?

____ Did you make a recommendation to the court as to the disposition of the case?

____ Did you state all the issues, facts, and analyses in an objective manner?

____ Did you use a consistent style throughout the memorandum?

____ Is the opinion free of grammar, punctuation, spelling, and citation errors?[19]

Additional Resources

◆ Calvert G. Chipchase, *Federal District Court Law Clerk Handbook* 26 (ABA 2007).

---

19. This checklist was adapted in part from a checklist found in Mary L. Dunnewold, Beth A. Honetschlager & Brenda L. Tofte, *Judicial Clerkships: A Practical Guide* 137-138 (Carolina Acad. Press 2010).

◆ Rebecca A. Cochran, *Judicial Externships: The Clinic Inside the Courthouse* (2d ed., Anderson 1999).
◆ Mary L. Dunnewold, Beth A. Honetschlager & Brenda L. Tofte, *Judicial Clerkships: A Practical Guide* (Carolina Acad. Press 2010).
◆ Federal Judicial Center, *Chambers Handbook for Judges' Law Clerks and Secretaries* (West 1994).
◆ Gerald Lebovits, *Judges' Clerks Play Varied Roles in the Opinion Drafting Process*, 76 N.Y. St. B.J. 34 (July/Aug. 2004).
◆ Joseph L. Lemon, Jr., *Federal Appellate Court Law Clerk Handbook* (ABA 2007).
◆ Eugene A. Wright, *Observations of an Appellate Judge: The Use of Law Clerks*, 26 Vand. L. Rev. 1179 (1973).

SAMPLE BENCH MEMORANDUM

To: Justices Bidwell, Darling, Farher, French, Morrissey, Park, and Sampson
From: Judy Clark, clerk
Date: October 10, 2002
Re: *The People of the State of New York v. Merritt Breshnahan*, Case No. 01-341

ORAL ARGUMENT DATE: October 17, 2002

ATTORNEYS:
Allan Kuusinen   Clyde Farnsworth
Assistant District Attorney   Attorney for Defendant-Appellant
1 Hogan Place   32 Fontanka Street
New York, NY 10013   Bedford Falls, NY 14218
(212) 555-1111   (914) 555-1111

LOWER COURT:
The Criminal Court of New York City and County (Judge Donovan Kane)

Issue and Short Answer

Did the trial court properly conclude that the People had presented legally sufficient evidence that defendant Breshnahan, a transsexual, was "disguised" in the manner prohibited by New York Penal Law §240.35(4) when she was dressed as a woman but had the reproductive organs of a man?

Probably not. Although the People demonstrated that the transsexual defendant Breshnahan is not legally a woman and nonetheless dressed as one, legislative intent warrants the implicit exception of transsexuals from the scope of the statute.

Procedural History

The New York City Criminal Court, New York County, convicted defendant Merritt Breshnahan of loitering in violation of Penal Law §240.35(4). R. at 471-72. After the close of evidence at trial, defendant Breshnahan moved for a trial order of dismissal pursuant to Criminal Procedure Law §§290.10 and 320.20 on the ground that the People had not introduced legally sufficient evidence that she had been "disguised" in a fashion prohibited by §240.35(4) when she was "wearing the clothing of one gender but ha[d] the reproductive organs of the other." R. at 467. The criminal court denied the motion, convicted defendant Breshnahan, and sentenced her to a fine of two hundred dollars. R. at 468, 470, 471-72. Defendant Breshnahan appealed the denial of the motion. R. at 477. The Appellate Term and the Appellate Division both affirmed, and this appeal followed. R. at 478.

Facts

Defendant Merritt Breshnahan, a transsexual, was arrested and convicted of violating Penal Law §240.35(4), which prohibits three or more individuals from being "masked or in any manner disguised by unusual or unnatural attire or facial alteration." When arrested, defendant Bresnahan was a biological male with a penis, testicles, and a scrotum, as were her two companions. R. at 110, 189, 373, 449. However, defendant Breshnahan was wearing a blouse, a skirt, stockings, high-heeled shoes, and women's undergarments. R. at 109, 187. Her companions were similarly dressed. R. at 3-5.

On the day of her arrest, defendant Breshnahan had been at work as a financial analyst for a stock brokerage firm. R. at 170. During her lunch break, she was walking to lunch with two other transsexuals. R. at 202-03. One block from her office, while standing at a street corner, defendant Breshnahan encountered the arresting officer. R. at 108-10, 114, 193-94. Because defendant Breshnahan and her two companions were dressed as women and effected feminine voices, inflections, gestures, and walks, the arresting officer initially believed them to be women. R. at 98-101. The officer testified that defendant Breshnahan and her companions "would have succeeded in fooling [him]" if he had not overheard a comment made by one of them. R. at 98. The substance of this comment was not made known at trial due to an objection by the defense. R. at 103.

Defendant Breshnahan has been diagnosed as suffering from Gender Dysphoria Syndrome ("GDS"), or transsexualism. R. at 81-96. GDS is a disorder in which the patient experiences "an

continues on next page

unrelenting and uncontrollable feeling that she or he is not the gender that matched the reproductive organs assigned at birth." R. at 389. Such beliefs generally manifest themselves at a very young age, and psychotherapy alone has proved ineffective as a treatment for the disorder. R. at 396, 401-02. The standard treatment for GDS is as follows:

> The patient is first given "an exhaustive psychological workup to confirm the diagnosis." R. at 419. Then, over a period of six months to two years, the patient is given hormonal injections which alter the body's appearance. *Id.* During this period, a clinic typically requires the patient to "live and dress as the gender the patient believes him- or herself to be. . . ." R. at 419-20. "At an appropriate point, the patient is provided with sex reassignment surgery, in which the original sex organs are replaced with those that are consistent with the patient's 'psychological gender.'" R. at 422.

Bl. Brief at 3-4. According to the medical experts, it would be an "irresponsible" medical practice to provide physical treatment for GDS without requiring the patient to "cross-dress" at the same time. R. at 326, 399. The patient must "cross-dress" to ensure that she is able to live the life to which sex reassignment surgery would commit her. R. at 326, 399. If the patient does not satisfy the requirement to live and dress as the gender the patient believes himself to be, treatment is halted "because sex reassignment surgery would not then be indicated as a permanent change in the patient's life." R. at 419-20.

Sex reassignment surgery is only one of "several stages in a sex role assimilation, and it must be preceded by a complete psychological and social assimilation." R. at 427. Thus, by the time the patient undergoes sex reassignment surgery, much of the patient's gender has already been transformed. R. at 426. Following sex reassignment surgery, a transsexual who was a born with male reproductive organs would have "an internal sexual structure like that of a woman who has undergone a total hysterectomy and ovariectomy." R. at 423-24. The transsexual would have a surgically constructed vagina, but she would not have a uterus or ovaries. R. at 374-75, 448. Furthermore, while such a transsexual would be considered medically a female, R. at 423, she would have male chromosomes for the rest of her life. R. at 448.

At the time of the arrest and at trial, defendant Breshnahan was in a long-term treatment program at the Gender Identity Clinic at Murray Hill Hospital, where she was under the treatment of a physician and a psychotherapist who specialize in treating individuals who suffer from GDS. R. at 81-96. Because her treatment plan required defendant Breshnahan to live and dress as a woman, R. at 81-96, 388-404, 409-444, she had dressed exclusively in female clothing and lived as a woman since the age of sixteen. R. at 178-79. Both defendant Breshnahan and her doctors were aware that the requirement that she live and dress as a woman could result in legal difficulties. R. at 179-80, 406, 442. Furthermore, while her pre-operative treatment plan required defendant Breshnahan to live and work as a woman, her doctors conceded that the plan "would not be 'significantly' disturbed if . . . [she] were to refrain, before surgery, from appearing in public with two or more . . . men in female dress." R. at 408, 449. Though defendant Breshnahan and her doctors testified that she intended to undergo sexual reassignment surgery, she had not had the surgery as of either the time of her arrest or trial. R. at 189, 197, 373, 449.

Standard of Review

This court reviews the question of whether legally sufficient evidence existed at trial to convict a defendant under the sufficiency of the evidence standard. Under the sufficiency of the evidence standard, the court must view the evidence "in the light most favorable to the People . . . to determine whether there is a valid line of reasoning and permissible inferences from which a rational jury could have found the elements of the crime proved beyond a reasonable doubt." *People v. Acosta*, 80 N.Y.2d 665, 672 (1993).

Analysis

Defendant Breshnahan first argues that the New York State Legislature did not intend for §240.35(4) to punish transsexuals wearing medically appropriate clothing as being "masked or . . . disguised." Bl. Brief at 13-14. Breshnahan supports her contention that the legislative intent does not include punishing transsexuals undergoing medical and psychological treatment with a history of the statute and its predecessors. Bl. Brief 13-14. Defendant Breshnahan also argues that, if this court upholds her conviction, it will be impossible in this state for a transsexual to receive a lawful medical treatment as prescribed by a physician or therapist. Bl. Brief at 9-12. Finally, Breshnahan argues that because her attire was medically appropriate and she had been living as a woman for her entire adult life, she therefore was not concealing her identity; nor was she masked or disguised. Bl. Brief at 9. Breshnahan asks this court to accept the position that medicine has accepted in determining her to be primarily a woman.

Ms. Breshnahan argues that construing §240.35(4) as prohibiting cross-dressing transsexuals from complying with prescribed medical regiments while in the company of other transsexuals would be an unreasonable result. Bl. Brief at 16. Defendant Breshnahan asks this court to imply that §240.35(4) affords the same exemption to

continues on next page

transsexuals as it affords masqueraders. Breshnahan relies on the canon of statutory interpretation that states, "It is . . . always presumed that no unjust or unreasonable result was intended and the statute must be construed consonant with that presumption." *Zappone v. Home Ins. Co.*, 55 N.Y.2d 131, 137, 432 N.E.2d 783, 786, 447 N.Y.S.2d 911, 914.

The People argue that Ms. Breshnahan was "disguised" as prohibited by §240.35(4), because she was, as a *pre*-operative transsexual, still possessed of male reproductive organs, male chromosomes, and other indicia of the masculine gender. R at 5. The People argue that §240.35(4) does not interfere with defendant Breshnahan's medical treatment because it does not prohibit an individual male from appearing in public dressed in female clothing but prohibits only three or more persons from appearing in public dressed in female clothing. R at 4.

The People also contend that Ms. Breshnahan's conviction under §240.35(4) was proper as comporting with the policy behind the statute. The People argue that the statute was enacted as a means of preventing crimes committed by disguised individuals wishing to gain improper access to private areas, such as washrooms, as well as to provide assistance to police in the identification and apprehension of suspects. R at 4-5. The People answer Breshnahan's claims by pointing out that in both *Archibald* and *Gillespi*, proving malicious intent was not required. *People v. Archibald*, 27 N.Y.2d 504, 260 N.E.2d 871, 312 N.Y.S.2d 678 (1970); *People v. Gillespi*, 15 N.Y.2d 529, 202 N.E.2d 565, 254 N.Y.S.2d 121, *amended*, 15 N.Y.2d 675, 204 N.E.2d 211, 255 N.Y.S.2d 884 (1964). R. at 6. In *Archibald* the Appellate Term rejected the claim that the People had to prove the defendant was disguised in order to commit an illegal act. *People v. Archibald*, 58 Misc. 2d 862, 863, 296 N.Y.S.2d 834, 836 (1968). This court affirmed the Appellate Term without opinion but cited *Gillespi* as the controlling precedent on which to rely. R at 6.

The People claim that the applicable canons of statutory interpretation require that this court interpret §240.35(4) in a manner consistent with upholding the conviction. The People argue that the Legislature purposely did not include language excepting transsexuals. The People rely on the canon that states, "[W]here as here the statute describes the particular situation in which it is to apply, 'an irrefutable inference must be drawn that what is omitted or not included was intended to be omitted or excluded.'" *Patrolmen's Benevolent Ass'n v. City of New York*, 41 N.Y.2d 205, 208-09, 359 N.E.2d 1338, 1341, 391 N.Y.S.2d 544, 546 (1976) (quoting Consol. Laws of N.Y., Book I, Statutes, §240 (McKinney 1971)). R at 8.

The trial court probably erred in concluding that defendant Breshnahan was "disguised" for the purposes of §240.35(4) although still possessed of male reproductive organs. Although the intent to commit a crime is not necessary to be in violation of the statute, the masquerader exception implies that the Legislature intended to create an exception where a "disguise" is usual and expected. In 1965, when the statute was enacted, masqueraders in general were expected to wear "disguise[s]," and cross-dressing transsexuals were rarely seen in public. Almost 60 years later, cross-dressing transsexuals make up a much larger demographic. They are frequently in public and should therefore be exempt from punishment under the statute.

Construing the statute as purposely omitting the exemption of transsexuals would produce an unduly unjust result for transsexuals in medical treatment. While strict construction of the statute would technically allow transsexuals to cross-dress in public, it limits their ability to socialize in public. This court is "justified in making an exception through implication" to canons of statutory construction where interpreting the plain language would produce unjust results. *Williams v. Williams*, 23 N.Y.2d 592, 599, 246 N.E.2d 333, 337, 298 N.Y.S.2d 473, 479 (1969).

Further, the People offer no practical reason for distinguishing between *pre*-operative and *post*-operative GDS patients. Nor do the People offer a reason why the presence or absence of genitalia affects the ability to provide assistance to police in the identification and apprehension of suspects. Since both pre-operative and post-operative transsexual/transgender patients born male dress as females, the People would need to provide a reason why the two classes are treated differently under the statute that directly relates to genitalia.

Moreover, from a practical standpoint, a transsexual born as a male would likely hinder the apprehension of suspects more thoroughly were she to dress as a man, returning thereafter to her regular style of dressing as a woman. The police would not be able to use the victim's description of a male attacker effectively in a subsequent investigation. The police would be looking for a male, and all those who could recognize the perpetrator would know her only as a female. Hampering the identification of perpetrators, as the People suggest, is one of the primary reasons that the Legislature enacted the statute. However, this supports rather than hinders an implication that transsexuals are omitted from the scope of §240.35(4).

Although a transsexual born as a male can gain access to private areas and washrooms, so can transgender patients. There is no reason to suppose that the same person poses a threat before surgery and ceases to pose that threat after the surgery.

continues on next page

Because the trial court construed the statute as purposely omitting transsexuals from exclusion under the statute notwithstanding the unreasonable result of such construction, the trial court erred in denying defendant Breshnahan's motion for dismissal pursuant to Criminal Procedure Law §§290.10 and 320.20. Even viewing "the evidence 'in the light most favorable to the People,'" no reasonable fact finder could conclude that defendant Breshnahan violated the statute as construed reasonably.

Recommendation

I respectfully recommend that the court reverse Ms. Breshnahan's conviction for violating §240.35(4), because holding otherwise contradicts Legislative intent to aid in victim identification. Further, construing the statute as purposely omitting the exclusion of transsexuals produces unreasonable results.

10

Drafting Jury Instructions

I. Introduction

While judicial clerks working for an appellate court will often be required to draft a bench memorandum, judicial clerks working for a trial court will often be called on to draft jury instructions. While the jury's duty is to decide the facts and reach a verdict, the judge's duty is to determine the rules of law that govern those facts. The judge must then charge the jury, communicating to the jury those laws and how they operate. The vehicle the judge uses to communicate the laws to the jury consists of written jury instructions that the court reads to the jury.

The judge can charge the jury at the start of the trial, at the end of the trial, or both. If the judge gives instructions to the jury at the start of the trial, he or she will do so after the jury has been sworn in but before the start of opening arguments by the parties. These initial instructions provide the jurors with basic information regarding the procedures the court will follow during the trial; the trial schedule and when the jurors are expected to arrive at the courthouse; the jurors' duties, including the duty to refrain from discussing the trial with others; and what constitutes evidence. Occasionally, the court will provide initial instructions about the law to give the jurors context for the testimony that they will hear during the trial and to aid the jurors' understanding of that testimony. These initial instructions might address the causes of action or crimes at issue, any defenses raised by the parties, and the burden of proof.

The final charge takes place following the close of the trial but before the jury begins deliberations. In the judge's final charge to the jury, the judge identifies and explains the law that the jurors must apply to the facts of the case and makes clear that the jurors must rely on that law when reaching their decision. The final charge also includes instructions regarding the verdict form and how to fill it out.

A. Preparing to Draft Jury Instructions

Drafting clear jury instructions requires mastery of the subject area. Because jury instructions are a major cause of reversals or new trials on appeal, it is of the utmost importance that the instructions be substantively accurate. To ensure the accuracy of the jury instructions, you must consult the record and the pretrial order, learn about the issues in the case, research relevant authorities, and prepare an outline of the relevant law. Additionally, you must review the requested jury instructions submitted by the parties.

Preparing an outline is an important step that you must not skip in an attempt to save time. In fact, an outline that helps you to grasp the legal issues and understand the pertinent law will simplify preparation of the jury instructions. Carefully outlining the issues will help you understand the law on a deeper level. Additionally, an outline of the relevant issues and law will suggest a natural organization for the instructions.

The judge should inform you whether the case will be submitted for a general verdict, a general verdict with special interrogatories, or a special verdict. It is important to note that the use of interrogatories with a general verdict or a special verdict may substantially affect the content of the jury instructions. The differences between these types of verdicts and their effect on the jury instructions are discussed in more detail in section C(1)(e)(iii).

A wealth of resources is available to make drafting jury instructions easier. The judge will often have standard or form jury instructions that you may consult. In addition to the judge's personal cache of instructions, the trial courts may have developed pattern or model jury instructions that serve as a helpful guide. In federal court, several sources are commonly relied on when drafting jury instructions, including the Federal Judicial Center's pattern civil and criminal jury instructions for each federal circuit,[1] Devitt and Blackmar's *Federal Jury Practice and Instructions*,[2] and the *Modern Federal Jury Instructions*.[3] Further, most states have developed their own pattern or model jury instructions. There are also form books that include jury instructions for specialized areas of law, such

---

1. Federal Judicial Center, *Pattern Criminal Jury Instructions* (1987), *http://www.fjc.gov/public/pdf.nsf/lookup/crimjury.pdf/$file/crimjury.pdf.*

2. Edward J. Devitt, Charles B. Blackmar & Michael A. Wolf, *Federal Jury Practice and Instruction* (6th ed., Thompson West 2006).

3. Leonard Sand, John S. Siffert, Walter P. Loughlin, Steven A. Reiss & Nancy Batterman, *Modern Federal Jury Instructions* (Bender 1984).

as trademark and copyright law,[4] employment law,[5] and criminal law.[6] Once you have identified the issues in the case, researched the law, and prepared an outline of the law, you should consult the pattern or model jury instruction for your jurisdiction.

While the court generally does not charge the jury until the end of the trial, procedural rules often require the judge to disclose the final jury instructions to counsel prior to closing arguments. Thus, jury instructions must be prepared quickly and efficiently. Once the proposed jury instructions are complete, but before the jury is charged, counsel must be given an opportunity to object to the proposed instructions. These objections are made on the record but outside of the jury's presence. If changes to the instructions are necessary following counsels' objections, the instructions are retyped and the final version of the instructions is filed in the record. Each version of the jury instructions, including the jury instructions requested by the litigants and the proposed jury instructions, are included in the record for purposes of appellate review.

B. Formatting Jury Instructions

Jury instructions should be printed on plain white letter-size paper and consecutively paginated. The first page of the instructions consists of the caption of the case and the title "Instructions to the Jury." The next page is titled "Table of Contents," and will identify each individual instruction and the page on which it begins. When you begin drafting the individual instructions, each instruction must be typed on a separate piece of paper. This will allow the judge to easily insert additional instructions, delete instructions, or reorganize the instructions. The top of each page must be labeled with a description. This description may be general, such as "Jury Instruction No. 1," or it may be more specific to identify for the jury exactly what the instruction addresses, such as "Direct and Circumstantial Evidence." You can determine which type of heading the judge prefers by examining jury instructions that he or she had previously written. Additionally, you must include citations supporting each instruction.

Once you have drafted an instruction, the next step is to improve the layout of the instruction so that it is easy to read. You can improve the readability of the instructions by using visual clues, such as tabulating lists and numbering the items in the list. Generous use of doubling spacing will also make the instructions easier to read. These two techniques increase the amount of white space on the page so that the judge's eye can more easily focus on what he or she is reading to the jury. This will improve the

---

4. *See, e.g.*, ABA Section of Litigation, *Model Jury Instruction: Copyright, Trademark and Trade Dress Litigation* (2008).

5. *See, e.g.*, ABA Section of Litigation, *Model Jury Instruction: Employment Ligitation* (2d ed. 2005).

6. *See, e.g.*, Kevin F. O'Malley, Jay E. Grenig & William C. Lee, *Federal Jury Practice and Instructions Criminal* (5th ed., Thomson West 2000).

judge's charge to the jury and make it easier for the jurors to understand the law.

II. Drafting the Jury Instructions

This section offers specific advice on drafting jury instructions. It provides some guidelines for communicating effectively with juries. These guidelines will address writing tips that are specific to drafting jury instruction, how to approach pattern jury instructions, advice on the types of instructions to include, and suggestions for how to organize the set of instructions.

A. Writing Tips Specific to Jury Instructions

When drafting jury instructions, it is imperative that you keep your audience in mind. Because jurors are drawn from geographical pools around the country, each jury will vary in terms of educational achievement and reading and comprehension levels. Thus, it is not feasible to draft jury instructions that all jurors will understand. Rather, the instructions should be written to effectively communicate with the *average* juror to assure that the majority of jurors will understand the law. You can assume that the average juror graduated from high school and can read and comprehend at a 12th-grade level. While this will not be true for all jurors, it will be true for most.

Thus, because you are trying to communicate with relatively "ordinary" folks, such as hairdressers, waiters, bank tellers, and sanitation workers, it is important to pay attention to your tone and vocabulary. Jury instructions are not the place to show off for the jury by using elevated and educated language. While jury instructions should be dignified, they should not be overly formal. Formal language reduces comprehension by individuals with little education. Furthermore, "formality creates distance between a speaker and the audience."[7] Since you want the jurors to feel as though they are part of the judicial system, and not as though they are being ordered about, it is important to avoid being overly formal. However, because jury instructions should be dignified to elicit respect for the judicial system and to remind the jurors of the seriousness of the situation, the use of slang is inappropriate. Your goal is to reach a happy medium—use a level of formality sufficient to remind the jurors of the importance of what they are doing without alienating them.

---

7. Peter M. Tiersma, *Communicating with Juries: How to Draft More Understandable Jury Instructions*, 10 Scribes J. Legal Writing 1, 3 (2005-2006), *http://www.ncsconline.org/Juries/communicating.pdf.*

Another aspect of formality involves how you refer to the parties to the litigation and other participants. Identify the parties and other participants by name rather than using abstract descriptive terms such as plaintiff or defendant. Not only does identifying the parties by name lessen the level of formality, but it also makes the instructions more concrete. The jurors are not deciding a lawsuit between some abstract landlord and tenant. They are deciding a lawsuit between John Smith, a landlord, and Bob Davis, a tenant. The actions of each are attributable to them as persons, not as abstract legal concepts. Making the instructions more concrete will increase the jurors' comprehension of the law and make it easier for the jurors to apply the law to the facts and reach a verdict. When "links between actions and goals are stated explicitly" and the law is linked explicitly to the specific facts of the case, communications directed to individuals who are inexperienced in the area are more effective.[8]

With regard to vocabulary, remember to avoid legalese and other legal concepts. You must translate those terms and concepts into ordinary English. Thus, instead of saying that Jones must prove by a preponderance of the evidence that Davis is the father of her child, you would say that Jones must prove that it is more likely than not that Davis is the father of her child. Consequently, you eliminate the unfamiliar legal term and explain the concept of "preponderance of the evidence" in language that the average juror can understand. You may wonder why you wouldn't include all those nifty legal terms floating around in your head. Each legal term has a precise meaning associated with it. Why would you even try to use other words to describe these complex concepts? The reason is simple: The vast majority of jurors do not know what you know because they are *laypersons*. They haven't attended law school; many have only a high school education. If you draft the jury instructions as though you were addressing other lawyers, then those instructions will fail to communicate the information to the jury.

A specific class of legal words that confuse laypersons are words ending in the suffixes -or and -ee. These words often come in pairs, such as lessor and lessee, mortgagor and mortgagee, assignor and assignee, or vendor and vendee. Because such words often confuse laypersons, it is especially important to replace them with less confusing words. For example, lessor and lessee can be replaced with the more commonly known words landlord and tenant.

You cannot, however, always avoid legal terms simply by substituting ordinary language. Some words are so firmly entrenched that lawyers and laypersons alike expect to hear it. Other legal terms cannot be explained in just a few ordinary words. The term "reasonable doubt" is an example of

---

8. Kevin O'Malley, Jay E. Grenig & William C. Lee, *Federal Jury Practice and Instructions* 819 (6th ed., Thomson West 2006) (quoting Dean E. Hewes & Sally Planalp, *The Individual's Place in Communication Science* in *Handbook of Communication Science* 147 (Charles R. Berger & Steven H. Chaffee eds., 1987)).

both types of words. In either situation, it is best to just use the term. However, when you use the term, you must define it for the jury. You do not want jurors looking up words in a dictionary during deliberations — such behavior is a type of juror misconduct.

Furthermore, some legal terms have a significantly different legal meaning than their ordinary meaning. When possible, you should avoid the term completely to avoid confusing the jurors. However, if avoiding the term is not feasible, you must alert the jurors of the difference in meaning and define the term. You do not want the jurors trying to guess the meaning of the legal term based on the ordinary meaning of words. For instance, based on the ordinary definition of "malice," jurors might assume that "malice aforethought" requires ill will despite the fact that the law of murder does not require that the defendant harbor ill will toward the victim. Therefore, an instruction on "malice aforethought" might read:

> Unlike its meaning in ordinary language, "malice" in the phrase "malice aforethought" does not require that the defendant have had ill will or bad feelings toward the victim.[9]

Other legal terms that jurors may incorrectly define based on the ordinary meaning of the words include negligence, reasonable doubt, personal property, filing a complaint, burglary, and mayhem. While jurors may be familiar with terms like negligence and reasonable doubt, they are familiar with those terms only in a general sense and are not aware of the nuances in meaning that result from years of refinement. Additionally, crimes like mayhem and burglary have significantly different meaning than the popular meaning of those words. While the crime of mayhem involves the cutting or mutilating of body parts, the popular meaning of mayhem refers to a wild party or anarchy. Given the confusion that jurors may experience when such words are used in jury instructions, it is advisable to avoid them when possible and to define them if necessary.

Moreover, you should use impartial language when drafting the instructions. You must not articulate the instructions in a manner that favors one side over the other. It is important to remember that jurors are alert to the slightest suggestion of partiality by the judge. Therefore, you must not use language that biases a party; suggests a particular outcome on an issue; or unduly emphasizes facts, issues, or law. Thus, while the parties submit proposed jury instructions, it is not wise for the judge to simply adopt the terminology suggested by counsel. When submitting proposed jury instructions, counsel is advocating for an instruction that favors his or her client rather than for a fair and objective articulation of the law. Therefore, while the judge should consider the language proposed by

---

9. Tiersma, *supra* note 7, at 6.

counsel, the judge should rephrase the language and put it into his or her own words — words that are impartial.

You must use neutral language when referring to the parties in a criminal trial. Generally, you should refer to the defendant by name rather than as "the defendant." Using "the defendant" should be avoided because some people object that the term has a biasing effect — it suggests that Mr. Jones actually committed the crime. Furthermore, the prosecution generally objects to being called "the prosecutor," likely due to its similarity to "persecutor." However, unlike the defendant, the prosecutor should not be referred to by name, as the individual did not bring the case against the defendant; the state did. Thus, you should refer to the prosecutor as "the state," "the commonwealth," or "the government." Whatever manner you choose to refer to the parties, remember to be consistent.

Furthermore, you should articulate the law in an impartial manner. For example, to avoid phrasing that assumes guilt or innocence, abstain from using "you should find" at the beginning of a sentence. For example, avoid drafting an instruction that reads, "You should find that the defendant failed to yield the right of way if. . . ." Many judges believe that such language directs the jury toward a particular outcome. A less biased manner in which to draft the instruction would be as follows:

> To determine whether the defendant failed to yield the right of way, you must answer the following questions. . . .
>
> If your answer to all of the questions is "yes," then you should find that the defendant did fail to yield the right of way. If, however, your answer to any one of the questions is "no," then you should find that the defendant did not fail to yield the right of way.[10]

Additionally, avoid putting undue emphasis on a particular fact, issue, or law. Doing so results in a subtle and unconscious partiality because it focuses the jury's attention on certain aspects of the case and draws it away from other aspects. The jurors may interpret such emphasis as indicating that the stressed information is more important or decisive than the other information.

Finally, each instruction should be written in short, simple sentences. Simplify complicated or convoluted sentences by splitting them into shorter sentences. For instance, divide a sentence that has more than one important point into two or more sentences. Each sentence should address only one important point, and when taken together, the sentences should explain the law in a step-by-step fashion. Making your sentences shorter is not merely an academic endeavor; sentence length affects the reader's ability to remember information. Because an individual can process a limited amount of information when reading a sentence once,

---

10. O'Malley, Grenig & Lee, *supra* note 8, at 819 (adapting Wis. Civ. J.I. 1157).

you do not want to pack too many ideas into a sentence. If you include too much information, the reader will forget some of it. Thus, you must limit the number of ideas in each sentence. Furthermore, writing shorter sentences aids the judge when he or she is charging the jury—the judge cannot take a breath until he or she reaches a period.

In summary, the instructions should be written in language that a layperson with a high school education could understand. Consequently, the instructions should be written in plain language, avoiding legalese and overly formal vocabulary. Furthermore, the instructions should be written in impartial language that refrains from favoring one party over another or unduly biasing a party.

B. Pattern or Model Instructions

As noted previously, a wealth of standard jury instructions exists. The Federal Judicial Center has devised pattern jury instructions for civil and criminal cases arising in each federal circuit, and many states have created pattern or model instructions.

It should be noted that these pattern instructions have not generally been approved by the appellate courts and so are not binding on the trial courts. Pattern instructions are merely helpful guides—suggestions meant to assist those drafting instructions so that they do not have to reinvent the wheel. However, if an appellate court has specifically approved a particular instruction, trial courts often will use that instruction in an effort to avoid reversal in the event the jury instructions are later challenged on appeal. But they are not required to do so. While the legal principle approved by the appellate court is controlling, the specific language approved by the court is not.

With regard to civil cases arising under a federal district court's diversity of citizenship jurisdiction, the district court may use the state's pattern jury instructions. However, the district court is not necessarily required to use a state's pattern instruction, even if a state court is bound to use that instruction. For instance, where a state's pattern instructions instruct that the instructions must be used, the state's courts are required to do so. However, because the pattern instructions are not law, federal courts are not bound to use the instructions. They will certainly take the pattern instructions into account, but they may modify the instructions or use other more appropriate instructions if the circumstances demand it.

Furthermore, when relying on standard instructions, remember that they are not "ready-made instructions."[11] They cannot be "swallowed whole."[12] While standard instructions provide a guide, the instructions must be tailored to take into account the particular facts of the case before

---

11. Robert L. McBride, *The Art of Instructing the Jury* §5.10 (W.H. Anderson 1969).
12. O'Malley, Grenig & Lee, *supra* note 8, at §7:2.

the court. In particular, the points of law that have been approved by appellate courts should be "couched in language appropriate to the facts and to the parties" in the current litigation.[13] Deletions and additions are always necessary to tailor an instruction to a particular case. However, use caution when altering pattern instructions, particularly in states that regularly supplement such instructions. Be sure to carefully consider the ramifications of departing from the language of the instructions; you do not want to fall victim to an error that the committee drafting the pattern instructions may have discovered.

C. Types of Jury Instructions

The purpose of jury instructions is to identify the issues in a case for the jury, explain the law applicable to those legal issues, and provide guidance to the jury on how to reach a verdict. Jury instructions not only define the issues in the case and identify the relevant law but also articulate the processes to be used in resolving those issues and identify the steps that the jurors must follow to reach a verdict.

The majority of the instructions will address subjects that should always be included in any set of jury instructions. These instructions are known as common general instructions. The remainder of the instructions will address the specific legal issues that arise during the case. These instructions are known as specific law instructions.

1. COMMON GENERAL INSTRUCTIONS

Common general instructions must be given in every case. Sometimes referred to as advisory or cautionary instructions, common general instructions explain to the jury the nature of the deliberative process and identify the jurors' responsibilities. These instructions are quite similar in all cases. They address a variety of subjects, including evidence, credibility, burden of proof, weight of the evidence, prejudice and sympathy, the function of the judge, and the duties of the jury. Common general instructions may also include a number of discretionary items that the judge may believe will be helpful to the jury or that may be necessary to address particular problems that arose during trial.

This section identifies and explains what should be contained in the individual instructions that are often included in common general instructions. However, this section is merely a guide. If a particular instruction is not applicable to the case at hand, omit it. If the judge wishes to articulate a particular instruction with different language or prefers a different organization of the common general instructions, you must do as the judge wishes. And, by all means, remember that the list of common

---

13. *Id.*

general instructions is greater than those included in this section. Only the most commonly encountered common general instructions are included. The circumstances of the individual case may demand the inclusion of other instructions.

a. Introduction

The first instruction includes a brief introduction. In this introduction, the judge provides an outline for what is to follow, essentially identifying for the jurors what he or she is going to tell them in more detail later.

SAMPLE JURY INSTRUCTION NO. 1

INTRODUCTION

Members of the jury, now it is time for me to instruct you about the law that you must follow in deciding this case. I will start by explaining your duties and the general rules that apply in every criminal case. I will also explain some rules that you must use in evaluating particular testimony and evidence. Then I will explain the required elements of the crime that the defendant is accused of committing in this case. And last, I will explain the rules that you must follow during your deliberations in the jury room and the possible verdicts that you may return.

---

b. Jurors' Duties

The introductory instruction should be followed by an instruction that identifies the jurors' duties and explains the differences between the functions of the judge and the jury. This instruction must inform the jurors that they are responsible for deciding what the facts of the case are based on the evidence that the jurors heard in court. The instruction should also inform the jurors that they should apply the law that the judge gives them to the facts of the case to determine whether the defendant is guilty in a criminal case or liable to the plaintiff in a civil case. The instruction should make clear that it is the judge's duty to decide what the governing law is and to explain it to the jurors. It should also make clear that the jurors are obligated to follow the law as the judge has explained it to them and that they must apply the law as it is, even if they disagree with it. The jurors should also be instructed that they are to perform their duties fairly and that they are not to allow prejudice or sympathy toward one party or another, or public opinion, to influence their decision.

SAMPLE JURY INSTRUCTION NO. 2

JURORS' DUTIES

You have two main duties as jurors. The first one is to decide what the facts are from the evidence that you saw and heard here in court. Deciding what the facts are is your job, not mine, and nothing that I have said or done during this trial was meant to influence your decision about the facts in any way.

Your second duty is to take the law that I give you, apply it to the facts, and decide if the government has proved the defendant guilty beyond a reasonable doubt. It is my job to instruct you about the law, and you are bound by the oath that you took at the beginning of the trial to follow the instructions that I give you, even if you personally disagree with them. This includes the instructions that I gave you before and during the trial, and these instructions. All the instructions are important, and you should consider them together as a whole.

The lawyers have talked about the law during their arguments. But if what they said is different from what I say, you must follow what I say. What I say about the law controls.

Perform these duties fairly. Do not let any bias, sympathy, or prejudice that you may feel toward one side or the other influence your decision in any way.

c. Burden of Proof

The next instruction should identify the burden of proof and tell the jury which party bears that burden. Because research suggests that jurors often do not understand the burden of proof or confuse different standards, such as preponderance of the evidence and beyond a reasonable doubt, your instruction needs to be as clear as possible. It should explain the burden in common everyday terms. Additionally, if it is acceptable in your jurisdiction, you should attempt to avoid possible juror confusion by distinguishing the preponderance of the evidence or clear and convincing evidence standards from the more commonly known reasonable doubt standard. Finally, the instruction should inform the jurors that they must consider all the evidence, regardless of which party produced the evidence.

Because the burden of proof is so important, it must be described in common everyday terms that laypersons can understand. For instance, when describing the preponderance of the evidence standard, you should inform the jury that the party who is trying to prove something must persuade the jurors that it is more likely true than not. Go on to explain that if the jurors cannot decide that something is more likely true that not, then they must conclude that the party did not prove it. Also, to avoid the jurors confusing the preponderance of the evidence standard with the reasonable doubt standard, just explain that while the reasonable doubt standard applies to criminal trials, the preponderance of the evidence standard applies to civil trials. California's jury instruction on the preponderance of the evidence standard is a good example:

Obligation to Prove — More Likely True Than Not True
A party must persuade you, by the evidence presented in court, that what he or she is required to prove is more likely to be true than not true. This is sometimes referred to as "the burden of proof."

After weighing all of the evidence, if you cannot decide that something is more likely to be true than not true, you must conclude that the party did not prove it. You should consider all the evidence, no matter which party produced the evidence.

In criminal trials, the prosecution must prove that the defendant is guilty beyond a reasonable doubt. But in civil trials, such as this one, the party who is required to prove something need prove only that it is more likely to be true than not true.[14]

Defining the beyond a reasonable doubt standard in common everyday terms is a little trickier. You might begin by explaining that proof beyond a reasonable doubt does not mean proof beyond all possible doubt and that possible doubts and doubts based on speculation are not reasonable doubts. After explaining what does not constitute a reasonable doubt, tackle what *does* constitute beyond a reasonable doubt. While the definition of the standard varies from jurisdiction to jurisdiction, the "firmly convinced" language used by some federal and state courts appears to be accurate and sufficiently explanatory:

When I tell you that a fact must be "proved beyond a reasonable doubt," it means that you must be firmly convinced, based on all the evidence that I admitted during the trial, that the fact is true.[15]

You might also describe this concept "as proof that is so convincing that you would not hesitate to act on it when making important decisions in your own life."

Because the definition of the standard varies from jurisdiction to jurisdiction, it is imperative that you determine how your jurisdiction defines the standard. If the definition in your jurisdiction is different from the one set forth above, either because the penal code defines the standard differently or the courts require that other language be used in instructing the jury, be sure to keep that in mind when drafting the instruction. You must retain the critical language required by the courts or statute. However, if the required language would be difficult for the jury to understand, you

14. Judicial Council of California, *California Civil Instructions* 200 (2003).
15. Tiersma, *supra* note 7, at 27.

may be able to make the definition of the standard more comprehensible by restructuring the definition, rephrasing negatives as positives, or simply providing a definition for the required language.

Furthermore, while examples are often helpful in explaining difficult concepts, they should probably be avoided when defining the beyond a reasonable doubt standard. Appellate courts have reversed judges for providing examples in jury instructions when the appellate court concluded that the example did not accurately reflect the law or was biased in favor of one party.

SAMPLE JURY INSTRUCTION NO. 3

PRESUMPTION OF INNOCENCE, BURDEN OF PROOF, REASONABLE DOUBT

As you know, the defendant has pleaded not guilty to the crime charged in the indictment. The indictment is not any evidence at all of guilt. It is just the formal way that the government tells the defendant what crime he is accused of committing. It does not even raise any suspicion of guilt.

Instead, the defendant starts the trial with a clean slate, with no evidence at all against him, and the law presumes that he is innocent. This presumption of innocence stays with him unless the government presents evidence here in court that overcomes the presumption and convinces you beyond a reasonable doubt that he is guilty.

This means that the defendant has no obligation to present any evidence at all or to prove to you in any way that he is innocent. It is up to the government to prove that he is guilty, and this burden stays on the government from start to finish. You must find the defendant not guilty unless the government convinces you beyond a reasonable doubt that he is guilty.

The government must prove every element of the crime charged beyond a reasonable doubt. Proof beyond a reasonable doubt does not mean proof beyond all possible doubt. Possible doubts or doubts based purely on speculation are not reasonable doubts. A reasonable doubt is a doubt based on reason and common sense. It may arise from the evidence, the lack of evidence, or the nature of the evidence. Proof beyond a reasonable doubt means proof that is so convincing that you would not hesitate to rely and act on it in making the most important decisions in your own lives.

If you are convinced that the government has proved the defendant guilty beyond a reasonable doubt, say so by returning a guilty verdict. If you are not so convinced, say so by returning a not guilty verdict.

d. Evidence

Since the jury must determine whether the burden of proof has been satisfied, it logically follows that the jury should then be instructed on what evidence is, how it should be considered, and how it should be weighed to reach a decision. This information spans several instructions.

i. Evidence in General

The first instruction should define evidence for the jurors. It should explain that their decision must be based only on the evidence that was presented in court and that they must not allow their decision to be influenced by anything that they may have learned outside the courtroom. The instructions should also inform the jurors that evidence constitutes only what the witnesses testified to while under oath, the exhibits that were entered into evidence, and any stipulations that the lawyers agreed to on behalf of their clients. The instruction should make clear that the lawyers' questions, objections, statements, and arguments are not evidence. Nor are the judge's comments, questions, and legal rulings considered evidence.

SAMPLE JURY INSTRUCTION NO. 4

"EVIDENCE" DEFINED

You must make your decision based only on the evidence that you saw and heard here in this courtroom and on the exhibits that have been admitted into evidence. Do not let anything that you may have seen, heard, or read outside of this courtroom influence your decision in any way.

The evidence in this case consists only of what the witnesses said while they were testifying under oath; the exhibits that I allowed into evidence; and any stipulations that the lawyers, on behalf of their clients, agreed to.

Nothing else is evidence. The lawyers' statements and arguments are not evidence. Their questions and objections are not evidence. My legal rulings are not evidence. And any comments I may have made or questions I may have asked are not evidence.

Make your decision based only on the evidence, as I have defined it here, and nothing else.

---

ii. Consideration of Evidence

With regard to the jury's consideration of the evidence, the jurors should be instructed to use their common sense when weighing the evidence and to consider the evidence in light of their everyday experiences with people and events. They should also be told to consider all the evidence that has been presented at trial regardless of which party produced it.

SAMPLE JURY INSTRUCTION NO. 5

CONSIDERATION OF EVIDENCE

You should use your common sense in weighing the evidence. Consider it in light of your everyday experience with people and events, and give it whatever weight you believe it deserves.

---

iii. Direct and Circumstantial Evidence

You will also need to instruct the jurors on direct and circumstantial evidence. Explain that direct evidence consists of evidence such as the testimony of witnesses or exhibits admitted into evidence at trial that, if believed to be credible, directly proves a fact. Circumstantial evidence should also be defined for the jurors. The instruction should explain that circumstantial evidence is essentially a chain of circumstances that indirectly proves a fact. Providing concrete examples of the two types of evidence would be helpful to the jurors as well. For example, if a witness testified that he saw it raining outside, that testimony would be direct evidence that it was raining. On the other hand, if an individual walked into the courtroom wearing a raincoat covered with drops of water and carrying a wet umbrella, that would be circumstantial evidence from which you could reasonably conclude that it was raining. Another example that can be used to differentiate between the two forms of evidence concerns a jet. For example, if a witness testifies that a jet flew across the sky, that testimony is direct evidence that a jet did indeed do so. On the other hand, if a witness testified that he or she saw only the white trail that jets leave, that testimony is indirect evidence, or circumstantial evidence, that a jet flew across the sky.

After explaining the difference between direct and circumstantial evidence, the instruction should inform the jurors that they must determine how much weight to attribute to direct and circumstantial evidence. The instruction should also note that the law does not differentiate between the two types of evidence in terms of the weight to be accorded to them; neither form of evidence is given greater weight than the other. Such an explanation is necessary because some laypersons are under the misconception that circumstantial evidence is weaker evidence than direct evidence.

SAMPLE JURY INSTRUCTION NO. 6

DIRECT AND CIRCUMSTANTIAL EVIDENCE

Now, some of you may have heard the terms "direct evidence" and "circumstantial evidence."

Direct evidence is simply evidence like the testimony of an eyewitness that, if you believe it, directly proves a fact. If a witness testified that he saw it raining outside, and you believed him, that would be direct evidence that it was raining.

Circumstantial evidence is simply a chain of circumstances that indirectly proves a fact. If someone walked into the courtroom wearing a raincoat covered with drops of water and carrying a wet umbrella, that would be circumstantial evidence from which you could reasonably conclude that it was raining.

It is your job to decide how much weight to give the direct and circumstantial evidence. The law does not make a distinction between the weight that you should give to either one, and it does not say that one is any better evidence than the other. You should consider all the evidence, both direct and circumstantial, and give it whatever weight you believe it deserves.

The law does require that before convicting a defendant, the jury must be satisfied from all the evidence in the case that the government has proved the defendant guilty beyond a reasonable doubt.

iv. Credibility of Witnesses

Another instruction should explain to the jurors that it is their duty to decide the credibility of witnesses. They should be told that they must determine how credible, or believable, each witness was and decide how much weight they think they should attribute to that witness's testimony. The instructions may also provide some guidance to the jurors on how to evaluate the witnesses' testimony. These suggestions could include having the jurors ask themselves a number of questions. These questions may include, but are not limited to, the following:

1. Whether the witness was able to clearly see or hear the events to which he or she testified
2. How good the witness's memory seemed to be
3. Whether anything may have interfered with the witness's ability to perceive or remember the events
4. How the witness acted while testifying
5. Whether the witness had any interest, bias, prejudice, or other reason for testifying that might cause the witness to lie or slant the testimony in favor of one party or the other

6. Whether the witness testified inconsistently while on the witness stand or at some other time with regard to an important detail

7. How believable the witness's testimony was in light of all the other evidence presented at trial

Additional instructions may be given when a witness is a police officer or a paid informant. These instructions are designed to help the jurors properly weigh the credibility of such witnesses.

SAMPLE JURY INSTRUCTION NO. 7

CREDIBILITY OF WITNESSES

Another part of your job as jurors is to decide how credible or believable each witness was. This is your job, not mine. It is up to you to decide if a witness's testimony was believable, and how much weight you think it deserves. You are free to believe everything that a witness said, or only part of it, or none of it at all. But you should act reasonably and carefully in making these decisions.

Let me suggest some things for you to consider in evaluating each witness's testimony:

1. Ask yourself if the witness was able to clearly see or hear the events about which the witness testified. Sometimes even an honest witness may not have been able to see or hear what was happening and may have made a mistake.

2. Ask yourself how good the witness's memory seemed to be. Did the witness seem able to accurately remember what happened?

3. Ask yourself if there was anything else that may have interfered with the witness's ability to perceive or remember the events.

4. Ask yourself how the witness acted while testifying. Did the witness appear honest? Or did the witness appear to be lying?

5. Ask yourself if the witness had any relationship to the government or the defendant, or anything to gain or lose from the case, that might influence the witness's testimony. Ask yourself if the witness had any bias, or prejudice, or reason for testifying that might cause the witness to lie or to slant the testimony in favor of one side or the other.

6. Ask yourself if the witness testified inconsistently while on the witness stand, or if the witness said or did something (or failed to say or do something) at any other time that is inconsistent with what the witness said while testifying. If you believe that the witness was inconsistent, ask yourself if this

---

continues on next page

makes the witness's testimony less believable. Sometimes it may; other times it may not. Consider whether the inconsistency was about something important or about some unimportant detail. Ask yourself if it seemed like an innocent mistake or if it seemed deliberate.

7. And ask yourself how believable the witness's testimony was in light of all the other evidence. Was the witness's testimony supported or contradicted by other evidence that you found believable? If you believe that other evidence contradicts a witness's testimony, remember that people sometimes forget things and that even two honest people who witness the same event may not describe it exactly the same way.

These are only some of the things that you may consider in deciding how believable each witness was. You may also consider other things that you think shed some light on the witness's believability. Use your common sense and your everyday experience in dealing with other people, and then decide what testimony you believe and how much weight you think it deserves.

SAMPLE JURY INSTRUCTION NO. 8

TESTIMONY OF A PAID INFORMANT UNDER A GRANT OF IMMUNITY

You have heard the testimony of John Doe. You have also heard that he received money from the government in exchange for providing information and that the government has promised him that in exchange for his cooperation, he will not be prosecuted for possession of a $20 rock of crack cocaine found on his person.

The use of paid informants is common and permissible. It is also permissible for the government to promise not to prosecute someone for a crime in exchange for his cooperation. But you should consider John Doe's testimony with more caution than the testimony of other witnesses. Consider whether his testimony may have been influenced by what the government paid him or what the government promised him.

Do not convict the defendant based on the unsupported testimony of such a witness, standing alone, unless you believe his testimony beyond a reasonable doubt.

SAMPLE JURY INSTRUCTION NO. 9

> ## TESTIMONY OF LAW ENFORCEMENT OFFICERS
>
> You have heard the testimony of Special Agents Jane Jones and Tom Taylor of the Bureau of Alcohol, Tobacco, Firearms, and Explosives.
>
> The fact that a witness may be employed by the federal government as a law enforcement official does not mean that his or her testimony is necessarily deserving of more or less consideration or greater or lesser weight than that of an ordinary witness. It is your decision, after reviewing all the evidence, whether to accept the testimony of these law enforcement witnesses and to give to their testimony whatever weight you find it deserves.
>
> Earlier, I talked to you about the "credibility" or the "believability" of the witnesses, and I suggested some things for you to consider in evaluating each witness's testimony. You should consider those same things in evaluating the testimony of the law enforcement officers.

In a criminal trial, other instructions may need to be given to the jury regarding the testimony of police officers and paid informants receiving a grant of immunity. An instruction may also need to be given with regard to a defendant's decision to refrain from testifying. If the defendant elected not to testify, it should be made clear to the jurors that the defendant has a constitutional right to not testify and that the failure of the defendant to testify may not be considered by the jury in any fashion.

v. Judge's Questions or Comments

An instruction should also address the judge's questions or comments during the trial and explain that they were not a comment on the evidence. The instruction should make clear that the judge was not trying to give the jurors his or her impression of the witnesses' credibility or which party should win the case.

SAMPLE JURY INSTRUCTION NO. 10

> ## COURT'S QUESTIONS
>
> As you probably noticed, I occasionally ask questions. I do have the right to ask questions if I think the evidence will be a little clearer once those questions are answered. If any of you have concluded from any of my questions that I was trying to give you my impression of which

continues on next page

witnesses were being truthful, or which party should win this case, that's simply not so. The credibility or believability of each witness is solely the function of the jury and not of the court.

e. Concluding Instructions and Verdict Form

The concluding instructions explain the deliberation process, instruct the jurors as to their duties with regard to the verdict, and provide the verdict form. The concluding instructions that address the deliberation process and instruct the jurors as to their duties address matters such as electing a foreperson, not conducting their own research into the case, not allowing prejudice or sympathy to sway their vote, deliberating, and not informing anyone of the verdict until it is announced in court.

i. Generally

The first of these instructions should inform the jurors that their first step when they return to the jury room is to elect a foreperson. The instruction should go on to explain the function of the foreperson. It should explain that the foreperson is responsible for ensuring that the deliberations proceed smoothly and in an orderly fashion by making certain that each juror is given the opportunity to discuss and vote on each issue. The instruction should also explain that the foreperson speaks for the jury when submitting questions to the court and when delivering the verdict. Finally, it should be made clear that despite the fact that the foreperson is important to the orderly progress of the deliberations, the foreperson has no more authority than any other juror, and the foreperson's opinion should not be given more weight than any other juror's.

Another instruction should remind the jurors that they are to base their decision only on the evidence that they saw and heard in the courtroom. It should instruct the jurors that they are not to conduct any independent research, reading, or investigation while deliberating. Yet another instruction should remind the jurors that they must not allow their decision to be influenced by sympathy or prejudice. The instruction should inform the jurors that, in fulfilling their duties as jurors, they must make every effort to reach a fair and just verdict.

You should also include an instruction that addresses the jurors' duty to deliberate and their conduct while deliberating. It should explain to the jurors that they must discuss the evidence with each other and make a reasonable effort to reach a decision. It should also instruct the jurors that they should keep an open mind and not hesitate to change their mind if they are later convinced that their original position was incorrect. Finally, the instruction should caution jurors not to change their minds just because other jurors view the evidence differently or just to return a verdict and conclude the case.

Another instruction should inform the jury how many jurors must agree to reach a verdict. In criminal cases, the decision must be unanimous. The instruction should explain that to find the defendant guilty, every one of the jurors must agree that the government has overcome the presumption of innocence with evidence that proves his or her guilt beyond a reasonable doubt. It should explain the opposite as well, informing them that to find the defendant not guilty, every one of the jurors must agree that the government has failed to convince them beyond a reasonable doubt that the defendant is guilty of the offense charged in the indictment. In civil cases, however, a unanimous verdict is not required. In civil cases, you should inform the jury of the exact number of jurors who must agree to reach a verdict. This number varies depending on the jurisdiction.

SAMPLE JURY INSTRUCTION NO. 11

JURY FOREPERSON, QUESTIONS FROM JURY

The first thing that you should do in the jury room is choose someone to be your foreperson. This person will help to guide your discussions and will speak for you here in court.

Once you start deliberating, do not talk to the court security officer, to me, or to anyone else except each other about the case. If you have any questions or messages, you must write them down on a piece of paper, have the foreperson sign them, and then give them to the court security officer. The officer will give them to me, and I will respond as soon as I can. I may have to talk to the lawyers about what you have asked, so it may take me some time to get back to you. Any questions or messages normally should be sent to me through your foreperson.

One more thing about messages: Do not ever write down or tell anyone how you stand on your votes.

SAMPLE JURY INSTRUCTION NO. 12

RESEARCH AND INVESTIGATION

Remember that you must make your decision based only on the evidence that you saw and heard here in court. All of the exhibits that have been admitted into evidence will go to the jury room with you, together with a copy of these instructions and the verdict form.

continues on next page

Do not try to gather any information about the case on your own while you are deliberating. For example, do not bring any books, like a dictionary, or anything else with you to help you with your deliberations, and do not conduct any independent research, reading, or investigation about the case.

Make your decision based only on the evidence that you saw and heard here in court.

SAMPLE JURY INSTRUCTION NO. 13

UNANIMOUS VERDICT

Your verdict, whether it is guilty or not guilty, must be unanimous.

To find the defendant guilty, every one of you must agree that the government has overcome the presumption of innocence with evidence that proves his guilt beyond a reasonable doubt. To find the defendant not guilty, every one of you must agree that the government has failed to convince you beyond a reasonable doubt that the defendant is guilty of the offense alleged in the indictment. Either way—guilty or not guilty—your verdict must be unanimous.

SAMPLE JURY INSTRUCTION NO. 14

DUTY TO DELIBERATE

Now that all the evidence is in and the arguments are completed, you are free to talk about the case in the jury room. In fact, it is your duty to talk with each other about the evidence and to make every reasonable effort you can to reach unanimous agreement. Talk with each other, listen carefully and respectfully to each other's views, and keep an open mind as you listen to what your fellow jurors have to say. Try your best to work out your differences. Do not hesitate to change your mind if you are convinced that other jurors are right and that your original position was wrong.

But do not ever change your mind just because other jurors see things differently or just to get the case over with. In the end, your vote must be exactly that—your own vote. It is important for you to reach unanimous agreement but only if you can do so honestly and in good conscience.

No one will be allowed to hear your discussions in the jury room, and no record will be made of what you say. So you should all feel free to speak your minds.

Listen carefully to what the other jurors have to say, and then decide for yourself if the government has proved the defendant guilty beyond a reasonable doubt or has failed to do so.

Juries sometimes ask to have portions of the trial transcript made available to them during deliberations. A trial transcript has not been prepared and therefore is not available to you. Instead, you, as jurors, must rely on your collective recollection of the testimony of the witnesses.

ii. Verdict Form

You must also include a verdict form with the instructions. A verdict is simply a written decision on the facts or the facts and law that the court submits to the jury. The verdict form should begin with the full caption of the case, which includes the name of the court that is hearing the case, the names of all parties, the case number, and the presiding judge. Next is the verdict itself. The appearance of the verdict will vary depending on the type of verdict that is to be submitted. Finally, the verdict form should include signature lines for the jurors as well as a date line. The first signature line should be labeled for the foreperson. The date line should be located directly below the last signature line, at the bottom right of the page.

You should, of course, instruct the jury that a verdict form has been included with the instructions. The instruction should tell the jury what to do with regard to the verdict form. This varies depending on the type of verdict to be returned. The instruction should also explain how many jurors must agree to reach a verdict. Finally, it should inform the jurors that each of the jurors who agree with the verdict must sign the verdict form.

iii. Types of Verdicts

Because the type of verdict may affect the jury instructions, it is important that you understand the difference between a general verdict, a general verdict with special interrogatories, and a special verdict. With a general verdict, the jury simply decides which party wins. A general verdict is a general answer — the defendant is guilty or not guilty, liable or not liable. A general verdict identifies in whose favor the jury found; however, it does not reveal how the jury decided the specific factual questions on which that decision was based. The jury's decision is generally articulated in a "yes/no" or a "check-the-box" fashion. For example, in a civil matter, a general verdict would be as follows:

> We, the jury, find for _____.
> (Insert party's name)

In a criminal matter, a general verdict would be similar to the following example.

> We, the jury, find the defendant, John Smith:
>
> ____ Not Guilty ____ Guilty   of Distribution of Cocaine Base, a Schedule II Controlled Substance, as alleged in the Indictment.

On the other hand, when the court requests a general verdict with special interrogatories, it asks the jury to return a general verdict that is accompanied by answers to questions as to specific factual issues on which the verdict depends. Thus, the court requires the jury to make specific factual findings, apply the law to those factual findings, and reach a general verdict. The function of these special interrogatories is to test the accuracy of the jury's general verdict by examining the jurors' reasoning process. If there is an inconsistency between the jury's finding to a special interrogatory and the general verdict, the finding of fact controls the verdict. Thus, the jury's factual findings may require a different judgment than that expressed by the jury in the general verdict.

A special verdict satisfies a more limited role than a general verdict or a general verdict with special interrogatories. In fact, when the court uses a special verdict, it completely dispenses with a general verdict. Rather than deciding the culpability of the defendant, a special verdict requires the jury to answer individual questions that arose during the case. This series of questions addresses all the issues in the case. The jury's *sole* function is to determine the facts or mixed questions of law and fact, depending on the jurisdiction. Once the jury has made its specific findings, the judge then decides the legal effect of those findings and makes the ultimate legal conclusion based on those facts. Because it is the judge who applies the law to the facts as found by the jury, the jury requires no instruction on the pertinent law.

Mixed questions of law and fact require some explanation. In some cases, one cannot clearly delineate between a question of law and a question of fact. For example, in a negligence case, deciding whether the defendant entered the intersection on a red light is a purely factual question on which the negligence case can be resolved. On the other hand, if the jury is required to decide whether a defendant's action complied with the standard of ordinary reasonable care, this requires the jury to consider the defendant's actions in light of the legal principles setting forth what constitutes ordinary reasonable care. This is a mixed question of law and fact.

So how does the use of a general verdict, general verdict with special interrogatories, and special verdict affect the jury instructions? A general verdict, general verdict with special interrogatories, and a special verdict in which the jury answers mixed questions of law and fact will be substantially the same. The jury must be instructed as to both the general law *and* the specific law that is needed to resolve the ultimate legal issue presented by the case. However, if the special verdict requires the jury to answer only *purely factual issues*, it is improper to instruct the jurors on the law or of the law's effect on their factual findings. Thus, the jury must not be instructed as to the specific law. Additionally, all three types of verdicts must ask pointed questions that elicit a simple yes or no answer or provide for checking the correct box.

Some differences exist between the instructions for a general verdict and those for a special procedure. Instructions when using a special procedure must provide directions to the jurors regarding when they must answer the special interrogatories or special verdicts and the methods they must use in coming to an answer. Thus, when using a special procedure, you must be sure to instruct the jury on the effect of its answers. For example, if the first consideration in a legal test is a threshold matter, your first question would ask the jury whether this threshold issue was satisfied. Then, you would instruct the jury regarding what it should do depending on its answer to this question. You might say something like, "If you answer yes to Question 1, answer Question 2. If you answer no to Question 1, skip Question 2 and answer Question 3."

iv. When to Use a General Verdict Rather Than a Special Verdict or Special Interrogatories

How does the court decide whether to use a general verdict, a general verdict with special interrogatories, or a special verdict? For the most part, the use of special verdicts and special interrogatories is within the discretion of the court.[16] The courts offer little guidance regarding when a judge should exercise its discretion by using the special verdict or special interrogatories. As such, the use of these special procedures largely depends on the individual trial judge's views of their usefulness and the proper role of the jury. However, these special procedures do not appear to be warranted when a case is relatively simple, such as a case involving only one legal issue or a basic automobile negligence case. On the other hand, judges have often exercised their discretion to use a special verdict or special

16. While the use of special procedures is generally within the discretion of the trial judge, in some states the use of special verdicts is firmly established and believed to be practical in all cases. Texas is one such state. Rule 49 of the Federal Rules of Civil Procedure permits a federal district court judge to use a special verdict or special interrogatories. The use of special procedures in federal court is entirely within the discretion of the judge. However, federal district courts tend to use special verdicts when the district court is located in a state where the use of the special verdict is prevalent. The district judge's instructions parallel to some extent the instructions required by the state in which the district court is located. When drafting the instructions, the district judge will use the same methods, forms of submission, and instructions used in the state in which the district court is located.

interrogatories in complex and difficult cases. For example, in civil litigation, the use of the special verdict has been found to be proper in

- actions involving multiple defendants;
- actions relating to damages for personal injuries or death;
- actions involving property damages;
- litigation involving insurance policies;
- cases involving securities fraud;
- antitrust cases;
- litigation over patents and trademarks; and
- cases involving discrimination and civil rights.[17]

A special verdict or special interrogatories may also prove useful in complex cases, such as where a plaintiff alleges numerous grounds of negligence. By requiring the jury to answer special interrogatories, the court can determine on which grounds the jury actually found liability. The special interrogatories clarify the issues not only for the jurors but also for the appellate court. Furthermore, a special procedure may be helpful in cases where the verdict depends on the jury's initial decision on determinative issues. Other examples of litigation where a special verdict or special interrogatories may be warranted include cases where

- the law is uncertain or developing;
- your client is likely to be the object of bias (e.g., a corporation or wealthy individual);
- contributory negligence is at issue;
- the passion or prejudice of the jury is likely to be excited;
- free expression is at issue; and
- a special finding as to intent or value is required.[18]

In criminal matters, the use of a general verdict is the norm; special verdicts and special interrogatories are highly disfavored. In fact, these special procedures cannot be used if a statute or rule requires a general verdict. Nevertheless, the use of special procedures is required in certain criminal cases and may be appropriate in several others. For instance, Federal Rule of Criminal Procedure 31(e) requires that in a criminal case in which the government seeks forfeiture of property, the jury return a special verdict indicating the extent of the property that is subject to forfeiture. Furthermore, for offenses where insanity, mercy, value of property taken, or a prior conviction must be specially determined, criminal codes often require the use of a special verdict.

Just as in civil litigation, special procedures may be useful in complex criminal cases. Thus, a special verdict or special interrogatories may be helpful in determining whether the defendant engaged in the requisite predicate acts in cases where the defendant has been charged with violating

17. O'Malley, Grenig & Lee, *supra* note 8, at §8:9 (footnotes omitted).
18. *Id.* (footnotes omitted).

the Racketeer Influenced and Corrupt Organizations Act or the Continuing Criminal Enterprise statute.

Special procedures have been found to be appropriate when the jury must determine issues such as

- the value of property taken;
- the type of weapon used in crimes of violence or drug trafficking;
- which statement was false in a perjury prosecution;
- the extent of harm in a carjacking case;
- the aggravating factors in a federal death penalty case;
- which photographs meet the statutory definition in a child pornography case; and
- whether both elements of an entrapment defense had been met.

Special verdicts or special interrogatories might also be useful in narcotics prosecutions. For instance, the use of special procedures can clarify not only the type of drugs but also the amount of drugs involved in the crime. This is particularly true when the amount of drugs may justify imposing a sentence that exceeds the maximum period of time authorized by the facts before the jury.[19] Special procedures might also be helpful in cases where a defendant is charged with crimes in the conjunctive. For example, when a defendant is charged with distributing or conspiring to distribute more than one drug, use of a special verdict would make it clear which of the criminal objectives it found the government proved at trial.

SAMPLE JURY INSTRUCTION NO. 15

VERDICT FORM

I have prepared a verdict form that you should use to record your verdict. If you decide that the government has proved the defendant guilty beyond a reasonable doubt, say so by having your foreperson mark the appropriate place on the form. If you decide that the government has not proved the defendant guilty beyond a reasonable doubt, say so by having your foreperson mark the appropriate place on the form.

Each of you should then sign the verdict form and put the date on it.

---

19. *See Apprendi v. New Jersey,* 530 U.S. 466, 488-490 (2000), in which the U.S. Supreme Court held that a fact that increases the penalty for a crime beyond the statutory maximum must be submitted to the jury and proved beyond a reasonable doubt. This rationale would extend beyond narcotics prosecutions to other criminal cases in which the penalty might be increased beyond the statutory maximum due to the nature of amount of particular element, such as a firearm. *But see United States v. Strickland,* 245 F.3d 368, 376 (4th Cir.), *cert. denied* 534 U.S. 894 (2001), where the court determined that appellate review of the case would be for plain error where the defendants failed to request a special interrogatory on drug qualities.

SAMPLE JURY INSTRUCTION NO. 16

IN THE UNITED STATES DISTRICT COURT
FOR THE SOUTHERN DISTRICT OF OHIO
EASTERN DIVISION

UNITED STATES OF AMERICA, :
    Plaintiff,   :   Case No. 2:06-CR-XXX
    v.   :   Judge Holschuh
JOHN SMITH,   :
    Defendant.   :

VERDICT

We, the jury, find the defendant, John Smith:

_____ Not Guilty _____ Guilty   **of Distribution of Cocaine Base, a Schedule II Controlled Substance, as alleged in the Indictment**

_____

United States v. John Smith

Page 2 of 2

_____

Foreperson

_____   _____
_____   _____
_____   _____
_____   _____
_____

                     Date: _____

2. SPECIFIC LAW INSTRUCTIONS

In addition to the common general instructions, the judge must instruct the jury on the specific law that applies to the legal issues that arose during the trial. The specific law will be different in each case and may concern any of the substantive areas of law. You should note that when drafting specific law instructions, the frequency with which certain subjects appear varies. Some subjects will appear often; others will appear only rarely. When dealing with an area of law that commonly pops up at trial, such as negligence, you may find the use of standard or pattern jury instructions helpful. You will, of course, need to modify such instructions to address particular issues that arose during the case before the court. If pattern instructions are not available, look for a case that addressed a similar problem. The trial judge's experience and the outcome of the trial may suggest potential instructions.

Drafting specific law instructions is much more difficult than drafting general common instructions. As stated previously, specific law instructions vary from case to case. You must clearly identify the issues in the case and set forth the applicable law in a manner that is understandable by the jurors. When drafting specific law instructions, keep the following advice in mind. First, you must have a clear grasp of the issues in the case and of the applicable law. A thorough understanding of the issues and the law will simplify the ordering of the instruction and the explanation of the law. Thus, when preparing specific law instructions, begin by carefully outlining the law governing the issues. During the outlining process, the law will fall into a recognizable pattern that suggests a logical arrangement for the individual instructions. The outline will also aid you in explaining the law.

Second, articulate the law in a concrete, rather than an abstract, manner. Generally, laws are stated in the abstract, so that they apply to any individuals and actions falling within their scope. However, at trial, the issue is very concrete. The jury must decide whether the *defendant* committed a crime or otherwise violated the law. Thus, the instructions should tell the jurors what they need to decide to reach a verdict. The instructions should (1) identify which party has the burden of proof, (2) identify the elements of the crime or cause of action in a list and explain that each element must be satisfied, and (3) tell the jurors what to do after they have decided whether the elements are satisfied. For example:

> You must find the defendant guilty of theft by larceny if the state has proven each of the follow elements to be true beyond a reasonable doubt:
>
> 1. The defendant took Mr. Smith's property without his or her consent;
> 2. The defendant intended to permanently deprive Mr. Smith of the property; AND
> 3. The defendant moved the property, even if only a small distance, and kept it for some period of time.

If, on the other hand, the jury must consider factors rather than elements, the instructions should be drafted somewhat differently. While all elements must be satisfied for a jury to find a defendant guilty of a crime or liable for a civil wrong, factors are merely considerations to take into account when reaching a decision. This distinction can be made known to the jury by presenting the factors as questions for the jurors to ask themselves. For example:

> It's up to you to decide whether to believe a witness. In evaluating a witness's testimony, ask yourself the following questions:
>
> 1. How well could the witness see or hear the things that the witness testified about?
> 2. How well was the witness able to remember and describe what happened?
> 3. Did the witness understand the questions and answer them directly?
> 4. Did the witness seem believable to you?

SAMPLE JURY INSTRUCTION NO. 17

DEFINING THE CRIME

That concludes the part of my instructions explaining your duties and the general rules that apply in every criminal case. I will next explain the required elements of the crime that the defendant is accused of committing.

But before I do that, I want to emphasize that the defendant is on trial only for the particular crime charged in the indictment. Your job is limited to deciding whether the government has proved each and every element of the particular crime charged beyond a reasonable doubt.

I turn then to the indictment.

SAMPLE JURY INSTRUCTION NO. 18

DISTRIBUTION OF COCAINE BASE (CRACK COCAINE)

Title 21 of the United States Code, Section 841(a)(1), makes it illegal "for any person knowingly or intentionally . . . to . . . distribute . . . a controlled substance." The indictment in this case accuses the defendant of knowingly and intentionally distributing more than 50 grams of cocaine base, commonly known as crack cocaine, a Schedule II controlled substance, in violation of this statute.

For you to find defendant guilty of this crime, you must be convinced that the government has proved each of the following elements beyond a reasonable doubt:

1. That the defendant distributed cocaine base, commonly referred to as crack cocaine, a Schedule II controlled substance;
2. That the defendant did so knowingly and intentionally; and
3. That, at the time of the distribution, the defendant knew that the substance distributed was cocaine base.

In addition, the government must prove that the alleged offense occurred, in whole or in part, in the Southern District of Ohio on or about June 22, 2006, the date alleged in the indictment.

If you are convinced that the government has proved each of these three elements beyond a reasonable doubt, and that the offense occurred, in whole or in part, in the Southern District of Ohio on or about June 22, 2006, say so by returning a guilty verdict on this charge. If you have reasonable doubt about any one of these elements, then you must find the defendant not guilty of this charge.

I will now give you more detailed instructions concerning each of these elements.

SAMPLE JURY INSTRUCTION NO. 19

DEFINITIONS

"Distribute"

The term "distribute," as used in these instructions, means to deliver or to transfer possession or control of something from one person to another. The term "distribute" includes the sale of something by one person to another.

"Controlled Substance"

You are instructed as a matter of law that cocaine base, otherwise known as crack cocaine, is a Schedule II controlled substance.

"Knowingly and Intentionally"

To act "knowingly" means to act voluntarily and with awareness of the nature of one's conduct and not because of ignorance, mistake, or

continues on next page

accident. An act is done "intentionally" if it is done deliberately with the specific intention to do the act that the law prohibits.

I want to explain something about proving a defendant's state of mind. Ordinarily, there is no way that a defendant's state of mind can be proved directly, because no one can read another person's mind and tell what that person is thinking. But a defendant's state of mind can be proved indirectly from the surrounding circumstances. This includes things like what the defendant said, what the defendant did, how the defendant acted, and any other facts or circumstances in evidence that show what was in the defendant's mind. You may also consider the natural and probable results of any acts that the defendant knowingly did and whether it is reasonable to conclude that the defendant intended those results. This, of course, is all for you to decide.

"On or About"

I also want to say a word about the date mentioned in the indictment. The indictment charges that the crime happened "on or about" June 22, 2006. The government does not have to prove that the crime happened on that exact date. But the government must prove that the crime happened reasonably close to that date.

"Southern District of Ohio"

The court takes judicial notice that Columbus, Ohio, is within the Southern District of Ohio. Because you as members of the jury are the triers of fact in this case, you are not required to accept the court's instruction that Columbus, Ohio, is within the Southern District of Ohio, and you may make your own determination of this fact.

SAMPLE JURY INSTRUCTION NO. 20

SUMMARY

Keeping in mind the above instructions regarding the applicable law, if you unanimously find that the government has proved beyond a reasonable doubt that the defendant did knowingly and intentionally distribute cocaine base, commonly known as crack cocaine, a Schedule II controlled substance, and that the alleged offense took place, in whole or in part, in the Southern District of Ohio, on or about June 22, 2006, then you must return a verdict of guilty.

> However, if you unanimously find that the government has failed to prove beyond a reasonable doubt any one of the essential elements of the offense, as I have explained those elements to you, then you must return a verdict of not guilty.
>
> That concludes the part of my instructions explaining the elements of the crime. Now let me finish by explaining some things about your deliberations in the jury room and your possible verdicts.

D. Organizing Jury Instructions

The organization of the instructions is solely within the discretion of the trial judge. No law controls the arrangement of jury instructions. The only rule regarding the organization of jury instructions is that they be organized so that they flow logically. The jury instructions must "prepare the jury for its work, guide it to its problem and lead it step by step through the issues and to an intelligent verdict."[20] While all jury instructions must be organized so that they flow logically from one to the next, the placement of particular instructions is not set in stone. There is no limit to the number of different approaches a judge may take when organizing jury instructions. The organization of jury instructions is governed by the judge's style and his or her own personal manner of processing information. This section identifies some of the more common approaches to organizing jury instructions and offers some practical advice for arranging them. However, if the judge wishes you to reorder the instructions or include different or additional information than that outlined above in the discussion of common general instructions, or if your jurisdiction has some precedent on a particular instruction, you must comply with those requirements.

Two basic organizational methods exist for organizing jury instructions. One method begins generally, providing common basic instructions and definitions before identifying the specific legal issues and pertinent law. The specific law instructions are followed by the judge's concluding remarks regarding the jury's duties during deliberation and in reaching a verdict. This organizational method works well for those who believe that it is more logical to define terms and general rules before addressing the heart of the case. This organization may also maintain the jurors' interest and prevent them from making premature judgments.

The other organizational method begins by outlining the legal issues and explaining the specific law. Common basic instructions, definitions of terms, and concluding remarks follow the specific law. This organizational method operates on the premise that the heart of the case should be addressed first, when the jurors are freshest.

---

20. McBride, *supra* note 11, at §5.03.

While the two organizational methods outlined above are the most common, other arrangements are acceptable if they proceed in a logical manner. To proceed in a logical manner, the instructions must present the information to the jurors "in progressive steps that increase their ability to comprehend each successive part of the instructions. It is like building a house; without a firm foundation everything that follows will collapse."[21] It will be easier for the jury to understand the instructions if they are arranged in a logical sequence that moves from one step to the next. Each subject should build on the previous one in a manner that makes it easier for the jury to understand the law. Additionally, the instructions should make it clear to the jury when one subject has ended and another has begun. This will enable the jury to more easily follow along with the instructions. Finally, to proceed in a logical manner, the instructions must discuss related topics together. Thus, the burden of proof, evidence, and credibility must be discussed in the same part of the instruction. The same is true regarding the specific law concerning a particular legal issue — all the law pertaining to that issue should be grouped together. You should take great pains to ensure that evidentiary and procedural rules are not discussed at points where they do not fit into the topical flow of the charge.

III. Editing and Proofreading

Finally, as with any other document drafted for the court, when drafting jury instructions you must edit and proofread them before submitting them to the judge. Jury instructions should be not only professional in appearance but also free of grammatical and typographical errors. Jury instructions are, after all, entered into the record for purposes of appellate review, and a "small" error, such as a misplaced comma, could lead to reversal. Furthermore, jury instructions must be easily understood by a jury of laypersons and free of ambiguity. This is no small task! It requires thorough revision, exhaustive editing, and meticulous proofreading.

IV. Checklist for Drafting Jury Instructions

When revising and editing jury instructions, and before submitting them to the judge or the staff attorney, consider the following questions to determine whether the instructions are complete and easy for laypersons to understand. To avoid feeling overwhelmed when revising the

21. *Id.*

instructions, divide the revision into steps. During each step, revise the instructions with one question from the following list in mind.

____ Have you placed each instruction on its own page and included a title at the top of that the page?

____ Have you included all necessary general instructions?

____ Have you identified the specific legal issues in each case and included the relevant instructions?

____ Have you correctly stated the law?

____ If you believe that the jury will misunderstand or misinterpret something from the trial, have you included an instruction that will prevent that misunderstanding?

____ Have you deleted all information that is irrelevant to the case before the court?

____ Have you personalized the instructions by adding the names of the persons, places, and things involved?

____ Have you substituted plain English for legal terms or elevated vocabulary wherever possible?

____ Have you defined all uncommon words or terms?

____ Have you structured each of the lists in your instructions logically and in parallel form?

____ Have you numbered the items in your lists and used tabulation to make the lists visually attractive and easy to follow?

____ Have you simplified complicated sentences?

____ Have you deleted all ambiguities from the instructions?

____ Have you used correct grammar and punctuation?[22]

Additional Resources

- Mary L. Dunnewold, Beth A. Honetschlager & Brenda L. Tofte, *Judicial Clerkships: A Practical Guide* (Carolina Acad. Press 2010).
- Federal Judicial Center, *Chambers Handbook for Judges' Law Clerks and Secretaries* (West 1994).
- Robert L. McBride, *The Art of Instructing the Jury* (W.H. Anderson 1969).
- Kevin O'Malley, Jay E. Grenig & William C. Lee, *Federal Jury Practice and Instructions* (6th ed., Thomson West 2006).
- Peter M. Tiersma, *Communicating with Juries: How to Draft More Understandable Jury Instructions*, 10 Scribes J. Legal Wrting 1 (2005-2006), *http://www.ncsconline.org/Juries/communicating.pdf.*

---

22. This checklist was adapted in part from a checklist found in Mary L. Dunnewold, Beth A. Honetschlager & Brenda L. Tofte, *Judicial Clerkships: A Practical Guide* 202-203 (Carolina Acad. Press 2010).

11 Legal Citation

I. Generally

A legal citation identifies a legal authority or reference work. Because a legal citation allows an individual to locate a source, such citations play an essential role in legal research and writing. Furthermore, like the use of proper grammar, using proper citation form gives your work product a more professional appearance and subconsciously reassures the legal reader that your legal research is thorough and your analysis thoughtful. Reasonably or unreasonably, sloppy citation form sets off alarms for a legal reader and results in skepticism regarding the writer's analytical abilities. Given that a judicial clerk is drafting a document for a judge, creating skepticism in the clerk's ability, or worse yet, in the judge's ability, is unacceptable.

A. Using the Proper Citation System and Complying with the Judge's Unique Citation Preferences

At this point in your legal education, you have likely been introduced to legal citation. Therefore, there is no need to review individual citation rules. However, what you may not realize is that there are many citation systems, and the format required by each may vary from the others by a little or a lot. The bench and bar have primarily adopted either *The Blue-book: A Uniform System of Citation* or the *ALWD Citation Manual: A Professional System of Citation*. *The Bluebook*, which Harvard publishes, is currently in its 19th edition. The Association of Legal Writing Directors (ALWD) publishes the *ALWD Citation Manual*, which is currently in its

4th edition. In addition to these two citation systems, some courts use neutral citations[1] or follow their own unique citation system. Thus, it is important to know which citation system is followed by the court where you are clerking.

Often, the court will have a local court rule that officially adopts one citation system. If the court mandates that one system is to be used in all documents that appear before it, then the citations in any documents you draft must comply with that system. However, if the court has not officially adopted a citation system, you must be much more observant with regard to citation format. You must determine whether the court has unofficially adopted *Bluebook* form, ALWD form, neutral citation form, or its own unique citation format. In the absence of an official rule adopting a specific citation system, *Bluebook* form is often a default since most judges learned citation from some edition of the *Bluebook*. Unfortunately, if a judge asks you to "bluebook" the citations in a document, this is not really indicative of what citation system the jurisdiction uses. The judge is not necessarily asking you to review the citations to ensure that they comply with *Bluebook* form. The judge may simply be asking you to review the citations for accuracy under the citation system used by the court. To "bluebook" is simply a generic verb that lawyers use to refer to cite checking or using proper citation format.

In addition to determining what citation system the court uses, you must also determine whether the judge for whom you are clerking has any personal citation preferences that do not comply with the required citation format. You should adopt the judge's citation quirks when drafting a document since all the documents you draft for the court must be written in the judge's voice. Examples of such quirks could include always spelling out a word that the citation system abbreviates (or vice versa), using a different abbreviation than that required by the citation system, or refusing to include the date parenthetical in a statutory citation. Even in jurisdictions that require *Bluebook* form, you must watch for the judge's personal preferences. The judge likely learned citation form from a different edition of the *Bluebook* than the one with which you are familiar. Thus, there may be slight differences in the judge's citation form that are attributable to the difference in edition.

1. Neutral citations are also referred to as public domain citations. This citation system was created so that the public would have free access to the court's opinions and orders via the court's website. Courts that use neutral citations assign a citation number to each case, which is used in place of the usual reporter citation or commercial electronic database citation. Also, the court numbers each paragraph in the case, which allows readers to include pinpoint cites in their documents. This is necessary since there are no page numbers in the court's electronic copy of the case. If the court in which you are clerking employs neutral citations, please remember to determine what citation form governs all other citations. Neutral citations only apply to cases.

B. Tips for Individuals Who Learned Citation from the *ALWD Citation Manual*

Because *Bluebook* form is the most commonly adopted legal citation form in the United States, those who learned citation from the *ALWD Citation Manual* may require a brief introduction to the *Bluebook*. First, it is important to note that some differences exist in the citation format provided by the *Bluebook* and that provided by the *ALWD Citation Manual*. The changes to ALWD form were made only to promote consistency or flexibility where it would not affect one's ability to locate the cited authorities.

The following examples are not all-inclusive, but they represent the types of alterations the authors of the *ALWD Citation Manual* made to citation form. For instance, the *ALWD Citation Manual*

- uses abbreviations with only periods rather than abbreviations with periods and apostrophes;
- permits pinpoint references to material on consecutive pages to be presented by dropping the repetitious digits or by retaining all digits on both sides of the hyphen;[2]
- when citing to a treatise or book, requires that the publisher be included in the parenthetical with the date, whereas the *Bluebook* does not include such information in the citation; and
- in regard to law review articles written by students, requires that the words "Student Author" follow the author's name.[3] The *Bluebook*, on the other hand, has a complex set of rules regarding how to identify a student author.[4]

Although there are some differences between the citation forms recommended by the *Bluebook* and those preferred by the *ALWD Citation Manual*, the changes made by ALWD to citation form are relatively few and insignificant in the overall scheme of legal citation. The citation forms provided by the two manuals are quite similar, particularly with regard to the types of documents you will be drafting for the court. However, while it is true that most attorneys will not be able to discern whether the citations in a document were drafted under the *Bluebook* citation system or that set forth in the *ALWD Citation Manual*, the fact that improper citation form may reflect poorly on the judge demands accuracy in citation. If the court in which you clerk requires compliance with *Bluebook* form, then that is the format you must use. If you use the citation format

2. *Compare* Association of Legal Writing Directors & Darby Dickerson, *ALWD Citation Manual: A Professional System of Citation* R. 5.3(b), 35 (4th ed., Aspen Law & Bus. 2010) *with The Bluebook: A Uniform System of Citation* R. 3.2(a) (Columbia L. Rev. et al. eds., 19th ed., Harv. L. Rev. Assn. 2010).
3. *ALWD Citation Manual, supra* note 2, at R. 23.1(a)(2), 202.
4. *Bluebook, supra* note 2, at R. 16.7.1. Rather than simply identifying the author as a student, the *Bluebook* identifies a student author in several different ways depending on whether the article is signed or attributed to the student and titled, simply signed, or unsigned but titled. *Id.*

provided by the *ALWD Citation Manual*, your citation format will appear sloppy to the discerning eye.

The first thing a clerk who learned citation from the *ALWD Citation Manual* should remember when required to cite in *Bluebook* form is *don't panic*! You will not be required to teach yourself *Bluebook* form. ALWD provides assistance with this endeavor in the form of handy charts that list the differences between the two citation systems and identify the rules in the *Bluebook* that correspond with those found in the *ALWD Citation Manual*. The "Comparison of Selected ALWD Fourth Edition and Bluebook Nineteenth Edition Rules" chart lists the differences between the citation systems set forth in the *Bluebook* and the *ALWD Citation Manual*. The "ALWD Citation Manual to Bluebook Conversion" chart identifies the most commonly used citation rules in the *ALWD Citation Manual* and lists the corresponding *Bluebook* rule. While the differences chart and the comparison chart are not located in the *ALWD Citation Manual* itself, they are located on the ALWD website (*http://www.alwdmanual.com/books/dickerson_alwd/authorUpdates.asp*).

Because these charts are quite helpful, it would be wise to bookmark the links on your computer or to print the charts and store them in the back of your *ALWD Citation Manual*.

II. Tips on Word Processing and Citations

A. Inserting Symbols Commonly Used in Legal Writing

Legal citation requires the use of several symbols, including the section (§) and paragraph (¶) symbols. To create a section or paragraph symbol in Word, go to the menu bar at the top of the page and select Insert → Symbol to open the Symbol dialog box. Once the box opens, select the Special Characters tab, select the symbol, click the Insert button, and hit the Close button to exit the dialog box. Many symbols can also be inserted using shortcut keys. To learn the shortcut key for a symbol, open the Symbol dialog box, and select the Special Characters tab. If a shortcut exists, it will be listed to the right of the character. A writer may assign a shortcut if no shortcut exists or if the writer prefers another, more memorable shortcut. For more information on how to assign shortcuts, go to the Help menu and type "symbols and shortcut."

To create a section or paragraph symbol in WordPerfect, go to the menu bar at the top of the page, and click on Insert → Symbol, or just hit the "Ctrl" and "W" keys at the same time to open the Symbols dialog box. When the box opens, select Typographical Symbols from the dropdown menu, select the symbol, and click the Insert and Close button to close the dialog box. The writer can also assign a symbol to a keyboard key by customizing the keyboard settings. For more information on how to assign symbols, go to the Help menu and type "symbols, assigning."

B. Disabling Default Settings That Interfere with Proper Citation Form

Because legal citation is so precise, the default settings of word processing programs affect citation in a negative manner. These default settings include automatic spacing following periods; automatic capitalization; and automatic replacement of words, symbols, and ordinal contractions. These settings can cause problems because the word processing program capitalizes letters that the writer does not type as capitals, inserts one or two spaces after *every* period, and converts ordinal abbreviations into superscripts. Therefore, to ensure maximum accuracy in citation, these default settings must be disabled. To disable these settings, start by selecting Tools on the menu bar and then selecting QuickCorrect in WordPerfect or AutoCorrect Options in Word.[5] Specific instructions on disabling each setting follow.

The automatic spacing feature is troublesome with regard to citation format because it inserts one or two spaces following every period, regardless of whether the period ends the sentence. To disable the automatic insertion of spaces following a period, in WordPerfect, go to the Format-As-You-Go tab, and make sure "Change one space to two spaces between sentences" is not selected. Word, on the other hand, does not have a default setting that adds one or more spaces after a period.

The automatic capitalization feature interferes with proper citation format because the feature capitalizes the first letter following a period. In WordPerfect, this feature can be disabled by selecting the Format-As-You-Go tab, removing the check mark from the "Capitalize next letter after end-of-sentence punctuation" box, and clicking the OK button. In Word, select the AutoCorrect tab, remove the check mark from the "Capitalize first letter of sentences" box, and click the OK button.

The automatic ordinal superscript feature also interferes with proper citation format. An ordinal denotes a series, and ordinal contractions such as "1st" and "4th" are commonly used in legal writing. The automatic ordinal superscript feature will place the letter portion of the ordinal contraction in superscript. The automatic ordinal superscript function can be disabled in WordPerfect by selecting the Format-As-You-Go tab, removing the check mark from the QuickOrdinals box, and clicking on the OK button. In Word, select the AutoFormat tab, remove the check mark from the "Ordinals (1st) with superscript" box, and click the OK button.

The automatic replacement of words and symbols may interfere with proper citation format because the feature will automatically replace one word or symbol with another. This automatic replacement feature is problematic in legal writing because it will replace (c) with © and (r)

---

5. Note that in Word 2007 and later versions, the menu bar differs. You will need to click the dropdown arrow next to the title bar at the top of the page and select More Commands. Select Proofing from the list on the left, and then click the AutoCorrect Options button to get to the dialog box mentioned in these instructions.

with ®. In WordPerfect, this feature can be disabled by selecting the QuickCorrect tab, choosing the undesired entry from the list, and clicking on the Delete Entry button. In Word, select the AutoCorrect tab, click on the undesired autocorrect option in the list so that it appears in the Replace With box, and click the Delete button so that the option is removed from the AutoCorrect window.

Additional Resources

- Association of Legal Writing Directors & Darby Dickerson, *ALWD Citation Manual: A Professional System of Citation* (4th ed., Aspen Law & Bus. 2010).
- *The Bluebook: A Uniform System of Citation* (Columbia L. Rev. et al. eds., 19th ed., Harv. L. Rev. Assn. 2010).
- Wayne Schiess, *Meet ALWD: The New Citation Manual*, 64 Tex. B.J. 911 (2001).

12
Applying for a Clerkship

Once you've externed for a judge, you may decide that you want to apply for a clerkship. Through your externship, you will have seen firsthand the excellent experience that you would receive from continuing to work in chambers. A clerkship allows you to continue and deepen that experience. Generally speaking, clerking will prepare you to be a better lawyer when you begin to practice law. Clerking provides additional training that further develops your research, writing, and analytical skills. It also broadens the areas of law to which you have been exposed in law school. Additionally, clerking at the trial level introduces you to civil and criminal litigation in a practical, rather than an academic, fashion, while appellate court clerkships introduce you to appellate procedure.

The further training you receive as a clerk will make you a valuable asset for many other employers, many of whom actively recruit former clerks. A clerkship is an essential credential if you plan to enter academia. Further, law firms value clerkships so highly that they are often willing to pay a bonus to an associate with clerkship experience or defer an associate's start date so that he or she can clerk before starting with the firm. Many government agencies, especially federal agencies such as the Department of Justice and the U.S. Attorney's Office, actively recruit former clerks. Because a judicial clerkship can benefit your legal career in numerous ways, competition to obtain a clerkship is fierce. Most federal judges receive hundreds of applications for a single clerkship position. Because applying for a clerkship is so competitive, it is important to be prepared for the application process; to research judges; and to know when to apply for available clerkships, what materials to include in the application packet, and how to apply for clerkships.

I. Getting Ready to Apply for a Clerkship

Which judges employ clerks? Federal magistrate judges, district court judges, court of appeals judges, Supreme Court justices, bankruptcy judges, tax court judges, administrative law judges, and state court judges at all levels employ clerks. Due to the variety of judges who hire clerks and the range of courts in which they sit, the hiring of law clerks is quite idiosyncratic. For instance, most judges hire clerks for one- or two-year terms. Many, however, have begun to employ at least one career clerk. Moreover, the timing of the hiring process can vary by judge, as can the materials required for completion of the application. Furthermore, while most judges require high grades and law review experience, not all judges do so. Some judges look for other traits in their potential clerks. For example, a district court judge in California hires only clerks who intend to practice public interest law. Thus, due to the idiosyncratic nature of the hiring process and the fact that judges look for a variety of traits when hiring a clerk, it would be wise to research the judges to whom you intend to apply.[1] The more information you know about a judge, the more you can emphasize any connection you may have to the judge or a trait that the judge may be interested in.

Several sources exist that you may consult regarding applying for clerkships. These sources provide information regarding the hiring procedure, including the deadlines for applications, the materials that should be included in the application packet, salaries, and more. Much of this information can be found at *http://www.judicialclerkships.com*, which serves as a central depository for information concerning judicial clerkships. The website also provides links to court websites and listings for vacancies. Additional resources to consult with regard to federal clerkships include the Federal Law Clerk Information System (found at *https://law clerks.ao.uscourts.gov*) and the *NALP Judicial Clerkship Directory*. With regard to state court clerkships, consult the *NALP State Judicial Clerkship Directory* and Vermont Law School's *Guide to State Judicial Clerkship Procedures*. You should also review any job posting for a clerkship that is located online or at your law school's career services department.

---

1. When initially deciding which judges you should apply to, if you feel overwhelmed by this level of research, know that it will be sufficient to research the geographic location of the court and the biographical information on the judge. However, if you are contacted for an interview with a particular judge, you should thoroughly research that judge to discover his or her idiosyncrasies in hiring and to assess the reputation of a judge and what it is like to clerk for that judge.

When assessing the reputation of a judge and what it is like to clerk for that judge, several resources are available. The most helpful of these resources include the *Almanac of the Federal Judiciary*, *The American Bench*, and the *Judicial Yellow Book*. Additionally, you may learn valuable information about a judge by contacting your own law school's alumni who have clerked for that judge.

II. Timing

A. Applying for Federal Clerkships

Each year, federal judges issue the Law Clerk Hiring Plan, which offers guidelines for federal judges with regard to hiring judicial clerks. The plan is designed to provide some uniformity among federal judges with regard to the timing of the hiring process. First, the plan's goal is to ensure that the hiring of judicial clerks will be done no sooner than the fall of the third year of law school. Second, the plan sets the dates when judges can begin accepting applications, when they can contact applicants to schedule interviews, and when they can begin holding interviews. Judges may begin accepting applications on the first Tuesday following Labor Day. They may begin contacting applicants for interviews that Friday. The first interviews may be held on the Thursday of the next week.

The plan is designed for all federal judges, including district court judges, magistrate judges, circuit judges, and bankruptcy judges. The plan does not, however, govern Supreme Court justices. Note that participation in the plan is not mandatory. Judges may voluntarily participate in the plan or not. Indeed, some judges elect not to participate in the plan. So how can you determine whether a judge is participating in the Law Clerk Hiring Plan? The Administrative Office of the U.S. Courts operates a website called the Online System for Clerkship Application and Review (OSCAR). OSCAR is a national database of federal law clerk vacancies. Judges have been encouraged to list their vacancies on OSCAR and to indicate whether they participate in the Law Clerk Hiring Plan. OSCAR provides the ability for potential judicial clerk applicants to obtain a listing of judges who are participating in the system and what materials those judges require in the application packet.

B. Applying for State Clerkships

With regard to clerkships in state courts, the application deadlines vary from state to state and from court to court. Because state court clerkships are not quite as competitive as federal court clerkships, state courts judges often begin hiring clerks a little later than federal judges. While some begin hiring clerks during the fall of the third year of law school, many do not begin hiring until the spring of the third year of law school. One method of searching for state clerkships is to check with the courts directly for vacancies. You should start by reviewing their websites for announcements. You could also call the judges' chambers to see if they have vacancies, when the deadline for applications is, and what materials should be included in the application. Remember to be polite and respectful when speaking with members of the judge's chambers. Depending on how you conduct yourself during such a phone call, you could gain a valuable contact in chambers or a less than enthusiastic voice.

Checking directly with the courts themselves works well if you are interested in clerkships in only one or two particular states. However, this method is cumbersome if you are interested in clerkships in a variety of states. A better approach would be to consult Vermont Law School's *Guide to State Judicial Clerkship Procedures*. The *Guide* is a valuable tool for researching state clerkships. Each year, the *Guide* collects information on clerkships from each state and provides a summary of the procedures, salaries, and time frame for hiring. While access to the *Guide* is not free, you can likely gain access through your law school's career services department.

III. The Application Packet

An application for a judicial clerkship generally consists of (1) a resume, (2) a cover letter, (3) law school transcript, (4) a writing sample, and (5) two or three letters of recommendation. It is important to remember, however, that this is a *general* rule; some judges may require more than this from their applications, while others may require less. For instance, some judges do not require a writing sample until they contact the applicant for an interview. Other judges require an applicant's undergraduate transcript as well as his or her law school transcript. Consequently, it is important to closely read any information for a clerkship that a judge has taken the time to offer, whether it is a post on the court's website, an announcement of the position that has been sent to your school, or information provided to the *NALP Judicial Clerkship Directory*. If the judge has not provided such information, you do not need to contact his or her chambers. Just fall back on the general rule of thumb offered above.

The rest of this chapter will discuss each component of the application packet and offer advice on how to create a successful application. Before examining the components individually, however, please note that each document included in the packet should be professional in appearance. This means that they should be free of grammatical and typographical errors. The documents should also be consistent, both internally and among the various documents. For instance, each document in your application packet should be printed on the same paper and use a consistent letterhead, font, and font size. Furthermore, substantively, you do not want your cover letter or law school transcript to contradict your resume.

A. The Resume

Your resume for a judicial clerkship should include the same types of general information that you would include in any other resume. This information should include your contact information, education, scholastic achievements, work experience, and publications. The primary difference between a resume for a judicial clerkship and one for another type of job is that a resume for a judicial clerkship should be retooled to emphasize your research and writing experience. Your resume should demonstrate your ability to research and write effectively, because the majority of a judicial clerk's time is spent conducting such work. In terms of length, work hard to edit your resume so that it fits on one page. However, if you believe that you have a number of skills that are relevant to a clerkship position that will not fit on one page, by all means include that information in your resume. Just be sure to thoroughly edit the document so that it is as concise as possible.

With regard to your contact information, include your e-mail address, as courts often use this mode of communication for contacting applicants. Generally, to be professional, you should use your official school (or work) e-mail address rather than a personal one. You do not want to reduce your chances for an interview with a creepy or weird personal e-mail address! Further, while the information that you should include in your resume regarding your education and publications is fairly self-evident, the information regarding your scholastic achievements and your work experience is a little trickier. Consequently, this section will look more closely at the latter elements of the resume.

1. Scholastic Achievement

What types of scholastic achievements should you include in your resume? With regard to your grades, at a minimum, you should include your grade point average. You should also include your class rank or the percentage of the class in which you fall (such as the top 10 percent) if it reflects favorably on you. With regard to the percentage of the class, anything within the top 25 percent seems to be helpful. You should also include any honors that you received during law school, such as being named to the dean's list or earning an award for a class. You should certainly include any awards that you received for earning the highest grade in a class, particularly for a legal writing class, drafting class, or clinic. In addition to traditional awards, if you are participating in a program to earn a certificate in a particular area of law, particularly legal writing, include that information in your resume. Furthermore, if you are a member of law review (or other law journal) or moot court, include that information on your resume. Your activities in law review and moot court demonstrate that you have had additional legal writing opportunities that required you to work without the direct supervision of a professor. You should also include information regarding any honor societies you have been inducted into, such as Phi Beta Kappa. Finally, with regard to scholarships, be cautious. Don't list all the scholarships you have received. Rather, only include those scholarships that were awarded on a merit basis. For instance, if you were awarded a scholarship based on your public service or for your outstanding undergraduate performance, include that in your resume. However, I would not suggest including scholarships that you were awarded due to your financial need or that were awarded based on criteria of which you are unaware.

2. Work Experience

With regard to your work experience, focus on those opportunities that provided you with legal experience, significant writing experience, or life experience. Legal experience can be gained from a variety of sources, including legal jobs (working for a government office or a private firm), legal internships or externships, research assistant positions with a law school professor, and law school clinics. Additionally, jobs that required significant writing experience do not necessarily have to be in the legal field. For example, if you were a journalist for a newspaper or magazine prior to law school, include that information in your resume. Finally, if you are coming to the law as a second career, and there is an extended gap between the time you attended college and your attendance at law school, include jobs that explain away gaps in your education. Inclusion of this information has an added benefit: It provides the judge some insight into who you are as a person, and if the judge finds this information interesting, it may help you obtain an interview.

When discussing your work experience, be sure to highlight your experience by being specific with regard to the areas of law that you dealt with and the types of documents that you drafted. For instance, let's say that you externed for a state supreme court justice. While it would be accurate to say that you "conducted legal research and writing on a variety of topics," this information is vague and does not really provide the reader with a sense of what you did while at the court. The reader has no idea what documents you may have written or whether your focus was on civil or criminal law. If, on the other hand, you stated that you "researched a wide variety of civil and criminal topics and drafted legal memoranda advising the judge as to the law and recommending whether the court should accept the appeal," the reader has a much clearer sense of what you did while at the court. Remember, vague descriptions of your job duties are not helpful to the reader. Be as precise as you can be (while still being concise).

3. Special Skills, Activities, and Interests

To provide some insight into who they are as individuals, students wish to include special skills, activities, and interests in their resumes. Often, the inclusion of such information simply consumes precious space that you could have used for more helpful information. However, when handled appropriately, the inclusion of special skills, activities, and interests can work to your advantage given that one of the primary concerns a judge has when hiring a clerk is whether the applicant will fit well with those already working in chambers. When in doubt with regard to whether to include a special skill, activity, or interest in your resume, consider whether it is unique enough to pique the judge's interest. Is it something about which the judge may wish to speak with you during an interview? If so, include it in your resume. If you don't think it is likely that a judge will be interested in the skill, activity, or interest, do not waste the space on it.

So what special skills should you include in your resume? To answer this question, one must first examine what is *not* a special skill. A special skill is *not* a skill that those working in the field are expected to possess. As a result, Westlaw and LexisNexis training are not a special skill. Lawyers expect every student graduating from law school to have acquired the ability to work with these research websites. On the other hand, mediation training that you received in preparation for a job as a mediator is considered a special skill. If you are fluent or close to fluent in a foreign language, you may wish to include this language skill in your resume. Note, however, that you should be fluent or close to fluent in a foreign language before you include it in your resume. Do not list a foreign language as a special skill just because you took classes in college. Additionally, musical skill is another skill that you may wish to include in your resume. If you sing opera or play the violin, the judge may be interested in this skill.

With regard to activities, be sure to include any community service activities that you have done. These activities do not need to be limited to legal service, though if you assist an attorney on pro bono cases, you would certainly include that in your resume! Include any volunteer work that you have done to benefit society, whether it was for a nonprofit organization or a government agency. There is one caveat with regard to activities or involvement in organizations that have political associations. Generally, it is advisable to omit references to organizations that have political associations (e.g., the Federalist Society, ACLU). Remember that you do not want to include any information in your resume that would result in your not making the cut for an interview. While the judge to whom you are applying may share your views, or at least not be negatively affected by them, remember that law clerks often review the applications first and make the first round of cuts. Since you have no way of knowing how a law clerk will respond to your political views, it is better to be safe than sorry. However, if you feel so strongly about your political views that you would not wish to work for a judge who does not share them, then you should include such information. A fit between you and chambers is essential to the judge-clerk relationship, and if you feel that this information is vital to that relationship, you should include it in your resume.

Finally, with regard to whether to include interests, keep in mind the goal of the resume — to make you appear qualified and interesting enough to earn an interview. Thus, you should not include generic interests such as reading, watching movies, attending concerts, hiking, cycling, and the like. Only include interests if you have a truly unusual interest, something that the judge may wish to ask you about during an interview. Examples of unusual interests include earning a pilot's license, climbing Mount Everest, playing an instrument in the symphony, and so on.

For examples of resumes drafted specifically for a judicial clerkship, see Sample Resume 1 and Sample Resume 2 at the end of the chapter.

B. The Cover Letter

Ideally, a cover letter invites the judge to read your resume and tells him or her why you are the best person for the clerkship. If a cover letter does its job, it makes the judge want to learn more about you by reading your resume and inviting you for an interview. Like the resume, it should be only about a page long.

1. TECHNICAL DIFFERENCES WHEN ADDRESSING A JUDGE

Some initial differences are involved when addressing the cover letter and envelope to a judge. In the name and address block, precede the judge's name with the honorific "The Honorable" and include the full name of the court in which the judge sits. For example:

The Honorable David C. Norton, Chief Judge
U.S. District Court for the District of South Carolina
P.O. Box 835
Charleston, SC 29402-0835

For the salutation line, address the judge as "Your Honor." Another option is to follow the salutation "Dear" with the judge's title (e.g., Judge, Justice, Chief Justice) and last name (e.g., Dear Judge Norton).

Another difference when addressing a judge rather than a government office or a law firm concerns how you refer to the office itself. If you wish to refer to the office when drafting a cover letter for a judicial clerkship, you must refer to the office as the judge's "chambers."

2. THE SUBSTANCE OF THE COVER LETTER

When it comes to the substance of the cover letter, there are three different approaches. These approaches range from a very brief letter that simply serves as a conduit for the application materials to a very detailed letter demonstrating your analytical skills. The first approach, advocated by Debra M. Strauss in *Behind the Bench: The Guide to Judicial Clerkships*, produces a very brief cover letter that essentially identifies who you are, your interest in a clerkship with the judge, the materials enclosed in the application packet, your references, and your contact information. This information is very general and includes:

- Your status as a law student attending X Law School and the year you will graduate.
- The term for which you are applying for a clerkship in the judge's chambers.
- The items enclosed in the application packet (e.g., resume, law school transcript, letters of recommendation, and writing sample).
- If you have not enclosed the letters of recommendation that individuals wrote on your behalf in the application packet, the names and contact information (including phone numbers) for those individuals as well as their relationship to you.
- Your contact information, including your telephone number, postal address, and e-mail address.[2]

Consequently, a cover letter using this approach would look like this:

Dear Judge King:

I am a third-year law student at the University of California, Davis School of Law and will be graduating in May 2012. I am writing to apply for the law clerk position that is available for the September 2012 term. I have enclosed with this letter my resume, law school transcript, letters of recommendation, and a writing sample.

Please let me know if you require any other materials. Thank you very much for your consideration.

Sincerely,

Jill Brooks

While there is nothing inherently dangerous about using this approach for drafting your cover letter, it is a wasted opportunity. It does nothing to make the judge want to learn more about you. It just introduces you to the judge and details the contents of your application packet.

The second approach, also identified by Strauss in *Behind the Bench*, is much more detailed than the previous one. In addition to including the more general information, this approach essentially requires you to research the case law produced by the judge and select an opinion that you think is excellent. Then, in the cover letter, you analyze that opinion. You go on to identify not only the skills that will make you a good clerk but also why you are a good match as a clerk for this particular judge.

This approach is overkill. The writing sample that you include in the application packet will demonstrate to the judge that you can analyze the law, so why try to do it in a cover letter that should be only about a page long? The risk is twofold. First, you risk that your analysis is overly

---

2. Debra M. Strauss, *Behind the Bench: The Guide to Judicial Clerkships* 111-112 (2002).

rudimentary due to the page constraint. Second, you risk seeming disingenuous. Either way, you risk alienating the judge and having your file put aside. Additionally, if you apply to a large number of judges (as you should), you will spend an inordinate amount of time drafting cover letters.

The third approach is midway between the two previous options. With this approach, you include the general information that the first option requires as well as information that demonstrates that you would be a good judicial clerk. Consequently, you highlight your research and writing experience, any experiences you have had working for a judge (e.g., as an intern or an extern), and any other experiences that you believe make you uniquely qualified to be a judicial clerk. When trying to demonstrate that you would be a good judicial clerk, avoid merely rehashing the information found in your resume. Refrain from simply telling the judge, "I did this, and I did that." The judge can see where you have worked and what you did by examining your resume. Rather, you should discuss your experiences in a way that shows how they, as a whole, make you an ideal candidate for a clerk.

A wide variety of information can demonstrate your prowess as a legal writer. You could show that you have a solid background in research and writing based on your receiving an award for a legal writing or drafting class, serving as a teaching assistant for a professor who teaches legal research and writing, participating in law review (or another journal), interning or externing for a judge, participating in moot court (if you were required to draft a brief or part of a brief), participating in clinic, or drafting documents for a legal job during law school. The selection of your student note for publication and your service as an editor for law review (or another journal) can also bolster your research and writing experience. Some nonlegal experiences that may contribute to a strong background in research and writing include a major in English during your undergraduate education or employment that was writing intensive (such as being a journalist or an English teacher at the high school or college level).

You may also apply for a clerkship with a specialized court, such as the U.S. Bankruptcy Court, the U.S. Tax Court, or the U.S. Court of Appeals for the Federal Circuit. If you apply for such a clerkship, you will need to tailor the cover letter even more to highlight your particular qualifications in that area. Highlight any courses that you have taken in the area and any other background that you may have in that area. Thus, you should mention working in that area during a summer clerkship or during the school year. You should also mention any CLE presentations or workshops that you have attended that concern that area of law. Further, you should also highlight nonlegal experiences that may benefit you when working in the area. For instance, if applying to work in the U.S. Tax Court, mention any accounting or finance experiences that you've had. If applying for the U.S. Court of Appeals for the Federal Circuit, include your technical and/or engineering background. In addition to your course work and work experiences, when applying for a clerkship with a specialized court, it is appropriate to express your interest in practicing in that area after graduation from law school.

You can also show why your experiences have made you wish to be a judicial clerk. Often, the experiences a student has as a judicial intern or extern contribute to his or her desire to work as a clerk after graduation. If so, include this information in your cover letter. However, if you wish to explain why you desire to be a clerk, the explanation should discuss how you could be a benefit to the judge. Avoid listing reasons that benefit you as a lawyer.

You may wish to include some other information in the cover letter as well. If, for instance, you have a personal connection with the judge, you could mention that connection early on in the cover letter. Additionally, if you have a geographic connection to the court that is not apparent from your other application materials, note that fact. For example, if you grew up in the state in which the court sits or you wish to practice law in that state, then by all means, emphasize that information. Furthermore, if the court is far away from your law school and you plan to be in the area at a particular time, include that information in the cover letter. Let the judge know the dates when you will be in the area. Judges will often try to accommodate you by scheduling an interview when you will be in town.

For examples of cover letters, see Sample Cover Letters 1, 2, and 3 at the end of the chapter.

3. Electronic Applications

The cover letter presents some difficulties when the application must be e-mailed to a judge's chambers. Should the cover letter be in the body of the e-mail itself? Or should you attach a PDF of the letter to the e-mail that you send? No hard-and-fast rule applies to this situation. If you e-mail the letter, it will not bear your signature, and a printout will not appear as professional as it should because it will potentially include the e-mail information (e.g., "to," "from," "date," and "re") at the top of the page. However, if you attach the letter to the e-mail, you will need to write something in the body of the e-mail itself. This will give those in the judge's chambers more to read. So what to do? You could contact the judge's chambers and ask what the judge prefers. Or, when in doubt, cover all the bases. Put the text of the cover letter in the body of the e-mail and attach a PDF of the letter with your signature. If you do this, be sure to let the judge know in the letter that you've also attached a copy of the letter to the e-mail.

4. Checklist for a Cover Letter

____ Did you address the judge as "The Honorable" in the name and address block?

____ Did you address the judge as "Your Honor" or "Dear Judge X" in the salutation line?

____ Did you introduce yourself as a law student attending X Law School and include the year you will graduate?

____ Did you include the term for which you are applying for a clerkship in the judge's chambers?

____ If you have a personal connection to the judge, did you make that connection known early?

____ If you have a geographical connection to the area in which the court is situated that is not apparent from your application materials, did you make that connection known?

____ Did you highlight your research and writing experience?

____ Did you highlight any experiences you may have had working for a judge?

____ Did you highlight any other experiences that make you qualified to be a judicial clerk?

____ Did you show how your experiences considered as a whole make you an ideal candidate for a judicial clerk? Did you do more than rehash your resume?

____ If applying to a specialized court, did you include your particular qualifications in the legal area?

____ Did you list the enclosures included with the cover letter (e.g., resume, law school transcript, letters of recommendation, and writing sample)?

____ Did you include the names and contact information (including phone numbers) for those individuals who wrote letters of recommendation on your behalf (if you have not enclosed those letters of recommendation in the application packet)?

____ If the court is in a distant locale and you will be in the area at a particular time, did you include the dates when you will be in town?

____ Did you include your contact information, including your telephone number, postal address, and e-mail address?

C. Writing Sample

Because strong research and writing skills are a must for a judicial clerk, it is crucial that you submit the best writing sample possible when applying for a judicial clerkship. Your writing sample must demonstrate your strong legal research, writing, and analytical skills. It must also be well organized, concise, and clear. Finally, it must be meticulous; it is imperative that your writing sample be free of grammatical and typographical errors.

1. WHAT TYPES OF DOCUMENTS MAKE A GOOD WRITING SAMPLE?

What types of documents make a good writing sample? The answer varies depending on the court to which you are applying. If you are applying to a trial-level court, then an appellate brief, motion memorandum, or office memorandum would be most appropriate. These documents generally deal with the types of concrete legal issues that you would be likely to encounter as a clerk in a trial court. More theoretical or policy-based documents (some appellate briefs to a court of last resort or law review articles) are appropriate when applying to clerk for an appellate judge.

When considering which document to select, you may choose from a variety of documents. You may select a document that you drafted for your legal writing classes or for a legal employer. You may also select your law review case note or comment (or those drafted for another journal). If you select a document that you drafted for a legal writing class, review it to make certain that it is a good example of your skill. Your research and writing abilities will have likely improved since your first year of law school. Furthermore, review the document for grammatical and typographical changes that can be easily corrected. Do the same for citation errors. You do not want to submit a writing sample with obvious errors in it!

If you select a document that you drafted for an employer, you must obtain the employer's permission to use the document as a writing sample. Additionally, redact the names of the parties and any other identifying information. When redacting information, it is better to replace the original names of the parties and locations with fictitious names rather than simply deleting names or blocking them out with black lines like the government does when redacting documents. The latter forms of redaction make the document difficult to follow. Finally, include a statement on a cover page or at the beginning of the document explaining that you have obtained the permission of your employer to use the document as a writing sample and that you have redacted the names of the parties and any other identifying information to ensure confidentiality.

Students who have interned or externed for a judge may wish to use an opinion or decision that they wrote for the judge as a writing sample; however, this is not appropriate. While everyone knows that clerks, interns, and externs assist the judge by drafting the early drafts of opinions and decisions, we maintain the fiction that the judge is the author of every opinion he or she issues. Thus, because the judges to whom you are applying may view your claim to authorship of an opinion or decision as unseemly, you should refrain from submitting a judicial opinion that you drafted for a judge as a writing sample.

You should generally avoid submitting your law review case note or comment as your writing sample. First, judges do not want their clerks to draft law review articles. Judges want clerks to draft memoranda and opinions that narrowly focus on the issues to be resolved. A legal memorandum or a brief is a better choice for a writing sample because it is similar to the type of writing you will do in chambers. Second, your writing sample should substantially consist of your own original and unedited writing. The final published version of your article is not the best example of your writing since it has been heavily edited.

Furthermore, since your resume will include the citation to the final published version of the article, the judge may access your article online if he or she wants to read it. You could also bring the reprint or final version of the article to the interview.

2. Proper Length for a Writing Sample

Your writing sample should be sufficiently long to showcase your organizational and analytical skills. How long is that? A general rule of thumb is 10 to 15 pages, though up to 20 pages may be acceptable. However, if the judge requires the writing sample to be a different length, you must comply with the judge's demands.

While a writing sample should be only 10 to 15 pages (20 at the most), many appellate briefs, motion memoranda, and most law review articles are longer than that in length. So what should you do? Submit an excerpt from the document that best demonstrates your analytical skills. Generally, with appellate briefs and motion memoranda, the argument or analysis section is the most important section. If this entire section is too long, submit the issues that provide the strongest analysis. Be sure to provide a brief introduction to the fact pattern with which you were working and to identify the legal issues that you were required to analyze. Furthermore, if you are providing an excerpt from a law review article, be sure that the excerpt you submit can stand on its own. To ensure that the excerpted material can stand on its own, you will need to establish context by providing an introduction to the issue that you wrote about, any necessary background the reader may require, and any further explanation that the reader may need to understand the excerpt. At the end of the excerpt, you may also need to provide a concluding statement.

D. Letters of Recommendation

Judges cannot really gain a sense of who you are from your application packet, even when that information is accompanied by an interview. Therefore, references are an extremely important aspect of the application packet because your recommenders are vouching for you as a person. Ideally, your letters of recommendation, coupled with your application packet, should show the judge that you are more than just an excellent student. They should show that you are an interesting person who is concerned with more than just your studies.

Generally, most judges require only two or three letters of recommendation. However, the number of recommendations required can vary from judge to judge. Thus, you need to determine how many recommendations are required by the judge to whom you are applying. If you are unable to locate any specific requirements for the judge, you should supply three letters of recommendation.

1. Who to Ask for a Recommendation

One way letters of recommendation benefit you is by demonstrating that you have good judgment in selecting individuals to write letters for you! Selecting an individual who has a big name but does not know your work demonstrates poor judgment. Rather, you should select an individual who will write a hymn of praise for your writing, intellect, personality, and work ethic. Only select recommenders with a big name or who have "connections" to the judge if those individuals know your work well and can address your strengths, particularly with regard to your legal writing skills. If a recommender does not possess a strong knowledge of your work, the letter that he or she writes will be mediocre at best. Instead, approach one or two law professors who are familiar with your work and ask them if they will provide a strong letter of recommendation. Ideally, you should ask for a recommendation from a professor in whose class you did well. Professors you should approach regarding a recommendation include professors for whom you drafted legal writing documents or seminar papers, professors from whom you took small classes, and professors for whom you served as a research or teaching assistant. Legal writing professors are often a good source for a recommendation because they have worked with you in a small class and have evaluated your legal research, writing, and analytical skills. A professor with whom you participated in a law school clinic would also be a good option for the same reasons.

In addition to law school professors, you could ask a legal employer to write a letter of recommendation. Again, be sure that the individual worked closely with you and can discuss your written work in some detail. If you interned or externed for a judge and made a favorable impression, you could ask the judge for a recommendation. Just be aware that some judges believe that the canons of judicial conduct prevent them from writing letters of recommendation. So do not be offended if you ask a judge for a recommendation and he or she says no. Additionally, if you did not work closely with the judge, he or she may not be the best individual to ask for a recommendation.

2. Approaching Those You Wish to Write Letters of Recommendation

You should approach the individuals you wish to write letters of recommendation far in advance of the deadline for the application packet. While not always possible, your goal should be to give your recommenders four weeks time to prepare the letter. You do this out of courtesy. Your professors and employers are busy people, and since you are asking a favor of them, give them as much time as possible in which to do it. Giving them plenty of time will also work in your favor because they will be more likely to agree to write a letter for you.

Provide those individuals who have agreed to write a letter of recommendation for you with certain materials designed to help them in drafting the letter. Obviously, unless you are using OSCAR, you should provide the names and addresses of the judges to whom you want the recommender to send a letter. Again, you are asking your recommenders to do a favor for you — make it as easy as possible for them to do it. Additionally, provide your recommenders with your resume, cover letter, and transcript. You may also provide your writing sample, though this is not as essential as the former documents. These materials may supply additional information with which your recommenders can work, helping them to offer a more well-rounded view of you.

Some recommenders will agree to serve as a reference for you but will require you to write the first draft of the letter yourself. While writing the first draft may make you feel awkward and uncomfortable because whatever you write will feel presumptuous, you should know that your recommender would not have asked you to do this unless he or she was confident that you could write an appropriate draft for him or her to work from. After all, who knows you and your achievements better than you do? When drafting the letter, adopt the point of view of the recommender and try to focus on the areas of your work that the recommender knows well. Furthermore, sing your praises; do not sell yourself short in the letter. Remember that you are writing a *first* draft. The recommender will alter the draft in any way that he or she sees fit.

E. Transcripts

Judges generally require that you submit your current law school transcript. Some judges also require that you submit your undergraduate transcript as well. While some judges require an official transcript, many judges will accept an unofficial photocopied transcript. Review the job announcement sent out by the judge to determine whether he or she requires submission of an official transcript.

Be sure to request your transcripts early so that you have no problem meeting the application deadline. Requesting and receiving transcripts sometimes takes more time than you anticipate. Not all schools allow you to request and pay for transcripts electronically. Additionally, the transcript must be mailed to either you or the judge's chambers through regular mail.

If your school uses an unusual grading scale, you must determine whether your transcript includes a key for understanding that scale. If it does not, obtain a key from the registrar's office and include that with your transcript.

IV. Using OSCAR

OSCAR is an online application program that allows you to select which participating judges you wish to apply to by simply checking a box. It also allows you to submit your application electronically to each judge by uploading the contents of the application to the website. You may upload your resume, cover letter, transcripts, and writing sample directly to OSCAR. You may also submit electronic requests for recommendation letters to your recommenders. Under the My Recommenders tab, see if your recommender's name is located in the dropdown list under Choose Existing Recommenders. For recommenders whom you do not see on the dropdown list, you will need to create them in the system yourself using the Add to My Recommender tab. You will also need to type in their e-mail addresses. OSCAR electronically invites the recommenders to log into the system to create and upload letters of recommendation on your behalf. While OSCAR allows you to submit electronic requests for recommendation letters, you should do this only as a formality. You should have already approached your recommenders and obtained their agreement to draft a letter on your behalf. OSCAR's electronic invitation will then serve as a nice reminder for your recommenders. Also, advise your recommenders each time you select additional judges to whom to apply. OSCAR does not always notify your recommenders when you have added judges, depending on how your recommenders have set up their OSCAR accounts.

Not all federal judges have elected to use OSCAR. If you become aware of judges whose names do not appear in OSCAR, it is likely that they do not use the system. You will need to conduct some research to see if those judges have vacancies. If they do have vacancies, you will need to determine the application deadline, as they may not abide by the Law Clerk Hiring Plan. Additionally, you will need to determine what materials they require in the application.

SAMPLE RESUME 1

EMMA A. BEARDSLEY
_____

801 First Street, Sacramento, CA 95616 • 501-652-1234 • e-mail: ebeard@law.mcgeorge.edu

EDUCATION	**University of the Pacific, McGeorge School of Law** JD candidate, 2002 Class rank: Top 5% Senior research editor, _McGeorge Law Review_ King Hall Pro Bono Certificate **University of Maryland College Park** BA in Anthropology, May 1999 (graduated with high honors) Thesis: "A Study of Lilliputtan Culture: Does Their Small Stature Affect Their Societal Attitudes and Reaction to War and Violence?"
EXPERIENCE	**Professor M. Sagi, University of the Pacific, McGeorge School of Law, 2000-present** _Research Assistant._ Research and draft memoranda about the intersection of law and culture, dissent within expressive associations, and the conflict of group and individual rights in freedom of association jurisprudence. **Herrick, Orrington & Heathcliffe, Sacramento, CA, Summer 2001** _Summer Associate._ Researched legal issues in a variety of practice areas. Drafted legal memoranda, client letters, jury instructions, court filings, and research papers. **U.S. District Court, Eastern District of California (Sacramento), Summer 2000** _Judicial Extern._ Judge Carl K. Lawrence. Researched and prepared memoranda on pretrial motions. Wrote bench memoranda and draft orders. Attended trials, hearings, and pretrial conferences. **U.S. Institute of Peace, Washington, DC, 1994–1998** _Public Affairs Assistant._ Coordinated public outreach efforts, including reports, press releases, press briefings, and public events. Developed and implemented the Institute's National Performance Review program as part of Vice President Gore's Reinventing Government Initiative. Wrote annual _Guide to Specialists_ and managed Speaker's Bureau. **Center for Population Options, Washington, DC, 1991–1993** _Production Assistant._ Provided support to project director of the National Adolescent HIV Prevention Initiative. Researched issues surrounding the risk of adolescent exposure to HIV and incidents of infection. Planned publication layout and design.

ADDITIONAL
EXPERIENCE

J.R.R. Publishing, Los Angeles, CA, 1993–1994
Desktop Publisher. Prepared publications for graphic design studio. Designed and created brochures, newsletters, and promotional materials.

Netstar Corporation, Ontario, CA, 1988–1991
Administrative Aide. Implemented computer network and electronic mail system, installed software, provided computer technical support to staff. Managed office's supply budget and ordering process, and assisted office manager with various projects.

Salvo & Associates, Ltd., Los Angeles, CA, 1987–1988
Legal Assistant. Provided sole office support for small law firm. Performed paralegal research; tracked accounts payable and receivable. Prepared and filed court documents.

SAMPLE RESUME 2

GIDEON A. HARP

| 166 Carol Court | Tampa Bay, FL 43132 | (614) 693-1943 | gharp@law.stetson.edu |

EDUCATION

Stetson University College of Law   Tampa Bay, FL
Juris Doctorate Candidate, May 1999
GPA: 3.650   Rank: 6/231
*USAA All-American Scholar Award
*CALI Award for Excellence in Constitutional Law, 1997

Florida State University   Tallahassee, FL
Bachelor of Arts   Major: English; Minor: Psychology; June 1996
GPA: 3.86, Summa Cum Laude
*Most Outstanding English Major 1996
*Phi Beta Kappa

**RELEVANT
LEGAL
EXPERIENCE**
8/98–present

Florida Supreme Court   Tallahassee, FL
Justice Erica Lundberg's Office
Extern
*Recommended whether the Court should hear cases based on review of jurisdictional motions.
*Drafted bench memoranda in which I briefed the parties' arguments, the status of Florida law on the matters in issue, and recommended whether the Court should affirm or reverse the lower court's decision.

8/97–present

Stetson Law Review   Tampa Bay, FL
Executive Articles Editor/Law Review Staff
*Selected and edited outside authors' articles for publication.
*Organized symposia on adoption law and medical malpractice mediation.

5/98–present

Stetson University College of Law
Research Assistant for Professors Kranz and Grover
*Conducted research regarding the juvenile court system for use during meetings of the Florida Juvenile Sentencing Commission.
*Researched various tax issues and edited drafts of an article regarding the tax opinions of Supreme Court Justice Sandra Day O'Connor.

5/98–present

Kranz & Kranz   Tampa Bay, FL
Law Clerk
*Researched and briefed complex criminal matters, including the conflict between confrontation rights and the admissibility of statements against interest for statements made by a codefendant who does not testify at the defendant's trial.
*Researched possible civil causes of action for torts arising from violations of constitutional rights.

5/97–present	***Night Prosecutor's Program***	Tallahassee, FL

Hearing Officer
*Mediated criminal misdemeanor complaints and attempted to resolve the problem.
*Received training in alternative dispute resolution.

8/97–5/98	***Stetson University College of Law***	Tallahassee, FL

Dean's Fellowship for Legal Writing
Teaching Assistant
*Assisted students in research matters, citation form, and format of legal documents.
*Edited grammar and corrected citation forms contained within student legal writing papers.
*Provided the professor with the most relevant case law regarding topics chosen for student papers and research exercises.

8/97–12/97	***Florida Attorney General's Office***	Tallahassee, FL

Capital Crimes Division
Extern
*Corrected the case record by delving through hundreds of documents and transcripts.
*Researched complex death penalty issues.
*Drafted memoranda and briefs for the Fifth Circuit.

NONLEGAL   ***Tampa Messenger Company***   Tampa Bay, FL
EXPERIENCE   Correspondent
6/98–9/98   *Wrote news articles regarding matters discussed at the Violet Township trustees' meetings. These matters included environmental issues and zoning issues.

PUBLICATIONS   *State v. Johnson: Social Discontent, Retribution, and the Constitutionality of Capital Punishment for Raping a Child*, 27 Stetson L. Rev. ___ (1998) (forthcoming).

SAMPLE COVER LETTER 1

166 Carol Court
Tampa Bay, FL 43132

August 12, 1999

Honorable Beccah Tazlit
United States Magistrate Judge
235 John P. Canary U.S. Courthouse
85 Marconi Boulevard
Tallahassee, FL 43215

Dear Judge Tazlit:

I am a recent graduate of Stetson University College of Law. I am writing to express my interest in the law clerk position that will be available in September 1999. I have included with this letter my resume, law school transcript, writing sample, and letters of recommendation.

I believe that I am qualified for this position for many reasons. Not only am I dedicated, hardworking, and able to juggle many tasks at once, but I also have a strong background in research and writing. My undergraduate degree in English provided a sturdy foundation on which to build my communication and legal research skills. These skills were developed in various ways. During my second year of law school, I was a member of the *Stetson Law Review*, and my article was selected for publication. In addition, I was selected for the Dean's Fellowship for Legal Writing, and I served as a teaching assistant. These experiences, as well as my experience as an editor for the *Stetson Law Review*, further expanded my understanding of the *Bluebook* and legal writing in general. However, my stint as a correspondent for a local newspaper throughout the summer of 1998 is proof that I have retained the ability to communicate with those who are not lawyers!

If you would like to arrange an interview, I can be reached by telephone at (614) 693-1943 or by e-mail at gharp@law.stetson.edu. Thank you very much for your consideration, and I hope to hear from your office soon.

Sincerely yours,

Gideon A. Harp

SAMPLE COVER LETTER 2

EMMA A. BEARDSLEY

---

801 First Street, Sacramento, CA 95616 • 501-652-1234 • e-mail:
ebeard@law.mcgeorge.edu

October 6, 2000

The Honorable Harry T. Stone
United States Court of Appeals
218 Oxbow Street
Suite 1140
Woolfork, CA 91367-3633

Dear Judge Stone:

Associate Dean Keith Jones and Assistant Professor Megan Sagi suggested that I contact you. I am a second-year law student at University of the Pacific McGeorge School of Law and would like to be considered for a position as one of your law clerks for the 2002-2003 term.

I am in the top 5 percent of my class at McGeorge School of Law. I am also a member of the *McGeorge Law Review*. This past summer, I sharpened my analytical and writing skills during an externship with the Honorable Carl J. Lawrence, U.S. District Judge, Eastern District of California. In that position I gained extensive experience with many kinds of cases and analyzed a variety of legal issues. This semester, I am further developing my research and writing skills as a research assistant for Professor Megan Sagi. I would be honored to have the opportunity to clerk for the Ninth Circuit in your chambers. After law school, I plan to pursue a career in public interest law, and I believe the experience I gain as a law clerk will help prepare me to be an effective advocate on behalf of my future clients. I have enclosed a copy of my resume, references, my first-year transcript, and a writing sample for your review. My writing sample is an excerpted copy of an appellate brief I wrote for my first-year legal writing class. The law school will send letters of recommendation from Associate Dean Keith Jones, Professor Megan Sagi, and Professor Bill Williams separately.

I will be in Los Angeles November 3 through November 6 and would welcome the opportunity to meet with you to discuss how my background and skills may fit your needs. If these dates are not convenient for you, I will be happy to schedule a meeting for a date that better accommodates your schedule. Thank you for your time and consideration. I look forward to hearing from you.

Sincerely,

Emma A. Beardsley

Enclosures

SAMPLE COVER LETTER 3

855 Huckleberry Way
Winston-Salem, NC 31201
864-555-5555
aeverett@gmail.com

September 22, 2009

The Honorable Daniel Norcross, Chief Judge
United States District Court for the District of South Carolina
P.O. Box 835
Charleston, SC 29402-0835

Your Honor:

I am writing to express my interest in a judicial clerkship beginning in May 2010. I am a third-year student at the Wake Forest University School of Law in Winston-Salem, North Carolina. As a South Carolina native, I intend to practice law in South Carolina, and I am particularly interested in a clerkship with you so that I may effectively utilize my research and writing skills in a setting that will allow me to serve that legal community.

Legal research and writing receive special attention at Wake Forest, and during the two required courses in this subject, I have researched and composed multiple legal memoranda and briefs. Additionally, in an effort to further hone my writing skills, I am participating in the Advanced Legal Research, Writing, and Drafting Certificate Program, which consists of both drafting courses and advanced research courses.

Outside the classroom, I have gained valuable research and writing skills as the lead articles editor of the *Wake Forest Law Review*. In this position, I am responsible for planning this year's symposium, which addresses tort reform. Additionally, I have been fortunate to have the unique experience of arguing before members of the Delaware Supreme Court when my moot team advanced to the final round in the Vale Corporate Law Competition. My writing and oral advocacy skills will be further refined this semester as I prepare for the National Moot Court Competition sponsored by the New York City Bar Association.

My experience working for Justice Anita Phillips of the South Carolina Supreme Court and Judge Leonard Hizzey of the Forsyth County Superior Court in Winston-Salem, North Carolina, afforded me an opportunity to refine my research and writing skills. However, I am most appreciative of the insight into the judicial system that these positions provided me. The clerks in both chambers introduced me to the "community" aspect of the profession, which solidified my desire to submit this application. I am certain that a clerkship position would provide me with a unique opportunity to engage in sophisticated and challenging work while fulfilling my desire to be of service to others.

Enclosed are my resume, law school transcript, undergraduate transcript, and writing sample. My writing sample is the legal argument section of an appellate brief that I wrote for my legal writing class and addresses the issue of First Amendment free speech rights of public employees. Also enclosed are letters of recommendation from the Honorable Leonard Hizzey, Forsyth County Superior Court; Dean Ella Mascarino, Wake Forest University School of Law; and Professor Delia Amsterdam, Wake Forest University School of Law. I am happy to provide any other information that would be helpful to you. Thank you for your consideration.

Sincerely,

Alexandra Everett

Index

Italic page numbers indicate material in figures.